NIGHT CLASS

NIGHT CLASS

A DOWNTOWN MEMOIR

VICTOR P. CORONA

Soft Skull  New York

NIGHT CLASS

Library of Congress Control Number: 2017940028

Cover design by Debbie Berne

ISBN 978-1-61902-939-2

Soft Skull Press
1140 Broadway Suite 704
New York, NY 10001
www.softskull.com

Printed in the United States of America
Distributed by Publishers Group West

1 3 5 7 9 10 8 6 4 2

*To Guadalupe, Victor M., Joel, and Talal, my family forever,
and to the memory of Jeannie Stapleton Smith, mentor and friend*

CONTENTS

NIGHT CLASS

PREGAME

My first step into New York nightlife was almost a disaster. For weeks my friends and I plotted how to sail past the velvet rope guarding the wild weekly party called Ladyland, a sparkly mix of twirling models, queer art kids, and glam rock devotees. Held at the Hudson Hotel, a trendy venue that had appeared on *Sex and the City* and *Gossip Girl*, their night pulled in hip downtown DJs and passed free booze and champagne around the modish crowd of teal hair, mesh tops, and designer leather. Debbie Harry, the blond downtown goddess herself, had stopped by to bless the affair, while magazines deployed their style photographers to document the chicly outfitted It kids. And they were ready—always ready—to pose, pose, and pose.

I did not belong there.

Three years of dissertation research with the US Army, plus a year of working in Washington, DC, produced a dowdy cubicle rat version of me. I wore wire-frame eyeglasses on a face dotted with acne and shaved my whole head down to shiny skin. My way too bony body was dressed in clothes plucked right out of the Gap's sales racks. Picture Gandhi in baggy khakis walking around the Pentagon. Finishing my PhD at Columbia and becoming a sociology professor had not exactly improved my outfit choices or aesthetic tastes.

Of all nights, my first outing to Ladyland happened on St. Patrick's Day, 2011, when most nightlife folks avoid the drunk bridge-and-tunnel mobs stumbling around, leaving in their wake green party hats and vomit puddles. But two friends dressed as frumpily as me insisted that *this* was the night we would finally make it into Ladyland. I wore a drab black polyester jacket from Macy's, a plain purple T-shirt, dark jeans, and clunky black loafers that made an already horrible look even worse, all while carrying a huge satchel that had no business being anywhere fabulous.

The party itself went on in the Hudson's darkly lit library, adorned with strangely chic posters of cows and a purple pool table in the center. The main organizer was Kelle Calco, a suave member of a downtown clique known as the Rivington Rebels, sort of a rock 'n' roll men's club. Their home base was the storied St. Jerome's bar on the Lower East Side, where Lady Gaga and her friends first stirred up their scene years ago. Brian Newman, another Rebel and Gaga's trumpeter and jazz bandleader to this day, often dropped by. I was especially eager to meet Darian Darling, an incredibly glamorous Ladyland hostess and old Gaga friend, who back then still reveled in a closeness to her downtown buddy turned global pop star.

Once my friends and I arrived at the hotel, the glowing neon lime escalator took us to a lobby filled with woodsy motifs and festooned with what was probably faux ivy. I approached the doorman at the library's velvet rope and shyly asked about Darian's party. Eyes narrowed, he gave us all the once-over. Clearly unimpressed by our nerdy selves, he pretended not to know what we were talking about. We foolishly assumed that we were at the wrong spot or that maybe the event had been canceled. But checking our phones, we saw everyone inside tweeting about just how fabulous the party was. So, we went back to him, this time being told to ask our supposed contact to come out and bring us in. One friend wondered if flashing our Ivy IDs might persuade the unwelcoming doorman. I glared at him. Eventually the doorman said that one of us could go in, find Darian, and have her come out to bring in the others. As the unofficial leader, I walked in to my very first big nightlife party alone, humiliated, and tasked with asking one of Lady Gaga's old friends to tell her doorman to let in my frumpy pals, pretty please.

I walked around the dark room as the music pounded away, recognizing this or that corner from all the Ladyland photos I had seen online. And there was Darian, in a corner, her vintage houndstooth jacket and blond Technicolor halo clearly visible amid her gaggle of young admirers: muscular models, colorful club kids, the Jerome's crowd. The boys hovering around her were very cute, making me even more self-conscious about my bargain bin clothes. But Darian was actually pleasant and chipper when I introduced myself and leaned in for a double air kiss, and against all odds the rest of the night flowed smoothly. My two friends were let in and, drinks in hand, we took in the fabulous scene.

Clearly that night's dreary version of me, pathetically pleading with the doorman, would not fly in clubland. Of course his rejections hurt, but it also pushed me to become a better version of myself. To some it all might just expose nightlife as a snobbish, sadomasochistic practice. But as I often tell my students, if they let just anyone into this school, your diplomas wouldn't mean anything. It's the filter, the gatekeeping, the conscious curation of a community inside that creates value.

Now zoom ahead five years to my thirty-fourth birthday. Watch me breeze into downtown hotspot The Box, a hub for A-listers and Wall Street millionaires where I had become a Friday night regular. My glittery red eye shadow matched my lacquered nails and the burgundy highlights in my hair, now grown down to my eyebrows. Accompanied by a friend in high heels, the beloved nightlife artist Muffinhead, I strolled right in, past the lines of people waiting outside, and dove into the outrageously chic crowd packed in front of the stage. Before long one of the hosts handed me a flute of champagne and I found my friends and some former students in the bouncing mass. For a few of them, it was their first Box night. They seemed overwhelmed by their immersion in flashy spectacle and maybe a little shocked at seeing their former professor wearing shimmering make-up and face jewels. A gorgeous friend had of course quickly been invited by some handsome finance guys to sit in their booth, while a fellow writer sipped on a Stella and relayed her thoughts about the crowd.

Bottle after bottle of champagne and vodka arrived at the hosts' table as combat boots and Louboutins crushed the limes and ice cubes spilled on the floor. Soon bow-tied staff members started marching through the crowd, asking everyone to sit down in preparation for the night's performances, which would include beautiful topless dancers' aerial contortions and, thanks to the great Rose Wood, raw shock and awe. Before it was over the stunning chanteuse serving as Mistress of Ceremonies hushed the crowd to announce that it was a special night for someone in the house. She called me up on stage and asked everyone packed in there to raise a glass and toast my birthday. On stage, at The Box, on my birthday. Gandhi had gone gaga.

Today it seems unbelievable that I could once see a future for myself in Washington's defense establishment. But like New York and Los Angeles, the capital's air is tinged with the residue of its métier. A palpable frisson of power emanates from federal corridors, alongside endless streams of bureaucrats pouring into and out of Metro stations. New York's electric and maddening pulse is often contrasted with the slower, heady, and chemical romance of Los Angeles, where wannabes' decayed dreams litter boulevards lined with palm trees reaching for the sky. But New York. The bite of its worn streetscapes and neon auras, a skyline mixing shiny glass and steel shards with ornate, squat housing stock, the endless collisions of noises, smells, faces, lights, and longings. I missed Gotham so much.

Although born in Mexico, I grew up just north of the city in Westchester County, where my brother and I devoured American pop culture. Our love of TV, film, and music videos was thankfully balanced by my parents' fondness for classical music and the fine arts. So I started exploring more of my cultural loves once I left Washington and was back in New York looking for teaching jobs. As I worked to inhabit the identity of a new professor, I can pinpoint for you the exact moment when I fell down a rabbit hole that would lead to these pages.

I was watching MTV as an episode of their tawdry reality show *The Hills* was ending. Credits rolled, and a snippet of Lady Gaga's "Bad Romance" viral video hit came on. I watched the crazy rush of diamonds and fire, bodies twisted into zombie dance moves, Alexander McQueen couture, and product placements peppering a slave rebellion storyline. I was hooked. Like most, I had heard previous hits like "Just Dance" and "Poker Face" but it was *this* video, set to an extremely catchy earworm of a song, that triggered a real curiosity about Gaga and what her rising star meant. She seemed so weird, so fresh, so ready to shock, finally breaking the pop cycle of bouncy bubblegum princesses.

I wanted to know more about who she really was, what on earth was behind the outrageous spectacle that made you stop and look, going well beyond the basic Top 40 to which American ears were accustomed. I started reading up on the music industry that Gaga seemed to be dominating, the fashion bigwigs that she was befriending, the bars and venues where she performed before her Fame, and her many visual references to Andy Warhol, Grace Jones, Leigh Bowery, Madonna, David Bowie, and others.

When I started developing and teaching my own culture curriculum, an arc emerged. The great silver specter looming over New York was clearly Warhol, with Michael Alig's club kids linking the Factory to Gaga's wacky pop aesthetics. They had all tapped into a power of self-invention nurtured by the theatrical style of downtown New York. This sensibility was grounded in a fragmented but very vibrant nightlife community, one that included failed innovators like Michael, scene queens like Susanne Bartsch and Patricia Field, and very lucrative nighttime hubs like The Box. The more articles and books I read and the more documentaries and archival footage I watched, the more obsessed I became with downtown's mystery—its power to nurture and destroy identities—and the more I wanted to meet and understand its people.

But my first Ladyland showed me that my Ivy League pedigree mattered little at the velvet rope. Savvy, swagger, outfits, and the right names were the keys into this world. So I started a new learning process, a fresh reboot. I jumped in, dug in, sipped a bit of the Kool-Aid. I grew out my hair and bleached or colored it from time to time. Blond, red, violet, blue—I tried them all. Skin treatments helped with my complexion. I started lifting weights, made a few trips to SoHo shops, experimented with glittery make-up, and eventually got Lasik. I transformed. In for a dime, in for a dollar.

After teaching class during the day, I continued my education at night, learning about how identity, fame, spectacle, and delusion are all interwoven south of Twenty-third Street. My training ground included neighborhoods like the Meatpacking District, Chelsea, the West Village, Greenwich Village, the East Village, SoHo, TriBeCa, and the Lower East Side, plus smaller areas like Chinatown, Battery Park City, and the Financial District. I plunged into a gritty world of very creative personas and thoroughly damaged egos. I scoped out gallery openings, museum parties, film screenings, and book launches. Like Warhol, I would go to the opening of an envelope if it meant discovering something new.

I sought out the downtown birthed by Blondie and Jean-Michel Basquiat, Edie Sedgwick and Viva, Lou Reed and Nico, Dorian Corey and Octavia St. Laurent, Kelly and Ronnie Cutrone, Marsha

P. Johnson and Diane Brill, Patti Smith and Robert Mapplethorpe, Fab 5 Freddy and the Ramones, the people populating all those black-and-white images that somehow speak to kids caught in the still silence of Idaho or New Hampshire or wherever. Their tiny towns are so very quiet but downtown sights and sounds pull them to be a part of New York's noise.

Downtown cradled the old bohemia that incubated icons whose reach is now global, as well as the delusional has-beens and bitter nearly-made-its who are always ready to tell you what went wrong for them. They're the people you'll meet in this book, those who shared their stories with me in living rooms, bedrooms, coffee shops, parks, diners, and bars all over the city, or sometimes over the phone, allowing me to probe their past and present even as they worried about their faults and futures. After our conversations, some helped me, some hurt me. But my goal was always to understand what their downtown fame games had to teach me about the stuff of being a New Yorker, being an American, being a person trying to find his way, just like them.

Downtown is the extinct CBGB, Motor City, St. Jerome's, and Patricia Field's boutique, the long gone Limelight, Tunnel, Don Hill's, and Mineshaft. It's now the flourishing 1OAK, Avenue, and The Box, mixing nobodies and somebodies, vodka drinks in hand, libidos raging. Or the celebrity shenanigans in the Boom Boom Room and Up&Down, and eager students at NYU or the New School filming scenes on stoops and doing photo shoots in alleys. It's a speeding cab ride from the Chelsea Hotel to the Pyramid. It's newer ventures like Milk and The Hole, and galleries like Howl! and Maccarone, selling the art of dead icons and impatient upstarts. And bars like The Cock and Boiler Room, haunted by the ghosts of last calls and hookups past. Or the Stonewall and Tompkins Square Park, where identity met rebellion and history was made.

It's the chic brand of street cool that feeds today's fashion trends and nurtures lifestyles performed on social media rather flamboyantly and sometimes obnoxiously. It's preparing a few lecture slides about *Sex and the City*, leaving your office to get a bagel, and walking right past a graying Chris Noth chatting on the phone, or rushing to class and running into Anne Hathaway trying hard to look incognito on Eighth Street. It's a summer night that starts on the roof of the super elegant, members-only SoHo House, surrounded by tanned, rich people swishing their feet around in the pool, and ultimately ends at the filthy, foggy Eastern Bloc bar, with raunchy gay porn on the screens and go-go boys in jock straps swirling around you.

Early on, many nights ended sadly, especially when I was unknown and treated miserably by gatekeepers. Despite tough moments I kept going, thanks to the stubbornness and stamina I inherited from my mother. Along the way I curated performance showcases, worked on magazines, helped people get gigs, and organized photo and film shoots. I learned what a truly deathly hangover was, as well as some useful remedies (dry toast and popcorn). I worked as Michael Alig's assistant during the summer after his release from prison, trying to understand the most pathological and exhausting human being that I have ever known. I go-go danced at a Hell's Kitchen gay bar, my flailing limbs illuminated by green lasers. I stared out at a twinkling skyline from the Rainbow Room but also waited in plenty of lines to use sticky urine-soaked bathrooms in Lower East Side bars.

Downtown is no idyll. It can seem like the playground of the white, the beautiful, and the rich. Standing at the velvet rope, not everyone is created equal. Hot looks or wealth will guarantee your entry into the haute spaces of the city, and without them, you will wait on line, watching others jump out of their cars and stroll in, all while you calculate how long your ego will let you stand there in shame. Awful things can also happen in the dark of night. Young women can be drugged, assaulted, or worse. Others may be robbed or get mixed up in bloody fistfights. And as shown by the tragedy of Michael Alig, addiction, death, and delusion may follow too.

My downtown story is about transformation, of the people I met, of me, and of the area itself. One ex–club kid told me about junkies passed out in parks with needles hanging out of their arms. He remembered an abandoned building between Avenues B and C with two buckets hanging from a dark and forbidding window. One was marked *C* for cocaine, the other *H* for heroin. You would put the money in the appropriate bucket, then up high it went, down the stuff came, and then up high *you* went. That downtown has largely faded, giving way to glistening luxury condos, sushi bars, artisanal ice cream shops, and outdoor farmers' markets selling fresh organic produce. The park junkies were replaced by happy hipster couples in flip-flops fussing over their little kids. The one constant—then, now, and forever—is probably the rats.

In trying to make sense of downtown tribes, I noticed a few other things that brought me to telling this story.

First, in a hypermodern era driven by tiny attention spans and viral micro-spectacles, downtown can preserve the primacy of the live moment. Think of how smartphone and social media technologies became the lens and filter of our cognition. Culture is now infinitely snarky yet somehow altruistic, crudely exhibitionist yet brimming with judgments of others. In the face of all this, New York holds on to the power of an unfiltered moment lived intensely. What performance art, theater, nightlife, and the city itself all have in common is that they can only be fully experienced in vivo. Video and photos can document a moment but can't duplicate it. The pages you're reading can reveal downtown's realities but can't reproduce them. When you finish my story, go see for yourself.

Second, I noticed that very similar social dynamics happen everywhere. Power, lust, ambition, fear, intrigue, jealousy, and that basic human need for identity animate all social worlds, whether your goal is to become a four-star general or a nightlife superstar. The flaws and foibles of downtown characters are found in any other sector of human activity. What's unique here is that these people chose to be part of a scene where the ultimate but only whispered goal is *apotheosis*. The pathologies of their glittering lives emerge because that elusive goal of iconicity is so rarely achieved. Who can truly stand next to Marilyn Monroe?

Finally, identity is so very malleable. My nighttime instructors included over eighty artists, performers, and impresarios who collided downtown, hungry for fame and glamour. The common thread among them is a transformative power offered by New York, one where you can author your own sense of self and test the limits of human ambition and appearance. Downtown is a petri dish for growing identities. Queer, trans, straight, glam, goth, punk, fetish, radical, butch, femme, preppy, spiritual, fairy, ambiguous, clown, absurd, and so on. They all mix and mesh downtown, from the scenes swirling around Warhol's Factory to Gaga's Lower East Side pals and today's nightlife hubs. The thrill and tragedy of the space reveal how dramatically identities can change, including my own. It's a classic New York idea—sung by countless crooners from Frank Sinatra to Alicia Keys—that you can find yourself here.

Downtown is where I sought a new education, where night classes held in clubs, bars, galleries, apartments, stoops, and all-night diners taught me about love, loss, and the real, living possibilities of identity. It's where a sociology professor managed to understand himself a little better and enjoy life a little more. As Petula Clark put it, the lights were much brighter there.

1

STEF INFECTION

Standing tiptoe made my legs ache, while I stretched to watch pop stars parade into the MTV Video Music Awards at Radio City Music Hall. I spotted someone stiffly step out of a limousine and kiss Kermit the Frog. She wore a sparkling gold mask, a feathered neck brace, and a huge black hat, a hint of pink hair peeking out. Behind me a young woman muttered, "That *has* to be Lady Gaga—only she would wear something like that." She was right. It was The Lady herself, meandering past red carpet camera flashes in her gilded Phantom of the Opera look, just a sidewalk away from the evening traffic flowing uptown on Sixth Avenue.

I really recommend trying this "stargazing" at least once. Yes, you're standing for a good two hours outside a gala, concert, or some other fabulous event to which you were not invited. Most of it involves waiting for the famous to come or go while you get elbowed and stepped on by sweaty and overly eager fans. Some start bickering. Potbellied paparazzi surround you and often block your view. You might get cursed out. Huge security men feel the right to grab and push in defense of their clients. All this while breathing in car exhaust. But within the bloated paparazzo and burly bodyguard hungry for a paycheck and the obsessed fan waiting to meet The Star, you see and smell up close the peculiar stuff of fame.

To M, a young friend from the St. Jerome's scene, stargazing was way too demeaning. Ambitious and brimming with entitlement, he wanted to strut on the red carpet himself and feel like a worshipped somebody, not be smothered by crazed young nothings. Despite being a young pop connoisseur who hung around Gaga's Lower East Side leftovers, M hated those pimply fans. They were usually a diverse lot, although if I'm being totally honest many are young girls who wouldn't be called skinny, plus their young gay BFFs that you can tell are just starting to experiment with make-up.

Check out their glittery lip gloss from CVS and a face just armored with foundation. Layer upon layer. If they're standing in the sun, watch what happens when their beloved celeb comes out. The boy's huge smile cracks the cakey armor and twenty-five dollars worth of aisle-two product slides off his face, encrusted with sweat. Meanwhile the world's most glamorous people walk by, sidestepping the crumbling human mess.

So overall, more *Freaks and Geeks* than *Gossip Girl*, capiche? And M just couldn't step outside of his ego long enough to marvel at this ugly but amazing New York circus, a morass that elevates a select few above the rest of us, always pushing the lunacy of fame to more perverse extremes.

There's also the sheer surreality of standing out in the street while Meryl Streep, Hugh Jackman, or Julia Roberts walks right past you, or yelling a hello to Anna Wintour, prompting her to actually smile and wave back. (All of this actually happened to me!) And if you try stargazing, watch and listen to the fans waiting out there day until night, leaning on the police barricades, iPhones at the ready. Look at their smiles and listen to their squeals of "YASSS KWEEN!" They're experiencing a very real joy, maybe the kind that others find in a religious service or at a political rally. They all fumble toward an identity in a world that offers less and less to believe in. As Richard Schickel put it, if we can't have common ideals, at least we can have common idols.

That night of Gaga-watching—my first glimpse of her in the fantastical flesh—fueled my fascination with how Stefani Joanne Angelina Germanotta used downtown to become one of the world's most famous people. But only much later did I meet the two ex–club kids from Michael Alig's Limelight scene that did Gaga's glittery make-up on that VMAs night. Some of their fellow clubland veterans, who also knew her back in the day, are now prosperous jetsetters, others practically destitute. Gaga's spunk and talent amaze those who still think of her as Stef but they also talk about how little she understood the downtown lineage that birthed her.

I also got to know Gaga's old friends, including her revered mentor Lady Starlight, responsible for nurturing Gaga's embrace of the weird and outré. And genderqueer cool kids like Darian Darling, Breedlove, and Justin Tranter, who taught her about music genres, street style, and underground performance, only to watch her ascend way on high while so many stayed behind.

Gaga's misfit crew took over the flame of fame from dwindling downtown tribes and magnified it even more. Then they rammed it down the throats of a younger generation, infecting them with visions of glittery glamour, love games that end in bad romances, and New York nights spent chasing the *scheiße* of stardom. Thanks to a small clique doing much of what Warhol's Factory Superstars and the club kids did, new ADHD-afflicted and smartphone-savvy youth came down with a very serious "Stef infection," to quote my friend Michael Womack, a pop fanatic himself.

The VMAs night wasn't the last time I saw Gaga in person. As I explored more of her story, I ended up at her Central Park concert televised on *Good Morning America* (in the VIP area thanks to some Interscope promoters), outside her foundation launch at Harvard, her New York Pride speech, and the big *ARTPOP* album launch in

Brooklyn. Being there or getting to know her frenemies felt so far away from those rows of gray cubicles back in Washington or theory classes at Columbia. And yet not totally surprising. Things that fascinate us when we're young usually continue to do so, in some way, when we're older: symbols, places, faces, images, bodies, objects, and desires. The impulses of our youth are rarely snuffed out entirely. They simmer and brew and somehow appear again later in life, all along hiding in our hearts like little monsters.

Each semester I end my courses with a sound-off session. Students can say or ask anything they want. After *RuPaul's Drag Race* exposed mainstream youth to the cheeky lingo and flamboyant cattiness of drag queens, I sometimes called the session our "Spill the Tea" time. This ritual became my traditional way of ending a class because I clearly remembered sitting in Yale classrooms feeling totally clueless and alienated, wondering who on earth these dowdy but brilliant people up at the podium were. I felt so overwhelmed, especially when sitting next to graduates of elite prep schools. When I started teaching years later I wanted to give my students a direct chance to ask me anything about their university, career building, and why I teach what I teach.

Some questions tend to repeat over the years. My arm tattoos peek out from the sleeves of my polos so I'm usually asked what they are. Most are references to favorite books of mine like *1984*, so this triggers a tangent about *why* they're my favorite books. Students are accustomed to everything being compared and ranked, so they ask about differences in teaching at Columbia versus NYU, Hofstra University versus the Fashion Institute of Technology.

There's always one student who can do a spot-on imitation of a professor—the same was true when I was in college. So they rib me about my expressions, like my visceral response when a student makes a really insightful comment during our discussions: "*Ex-*

treeemely interesting." Or my persistent use of an idiom to stress the supreme importance of investing real effort in their work, repeated to them ad nauseam throughout the semester: *the proof is in the pudding*.

The most common question is about why and how I ended up a professor. It's a good one, because it's tied to the whole point of my sociology classes and the eventual education I would get downtown: the complicated yet very malleable nature of human identity. We all carry around bundles of stories that we tell ourselves about our lives and the people around us. They guide us in chasing the things that we need and want, like what occupations we choose, how we dress, or whom we date. And no one alive at this very moment can escape these very basic questions about how we exist in the world and relate to others.

As I tell them, growing up for me was an interstitial thing, unfurling *between* identities and not fully grounded in any. My parents and I left Mexico when I was a year old and came to the United States, only legalizing our status when I was in fourth grade. Despite never finishing college, my mom and dad were clever and curious caregivers, raising my brother and me as god-fearing Catholics while still being open-minded and not dogmatic. We were never anything near rich but also never starved. I knew early on that I wasn't straight but I did have relationships with women, even later dating one for two years and almost asking her to marry me. Living in White Plains—a thirty-minute train ride from New York City—meant that we could immerse ourselves in noisy Manhattan bustle for a day and then retreat back to a quiet suburban street.

After I was born in January 1982, my first home was in a small town smeared on a dusty, jagged hillside outside Mexico City. Several forces came together to push my parents to leave our neighborhood of unpaved streets and stray dogs, particularly the peso devaluation crisis, the death of my mother's aunt, and my grandmother's back surgery. She was already employed here legally, obtaining permits to work as a live-in maid for wealthy families. Using tourist visas, my parents and I flew over in May 1983 and stayed with a friend whom my grandmother met while working at a local hospital.

Within a few days of arriving my father started working at a bakery—in violation of the visa—and we stayed beyond the allotted time, beginning a period of living in constant apprehension about doing basic things like getting a driver's license. One slipup, my mother worried, and we'd all get tossed back to our shithole Mexican hometown. As a kid I avoided talking about our illegal status, refusing to feel even more different from my classmates. And it all seemed so totally out of my control, so why bother poking around it?

My parents tried two different tracks to legalize our status. My mother had studied English in Westchester during her high school years, and the family she lived with put her in touch with a lawyer. My father pressed his boss for help with paperwork and also sought out legal assistance. His pursuits panned out first and when I was in fourth grade, we all flew to Tijuana to sort out Resident Alien papers. We started the naturalization process as soon as we could and a month before the 9/11 attacks I proudly became an American citizen. As I tell my students during our Spill the Tea time, the best thing that my parents ever did was leave Mexico.

In Westchester, growing up between categories meant that I never had a sturdy identity to define me. And so I've spent most of my life in search of one. It's no surprise that I ended up in a profession where it's my job to study other people's identities. This null sense of self makes me really curious about people's mannerisms and lingo in certain settings, the ease and flourishes with which some speak. This mastery of the rules of a particular social game is what my college sociology professors would describe as part of Pierre Bourdieu's concept of *habitus*, and I would eventually confront the challenges of learning these social rules in extremely different contexts.

Eat with me at a restaurant and you'll probably get annoyed at me, like most of my friends and family do. They assume that I'm not paying attention to them because I am *always* looking around, watching people come in, noting how they're dressed, seeing them flirt or argue, trying to figure out their story. I can't stop. It's the diversity of habitus on vivid display.

As I tell my students, being a sociologist for me means being a professional voyeur, a practiced eavesdropper on city streets that offer their own tragicomic brand of nonstop public theater. Throwing in some very famous people makes it especially fun. Hang out with me sometime and you'll witness my laser-guided, digitally enhanced Terminator vision, my StarGaze™ mode quickly able to spot a notable. Scan . . . Scan . . . Zoom . . . Identity Confirmed. Tony Danza on Columbus Avenue. Anjelica Huston at Broadway and Seventy-ninth. Mandy Patinkin at Best Buy. Fab 5 Freddy, Rose McGowan, or Sam Smith at The Box. Russell Simmons at Thailand Café on Second Avenue. (Try their Long Island Thai Iced Tea. But two at most. Trust me on this.)

I have always been obsessed with spectacle and drama, whether in Hollywood's hero vs. villain epics or in the tortured history of our civilization. Like I said, it's not that huge a surprise that I was pulled toward downtown's art and nightlife worlds. Lasers, glitter, fireworks, flags, things that shine and sparkle and glisten. No difference if it's the stars, eagles, or colorful combat decorations on an olive green officer's uniform or the sequined dress, bright purple lip, and glitter eye shadow of downtown's best drag queens. I admire things that speak to human ambition, to the will to become something and fight for it.

As kids my brother Joel and I absorbed American pop culture. To this day we obsess over comic book movies or the *Star Wars* series. When a new trailer premieres, we text each other about it. We were at the red carpet opening of *The Dark Knight Rises* in Manhattan and Joel even traveled to Pittsburgh to be an extra during Bane's stadium takeover. Four years before that I climbed a lamppost on Broadway to watch stars arrive at a mournful *Dark Knight* black carpet. But history itself is just as grand. Long before the age of Netflix and Hulu I loved going to the public library and renting VHS cassettes of Frank Capra's World War II propaganda films, spinning those epic narratives about the Allied nations' crusades against the Axis invaders.

But as I started high school, consuming stories wasn't enough. I started rabble-rousing, getting involved in activism and disruption, hoping to actually *be* a character in something epic.

At a state education program for differently abled and autistic children, my father worked with Margaret, a veteran member of a local activist group, a frayed relic of the "make love, not war" hippie movement. She'd end up breathless after furiously ranting about Reagan, Nixon, or Kissinger. One afternoon I came home from school and like most teenagers just wanted to sleep. My father woke me up, saying that Margaret had invited him to a screening she organized about the 1994 armed uprising by Mexican rebels in the jungles of Chiapas. He nudged me to get up, saying that if I was truly interested in history and politics I should actually go and learn more about it.

I left the event almost ecstatic. A postmodern jungle revolution led by a Mayan socialist army pumping out poetic communiqués? The black balaclava masks of the rebel leaders (years later reappearing in Pussy Riot's neon hues), a mysterious Che-like spokesman called Subcomandante Marcos, and black flags with red stars? How sexy is that? I was sold. Before that, Mexico only hovered in my consciousness as an extremely poor and dilapidated place that we had escaped, an ugly land that I didn't understand and that didn't understand me. The Chiapas rebels gave me a different way to relate to the place of my birth. It gave me an identity.

Finally, a respite from my rote suburban life. So I showed up at meetings organized by Margaret's activist group, learning about the political issues that they had worked on for years: protesting the local nuclear power plant, police brutality, pollution in the Hudson River, and, of course, US military involvement overseas. I protested and chanted against the same military-industrial complex that years later would employ me, help me pay off my college loans, serve as the basis for my doctoral dissertation, and provide yet another identity.

Rather than hang out in parking lots smoking weed, I became that snotty kid in high school, the one with a backpack covered in political pins, the one ready to question every damn thing the teacher said, not realizing how sanctimonious he sounded. Instead of getting high, I went left, spending countless after-school hours with Margaret and our comrades in meetings, dreaming up lofty plans, watching people several decades older than me actually believe that the great radical upheaval they wanted was just around the corner. But what choice did they have? The blind belief might have been a decaying and futile identity, but it was also their Saturday morning potlucks, memories of marches past, and the faded bumper stickers on their cars. *It was them.*

Sometimes I wonder what Margaret would say about my time in New York, about its downtown fame game, which creates an abundance of losers and rewards only the very few. Heartbreak and resentment are its dividends far more often than glamour and glory. The players are definitely more fabulous than the comrades with whom Margaret and I worked, but they can be just as delusional. And yet there is never a lack of eager players ready to roll the dice. The whole game can seem like one endless horse race in some grotesque arena tucked into Dante's *Inferno.* You look out at the racetrack and wonder which animal has the raw ability and willpower to win. The initial favorite might tire out and end up a broken heap in the mud. The slow starter might go nitro and in a flash charge to the lead. Therein lies the rub: determining the dynamo versus the dud. What's needed aside from innate talent and hard work? And what's luck got to do with it?

The plain-Jane brunette you see singing in a dingy bar on Bleecker Street could end up one of the most famous people on the planet, or she could be stuck forever, never finding the spark that thrusts her way up high. You see your nightlife performer friend profiled in *Interview* or *VICE* and a range of emotions flitters through your mind: joy, pride, surprise, seasoned with a dash of envy. But years later they're doing the exact same kinds of parties, maybe at a different venue, but they're a little thicker around the middle now and more concerned with raising a family than their media profile.

Some players in the game work harder than others, honing their craft while peers drown their ambitions in hookups and highs. You really should stay in and work or get a good night's sleep, but phone calls, texts, and FOMO beckon you out into the night. Oh and what if bae shows up? So then come the shots and the bumps and before you can finish a slurred sentence, it's four in the morning and you're being shooed out of a club that is now cruelly, clinically illuminated. The bright fluorescent lights seem to beg the question, "Was it worth it?"

Virtually everyone said that The Lady was of the first downtown breed, a meticulous perfectionist devoting herself fully to her work, only occasionally pulled in adverse directions by the loves of her life. Somehow the celebrated L. A. Reid missed it and Gaga was dropped from her first label, Reid's Island Def Jam. But she persisted and would go on to sign with Interscope (incidentally, it's owned by Universal Music Group, which also owns Island). And her hyper-ambition was always ready to jettison those who became inconvenient, whether early collaborators, past lover Lüc Carl, or former manager Troy Carter. No one with whom I spoke would say that she didn't deserve her success or that she's untalented. What they resent is her careful curation of a persona and the questions it raises about an artist's authenticity.

For basic, brunette Stef to become blond pop queen Gaga, she observed the lineages and looks of other stars past and present, deftly extracted samples, and with her Haus of Gaga team constructed a beautifully monstrous new chimera. Gaga surpassed Victor Frankenstein, actually *becoming* her monster and then birthing a progeny of similarly obsessed, if less talented, wannabe stars. Like a pharmaceutical company, Mother Monster profited brilliantly from her applied research. Her cultural synthesis is even more common now, thanks to the massive archives of art and fashion history easily accessible with a few swipes and taps of a phone. She just planted her flag first and most fabulously. With her mentors to guide her, Gaga shrewdly sashayed through the scene, sucking downtown's soul and eventually selling it to the world.

Something really remarkable always happened when I chatted with Gaga's friends, whether on or off the record, from the very start of my downtown nights. When the conversation finally turned to their famous friend, her name was never said. They would just murmur *She* and it was immediately understood that we had pivoted. If drinking, they might utter "Stef" or "Gags" later on. But inevitably they spoke more quietly and sometimes fidgeted or looked away as they conjured the Gaga ghost hovering over us, before dishing about She-Who-Need-Not-Be-Named.

The sketch of Gaga's past has been told over and over in unauthorized biographies and media reports. A brunette of Italian heritage demonstrates enormous musical ability and moxie early on, a talent earnestly supported by her affluent Upper West Side parents. She goes to school across Central Park at the elite Convent of the Sacred Heart, whose alumni include progeny of the Mortimer, Kennedy, and Hilton clans.

It's here that the young Stef may or may not have been bullied, depending on whom you ask, but nonetheless triggered the misfit mythos that would reach its apogee in her *Born This Way* era. She went to the Tisch School of the Arts at NYU until she dropped out, throwing herself into the Lower East Side's rock 'n' roll scene and exploring every bit of downtown that could mobilize her career. And like her forebears, Warhol and Michael Alig, Stef possessed enormous commercial savvy. The memoir of her old friend and DJ collaborator Brendan Jay Sullivan claimed, "This little girl had the business acumen of a mafia don."

She soon captivated the gays and the gaze of critics eager to understand her persona, like the celebrated gender theorist Jack Halberstam. In my culture and sexuality classes I assign Jack's *Gaga Feminism*, where The Lady represents a new feminism "of the phony, the unreal, and the speculative" wrapped in "punk aesthetics." Just as Warhol was a nexus for a new cultural moment, Halberstam wrote, "Gaga feminism is a politics that brings together meditations on fame and visibility with a lashing critique of the fixity of roles for males and females. It is a scavenger feminism that borrows promiscuously, steals from everywhere, and inhabits the ground of stereotype and cliché all at the same time." At its best, Gaga's pop performance art brims with the possibility of pointing us toward "the end of normal," a post-gender world that explodes labels and celebrates freed, ambiguous identities.

But Gaga paid a high personal price for this grand role, particularly in her deeply problematic relationship with Lüc Carl. The crux of the problem is captured in "Paparazzi," the song featured during her bloody VMAs debut on the night that I first saw her. The song's role reversal is classic Gaga: even as The Lady becomes hounded by photographers and obsessed fans, she sings about being someone else's "biggest fan" and pursuing a reciprocated love from the Rock Star. The subject is Lüc, a Nebraska native turned bar manager, who as a hard core rock 'n' roll scenester glibly looked down on his girlfriend's pop ambitions.

She tried very hard to impress him, to make him return her love, ending up caught in the colossal irony of alienating success. As Brendan Sullivan told me, "He didn't respect the work she was doing at the time. He thought it was just, you know, asinine and silly and foppish. [. . .] The song 'Paparazzi' is about the idea that in her life, he is the star but in order to keep his attention she needs to create music that he will respect. But the harder she works on her music the more the music takes her away from him." Brendan's far-off stare indicated that his mind had drifted elsewhere as he remembered the quiet agony of Gaga's catch-22.

At the popular bridge-and-tunnel hub called Hotel Chantelle, former Limelight director Steve Lewis introduced me to Lüc, who had a gorgeous model-groupie on each arm. Lüc is a "larger-than-life rock personality," Steve had told me earlier. *"God knows what he actually does but he's unbelievable."* Upon hearing from Steve that I was a sociology professor, Lüc seemed curious enough to pull away for a quick chat with me. When I later asked him to speak on the record, he quickly emailed me back but I didn't get very far. He wrote, "Assuming your book mentions my ex girlfriend Ill [*sic*] have to politely decline."

Gaga's real-life "I won't stop until that boy is mine" project finally did stop when Lüc couldn't handle being a sideshow to his famous girlfriend's stardom. His dreams of badass rock fame had come to nothing in New York. How did it feel? To have this wild Lower East Side adventure and then flee? To never escape an ex who devoted so much of her early self to you, long before the wacky talk of fame monsters, swine, mermaids, and government hookers. To watch her win a Grammy, to see her name flashing on a Madison Square Garden marquee, to join the whole world in staring as she jumps and flips all over a Super Bowl stadium?

Until it closed in 2016, Lüc's old bar, St. Jerome's on Rivington Street, was a mandatory stop for any Gaga fan. She even namechecked the bar in "Heavy Metal Lover" and while open it was still home base for old friends like the Rivington Rebels. When she talks about her early years, Gaga conjures visions of her crowd getting wasted on Jameson shots while DJs in ripped Ramones shirts played Bowie and Blondie. Gaga and her mentor Lady Starlight once go-go danced at the bar, and pal Breedlove hosted his extremely fun Magic Mondays there.

But roping in the Jerome's rock crowd was insufficient for Gaga's

Fame. Whether to make social progress or pop stardom, it does take a village, so early on she sought out the legitimacy of gay clubland. But some nightlife contemporaries have called her out on the more bombastic elements of the early mythos. As scene queen and event producer Ladyfag told *New York Post* journalist Maureen Callahan, "It's not like she was some kid who ran away from home and was hanging out in all the gay clubs, 'cause that's so not true." Alongside event producer pal Josh Wood, Ladyfag and ex–club kid Kenny Kenny booked Gaga to perform at their Sebastian party as "The Lady Gaga Revue." Years later, when the two Ladies met in Paris through Gaga's former fashion director Nicola Formichetti, Gaga described the gig as her "first real show."

The week before her performance, Gaga had gone to Sebastian with Lady Starlight, whom Kenny already knew from hanging around downtown and her work with M•A•C Cosmetics. "She's a great girl," he said about Starlight. "Really like her." And Gaga liked his party so Kenny agreed to book her the following week for a whopping one hundred dollars, billing her on the flyer alongside clubland stars Amanda Lepore and Sophia Lamar.

But some doubts lingered in the mind of the legendary downtown doorman. On the night of the show, while she did her makeup, Kenny remembered stopping by. "I was like, 'You sure you want to call yourself *Gaga*?' She said, '*No, I'm absolutely positive.*' And I was like, 'Sounds a little weird.'" Oddly named or not, the starlet packed the club and record industry folks and family came ready to buy bottles. "She did it and everybody loved it and immediately everybody was like, 'Who's that girl?' And all of a sudden, I was like, 'Kinda don't know,'" Kenny recalled, laughing at the breakout star unexpectedly born under his nose.

But for Ladyfag, Gaga's lineage to downtown circles is a thin one, telling me, "She takes from underground culture but there's nothing underground about her." Gaga's Fame needed the gay scene, Ladyfag said, "Like Madonna too, she had to be a part of gay culture.

She had to, like, kind of steal from it, be a part of it, make sure she's connected to it." At a 2011 nightlife panel at the Museum of Arts and Design, Ladyfag said something similar about Gaga's stated links to gay club culture. "In my opinion, and if you speak to any of my friends, they'll tell you that is a lie," she told the audience. "Because she wasn't there, and we all were."

Having known her from those early years, she adds a personal insight into The Lady who would tell a generation to love themselves because they were born that way. Ladyfag pointed out, "I'm sure she has lots of insecurities, first of all, it's clearly obvious."

Former members of Patricia Field's downtown fashion house backed up Ladyfag's claim. Jojo Americo, as part of The Ones, even opened for Gaga at the Highline Ballroom alongside Amanda Lepore. "You know, she's not this like cool downtown person at all," he said. "She's a rich kid who said she traveled through the New York club scene. I don't remember seeing her." House of Field drag queen and renowned wig stylist Perfidia corroborated, "No, no, it wasn't like Lady Kier, where everybody knew her and then she became world famous."

Gaga understood what marketing strategists know all too well: no matter how great the product, it needs a powerful story that's heroic, even messianic, spiced up with grandeur or mystery if possible. One of Gaga's closest friends from Jerome's is Brian Newman, who continues to tour the world with Gaga as her trumpeter and jazz bandleader. Darian Darling introduced me to Brian on a Ladyland night. He was and continues to be one of the most courteous scene people that I have met. In the fall of 2015, Brian visited my culture class at Columbia, where he spoke frankly about Gaga's understanding of the needed Fame ingredients. "Like Stef always—*I mean, LG*—always says," Brian told my students. "You really don't get to that point in your career that she did until she really changed someone's life."

Change lives Gaga did, including mine. Because of her, I ended up on a bridge connecting Cambridge and Boston on a pale gray day in February 2012. I walked toward Harvard Business School's opulent campus, separated from the rest of the university by the Charles River. Gaga was in town to launch her Born This Way Foundation alongside her mother, Cynthia, and Oprah Winfrey. I was scheduled to meet with Anita Elberse, a Harvard professor who wrote case studies about Gaga's career and had invited former manager Troy Carter to speak to her class about the entertainment business.

Despite my best efforts, I couldn't get into Gaga's Foundation launch that day, so I thought about catching an earlier bus back to New York before a snowstorm hit the area. But I also wanted to see the fans swarming around Gaga's Born To Be Brave bus. Flurries started to fall while I took a few photos, watching fans dressed in Gaga-garb freeze in their black shredded looks. Suddenly they all turned in my direction and started stampeding toward me. I spun around and saw a caravan of black SUVs loop around and pull up right in front of me. About five feet from me. There I stood, mouth open, as brawny security men got out and opened a door. The Lady emerged and stood right in front of me. Umbrella in one hand, BlackBerry in the other, I could see through her requisite sunglasses and stared right into her eyes for about four solid seconds. The stampeding fans then bum-rushed her, frantically begging for photos.

Gaga's Harvard gambit echoed another powerful blond ambition, the Argentine first lady Evita Perón and her social welfare organization. As her character crooned in Andrew Lloyd Webber's *Evita*, "Everything done will be justified by my foundation." Images of Evita handing out food, clothing, and land deeds to the poor firmly installed her image as their high flying, adored savior. With the Born This Way Foundation, Gaga gambled on somehow saving her hordes of fans from cruel bullies through her Fame, youth advocacy, elite Ivy resources, celebrity friends, and a powerful branding effort.

The full story of her Foundation could be the subject of a whole other book. But I bring up this story to make clear the symbolic distance between her day in Cambridge and the downtown scene she absorbed. And yet the latter enabled the former. Starlight and others clocked Gaga's enormous potential early on, but could even they have dreamt of such heights? While they tossed back whiskey shots and danced at Jerome's could they have ever imagined a packed Harvard lecture hall? A national youth foundation? Oprah?

Time and memory are funny, spongy things. My all-time favorite book, George Orwell's *1984*, is about the mutability of the past and the disposability of everyone. In Big Brother's nightmare of a nation, when all records of a life are tossed into a memory hole, a person can be completely erased from existence: "lifted clean out from the stream of history." Orwell is clearly commenting on attempts to bend and twist human consciousness to fit the aims of a small group of despots. From the Spanish Inquisition to Nazis and Communists, the ambition to seize and hold absolute power has depended on the ability to mute the past, to mold perception as the dictators see fit. But in any culture, and in any life, bits of our pasts are bound to fall down the memory hole. The question is who or what gets tossed in.

Veteran downtown performer Penny Arcade has crafted a whole career out of furious harangues about the "erasure" of history. Her archnemesis is Carrie Bradshaw, or rather the whole *Sex and the City* model of urban femininity fed to the bridge-and-tunnel stiletto crowd, which now feels at ease on a Lower East Side corner previously home to junkies. Alongside *Gossip Girl*, the myth of Carrie Bradshaw has fed a very profitable and shiny urban lifestyle, expressed in the visual vocabulary of Birkins, Manolos, cosmos, cupcakes, and chunky jewelry. Films like *Breakfast at Tiffany's* and *The Devil Wears Prada* similarly feed the hunger for flashing lights, fabulous revelry, and popping champagne bottles.

People like Penny reject this vision of New York entirely and are nostalgic for a vanished city, imagining the raw roar of a pre-Giuliani Gotham that was grittier and more authentic to them. Think of the derelict neighborhoods of Jean-Michel Basquiat's *Downtown 81*, where, he said, "It looked like we had dropped the bomb on ourselves." For others, this old spirit is conjured by CBGB's punk concerts or bars like Motor City and Jerome's. Or it may be the original Copacabana, Studio 54, or the club kids' Outlaw parties. Pick your nostalgia. You'll find someone in New York who shares it.

I understand Penny's outlook and I can see where she's coming from. In the Jackie Curtis homage *Superstar in a Housedress*, she actually contextualized her world beautifully: "Our world, the Lower East Side downtown art scene, was filled with wildly talented people. There was an awareness of sadness. There was never any question that there were enormous wounds. But it was, like, let's put on a show to cover up all of this despair and misery. Our lives were bleak, so we filled them with glitter." Penny justifiably rages against gentrification, the vanishing of our favorite venues, and the penniless withering away of her queer friends while Caitlyn Jenner is awarded "icon" status overnight. The issue, though, is that only Penny's version of downtown history gets to endure and avoid the memory hole. Penny appointed herself the Erasure Sheriff and now she decides. But in the wild maelstrom of downtown culture, not everything is worth remembering.

Penny lives near Gaga's old Stanton Street apartment, so you can imagine her seething hatred at fans that leave notes or flowers for their adored Lady. When I first met Penny at a café, she hadn't even sat down before she unleashed a resentful rant about "that no-talent cunt." (Never mind that Howard Stern—not exactly known for genteel pleasantries—called Gaga one of "technically the best singers I've ever heard.") Penny has criticized me for writing about Gaga or other downtown figures, basically anyone not named Penny Arcade.

Penny's downtown badassery sells well overseas, where it's seen as "authentically" New York, but it's tough to swallow here. When I asked cult film star Joe Dallesandro about Penny, he spat out, "An-

gry little bitch . . . I don't know why she's such an angry person."
Party Monster Michael Alig remembered Penny demanding to be
paid to show up at his events. "She was not very fabulous, not very
personable," he told me as we sat in a Starbucks filled with Columbia
students sipping lattes and clacking away on their laptops. "If she was
sitting in here she would look just like one of these regular people."

And yet Penny stands ready to snidely insult any and all perceived
enemies. The funny part is that I agree with some of Penny's analyses. She even reminds me of Margaret and my old Westchester comrades. But in choosing to scold ad nauseam as downtown's Erasure
Police, is Penny just angry that others managed to more lucratively
mobilize downtown's auras than she was? The true magic of winning
the downtown fame game lies in making it "up there," as Warhol
would say, and avoid getting thrown down a memory hole.

At a certain point The Lady developed a slightly poetic but sometimes baffling Gagaspeak. The liner notes of her *Born This Way* album begin with a rather fluffy acknowledgement: "I would like to
thank The Road, The Highway, and the wind in my Hair as we
surged down the freeway of life." But maybe it was inevitable that old
friends would fall by the wayside during the long trek of Gaga and
her Hair on that Road. Some, like Brian Newman, she has always
kept close, still performing with him and even becoming godmother
to his daughter. As Brian told my Columbia students, "I think she's
very much that same girl that was go-go dancing at St. Jerome's."

Maybe not everyone would agree.

The night I stood on Sixth Avenue watching Gaga was also the
first night that much of the world saw her on their screens. Her "Paparazzi" performance marked a big, glittery signpost on The Highway to true global stardom, reaching new heights with her "Bad
Romance" moment a few months later, when I myself would jump
down her rabbit hole. Watch the 2009 VMA footage. See P. Diddy

engrossed by her spectacle. That night's performance of her bloody demise, accompanied by accessories of rehabilitation like a metallic crutch and a bedazzled wheelchair, birthed a recognition of her powerful vocals and mesmerizing stage presence.

But watch the footage a second time. When she wins her very first VMA, she tightly hugs her then-manager Troy Carter, with whom she would break in a few years' time, allegedly due to "creative differences." Watch Perez Hilton jumping up and down, literally becoming her cheerleader when Gaga wins. Much later they will have an extremely explosive and public break, with her calling him "sick" and "fake." Two key Haus members would eventually spiral out of her orbit too. Haus choreographer Laurieann Gibson would split with her in a messy episode that roiled her fanbase. Past lover and Haus creative director Matthew "Dada" Williams would be more delicately eased out. Lady Starlight would go on to tour the world with Gaga but eventually make Germany the home base for her DJ gigs, far from the Malibu mansion and Central Park South apartment where her old protégée would perch.

The question of who gets tossed into the memory hole is a recurring feature of the fame game, as stable a staple of stardom as makeup and camera flashes. What is owed to the people who knew you way back when? Those who listened to you whine about break-ups or spin those big dreams of red carpets and award shows? Or who inspired a song or helped you book a gig? Gaga has provided opportunities for her friends to shine and join in her pop parade around the world. But if they can't muster the right mettle, what to do?

Her old DJ Brendan Sullivan was at least savvy enough to understand that his time at the brink of Gaga's memory hole would eventually come. According to his memoir, as Interscope prepared Gaga's first album drop he told her, "There is going to come a time when you are going to leave me behind. And when you think you've gotten to that point, I want you to do it." She understood, agreed, and, of course, eventually did it.

Now let me offer a night class case study.

Imagine that early on you're applauded for your amazing musical talent. But you also want to blur gender boundaries, pushing beyond glam rock toward a more raw, queer, and provocative intersex terrain. You pull together a collection of flashy looks and a band of hot guys, ready to pull stunts like changing your outfit in the middle of your concert set, right there on stage. You find a younger, kindred spirit who professes her fandom for you and one night she opens for you at a show. You score a major record deal, start building buzz and a fanbase, and book more gigs. Publicity shoots up.

But zoom ahead a few years and somehow, through the twists and turns of the fame game, there's a role reversal. Now *you* are opening for *her*, not at a small Lower East Side showcase, but on a global sold-out arena tour. She has picked from your gender-bending toolkit of stage antics, borrowed from your gospel of glitter and grit. And now *YOU* are the second banana, the sidekick, a character in the glamorous entourage of one of the biggest pop stars on earth.

What do you do? You're thrilled to be so proximate to such an impressive Fame but part of it must trigger some rotting of the soul. And who can really blame you? Why *her* and not *you*?

This is essentially the saga of Justin Tranter, the former frontman of Semi Precious Weapons, credited alongside Lady Starlight for pushing Gaga to embrace her provocative style and downtown mythos. When I first met Justin at Jerome's in 2011, he was at the height of his hope for a global stardom comparable to Gaga's. The possibility of becoming a household name seemed within reach and having just filmed a VMAs promo with Gaga, he was understandably on cloud nine. So when I introduced myself, Justin gave me a quick once-over and a dismissively shady "Yeah, OK, uhuh." I wasn't blond or cute, so what possible appeal could I have to Mama Precious, the lanky leader of the so-called Precious Empire?

Eventually his band would be dropped by their record labels and he would leave New York, the place that spawned his image. This was perhaps the darkest time, when they had to find a way Up There without an attachment to The Lady. As Brendan Sullivan told me: "They're such a great band, they don't have to open for her for the rest of their lives. [. . .] And I'm sure they loved leaving the tour, having new fans, and then headlining their own shows where everybody was there to see them, *not everybody was there checking their phones until Gaga went on.*"

Justin's story seemed to have a happy ending, just not the one that he might have foreseen back in the day. Out in LA he would rally to become one of the most sought-after songwriters in the industry at the time of this writing, working with Justin Bieber, Selena Gomez, Britney Spears, Gwen Stefani, and other global stars. This all happened well after I caught up with him, when we spoke a lot about how little he missed New York and his long history with Gaga and their misfit crew. But precisely when I asked about what he taught Gaga, who felt like a glimmering ghost hovering over our whole conversation, Justin asked that I turn my recorder off.

Downtown taught me to notice the abundant contradictions in its people and Justin is no exception. An early metal rock initiation from his older brothers was matched by an equally powerful obsession with *Annie*, *The Little Mermaid*, and tennis. Yup. Tennis. The man sitting in the diner behind Beyoncé in Gaga's "Telephone" video was once a young tennis champion. And although Justin declared, "The world is run by beauty," his favorite Warhol Superstar is Brigid Berlin, the frumpy, thickly built, and rather unglamorous Hearst heiress.

Justin identifies as "in-between" genders, so when he at last "put on a pump," his life changed, thereby cementing his "super femme androgynous look." While trying to build up Semi Precious Weapons in New York, he heard that Starlight and Gaga were among his fans. So he looked up Gaga on MySpace in early 2007 and had them open a show for them. Once Gaga's rise to Fame began revving up, Justin loved convening regularly with Starlight, Darian Darling, and Breedlove, although he was routinely harassed in public for his genderfuck looks, telling me he was once "held over subway tracks." His response? To avoid the subway and just walk everywhere, even in his heels.

Although he definitely seemed happier in LA than he was back in the city, there were whiffs of resentment, like when he mentioned that Semi Precious Weapons won *Village Voice* readers' best New York band polls but the paper itself never wrote about them. The weekly has largely waned in any relevance, I told him, and he shrugged it off, saying, "Good riddance. Who cares?"

One would imagine that by now there would be a manual somewhere for how to become famous, *Stardom for Dummies* or the like. Justin could submit a strong proposal. Several ingredients featured in his mix: "talent and clear vision" are paramount, he said, but must be buttressed by money, luck, and connections. Determination is key too, willing to try a hundred times if need be, to find your own Road to the enduring stardom you seek.

So go to the Lower East Side sometime and ask around about the pop star that many knew simply as Stef. You might get a grimace or a roll of the eyes. You might sit through a whole tirade about what she supposedly stole from whom. But ask about her mentor and performance partner and you'll hear something very different: reverence for the great Lady Starlight (Colleen Martin) instead of a rant.

It was on my thirtieth birthday that I met Starlight while she DJed at the now shuttered W.I.P. club attached to Greenhouse. We were introduced up in her booth by M, who revered her as much as he disliked her basic fans. Like Gaga and me, Starlight's nose dominates her face, although her huge smile and self-effacing humor will quickly disarm you. When we met the music was so excruciatingly loud that I was yelling into her ear at the top of my voice, big veins surely bulging from my neck and face. From Starlight all I could hear was, "WHAT?!"

Starlight's likeability complemented a deep and encyclopedic love of musical genres, a flare for vintage shopping and dressing up, an expert talent for make-up looks that emulated Ziggy Stardust or Peggy Moffitt, and a true devotion to Warholian spectacle. Nightlife promoter Twig the Wonderkid remembered meeting Starlight at one of her early parties. "They covered everything in aluminum foil," Twig told me, laughing out loud. "Up to that point I had never seen anyone put that much effort into transforming the room. I think they wanted to make it look like the Factory."

What Starlight lacked was her mentee's voice, steely stamina, and affluent upbringing. Nonetheless, she quickly won over a diverse and influential set of club owners, DJs, bar staff, and upstarts. Different allies and lovers rotated through Gaga's life, but the key figure was the fellow lady who unleashed Gaga's theatricality and bestowed downtown legitimacy. As Starlight crowed in a 2010 *Daily Mirror* article titled "The Woman Who Invented Lady GaGa," "As I'm eleven years older than Gaga, I do see myself as her mentor."

If you watch the 2011 HBO special about Gaga's Monster Ball tour, it begins with Gaga outside a Lower East Side bodega, hanging out with Starlight, Darian Darling, Breedlove, and her choreographer Richy Jackson. After she buys gum and coffee they all hop into a massive black SUV and blast off to her sold-out Madison Square Garden show. Backstage Gaga warms up her voice, greets a gushing Liza Minnelli, and gets into costume, gradually becoming bouncy with excitement. "Oh I hear them screaming! Let's go!" Before strutting out to sing and dance for a massive arena show, Gaga huddles with her dancers and staff, but then stops. "Can Colleen come in here?" Into the frame rushes a thin woman in a tight T-shirt with a blurred out print that's probably Metallica or some hair metal group. Beaming, Starlight squeezes in next to Gaga.

In the HBO show, Breedlove is still in his "dress to depress" phase, a slightly vaudevillian spin on an Eeyore-like loser, The Dude visits the Lower East Side. This phase for him involved huge eyeglasses, long hair, shaggy beard, a XXL T-shirt with his own mopey image, and glum repartee about being a loner looking for friends. In his daytime life, he's the make-up coordinator for *Wicked*, the hit Broadway musical about the two warring witches of Oz. Backstage at the Garden, he and Darian smile as they watch their old friend now swept up in the backstage swirl of a global pop tour.

Gaga's old friends enjoyed an initial bump in their fortunes when Gaga became famous, but sometimes struggled to build an independent fanbase or clientele in the way Brian Newman did. When I asked Ladyfag about Darian Darling and other Gaga friends hosting parties like Ladyland, she quickly interrupted, *"Based on her name,"* meaning Gaga's. I asked if Ladyfag believed that a relationship with Gaga had driven the success of Darian and others. She replied, *"Totally,"* which is fine, that's how it works. All you need is one shout-out from one famous person and suddenly you're associated with them."

At the cool rococo Lillie's in Midtown, I met Darian for dinner, joined by another old Gaga pal, Veronica Ibarra. Since I was profiling Darian for a magazine, I asked about her blond bombshell branding. She explained, "I'm playing with blond archetypes," including vintage Barbie, Marilyn Monroe ("a mess, and really sad and tragic"), Debbie Harry ("a drug addict but fabulous"), Madonna (an "over-ambitious bitch"), and her namesake, the trans Warhol Superstar Candy Darling ("always living in a fantasy world"). Like her famous pop star friend, Darian was an amalgam: "I've taken like a little bit of all of it together and mushed it into one big thing and kind of made it my own." After an encounter with Darian, club kid legend Walt Paper (Walt Cassidy) rightfully concluded, "She's very pretty and seems very cool but, you know, she's very derivative." Exactly. This was Darian's own synthesizing strategy for playing the fame game.

While Breedlove is still working to build a music career, I have always loved the Magic Monday songs he performed at Jerome's. Tracks like "I Never Had" and "New York City Rooftop" are extremely catchy, although my favorite will always be "Oh Pierre," his homage to make-up legend Pierre LaRoche, a riff on the tough learning curve of doing make-up right. Think back to the crumbling stargazing fan boy I mentioned. He'll get the hang of things soon enough, figuring out what kinds of hues and mixes work best for his skin type. Make-up is also the common denominator among Gaga's gang, as Darian observed during our dinner, remembering how the Starlight circle emerged through a love of cosmetics. And so Breedlove sings, "Oh Pierre, look what you've done / Making-up can be lots of fun / *I learned it from watching youuuuu.*"

Like other Starlight acolytes, Breed spoke about her deferentially, even as his "third parent." He said, "She unlocks the magic in people. And she did it for me, she did it for Gaga, she did it for Annaleigh Ashford, who just got nominated for a Tony this year for *Kinky Boots.*" Starlight collects vinyl and sound modifiers, but also identities, making her "a curator of all things, including people," he said.

When we talked about his downtown past, Breedlove remembered Starlight making it known that she had met a kindred spirit in Gaga during one of her DJ sets. In line with her knack for social curation, she announced to her crew, "I'm going to start performing with this girl." Ex–club kid Lila Wolfe saw the intensity of Starlight's influence on Gaga. Now a platinum blond Wall Street chiropractor, Lila admired Starlight—"Cool all around and always had good style"—and saw how Gaga absorbed her mentor's tutelage: "She is the product of [Starlight]." So as "Lady Gaga and the Starlight Revue," gigs were booked, flyers were printed, MySpace notices posted, talent scouts and managers cycled through. "And then," Breed thought back, "[Gaga] became the biggest pop star in the world."

When did he realize that it had actually happened? Fashion bible *Women's Wear Daily* was delivered to his building. One morning there was a still-brunette Gaga on the cover, wearing a mirrored bra and Dolce & Gabbana briefs, and Breed knew that she had made it Up There.

Oh Starlight, look what you've done. *She learned it from watching you.*

Longtime DJ and promoter Michael T first met Starlight at Bar 13 near Union Square. Seeing Starlight in one of her looks, he thought, "Who is this freak?" Soon enough he too thought of her as "a great person," as Michael told me in a Beauty Bar bathroom. While I leaned against the sink, Michael T sat on a closed toilet, chatting as casually as if he were perched on a porch swing. Always stylish and chic, Michael was maybe best known in certain circles for the hit parties Squeezebox and Motherfucker. Although the latter was Gaga's big debut as a nightlife host, he didn't bring up Gaga once while he sat on that toilet.

Astro Erle, a crusty ex–club kid with a face covered in faded punk tattoos, told me, "She used to go out to all the clubs that I used to work at," tagging along with Starlight. "But I remember her, like, observing, just sitting back and watching," he said. "Stefani was more a little reserved, a little quiet," he acknowledged. "She would steal, like, my accessories off of me, whatever it was I would be wearing. I'd be like, '*GORGEOUS*, honey, work it out.'"

Still, Astro had something to say to Gaga about her *Fame Monster* album cover, which some clued-in downtown denizens saw as a direct rip-off of a Kenny Kenny wig. "*That was my look*," Kenny insisted, "because [Gaga] said on *Oprah*—Oprah had her on when she became big—and she said, 'For the cover of my album I wanted to be blue but my make-up artist said no.'" That's not exactly what Gaga told Oprah, but in Kenny's original photo with the wig, his face is indeed totally made up in blue.

A drunk Astro Erle, who cut Kenny's original wig (often called "hats" by stylists), actually called Gaga out on it, Kenny claimed, relaying a story that he said was confirmed by Darian. At some dive bar, Astro screamed at Gaga, "*You took Kenny and mine's hats!*" She casually replied, "I know, old club kids." Kenny wasn't really bitter, remembering that Gaga's team wanted him to work on her tour and throw parties. Alas, he was too heartbroken over a failed relationship and turned the offer down. Still, he didn't let her off the hook: "The looks are authentic, but they didn't look authentic on her."

For Gaga's initial burst of bizarre alien fetishy looks during her breakout moment in 2009, she turned to the ex–club kids who managed to migrate from their dwindling downtown tribe into an affluent professional elite.

Aside from RuPaul, Kabuki Starshine is maybe the most successful ex–club kid alive today, having used his painterly ability to become a wealthy giant of the make-up industry. His client list is as supremely A-list as it gets, including everyone from Iman to Lana Del Rey to FKA twigs, painting Rihanna and Katy Perry for their artsy music videos, and Michael Jackson himself for his very last two photo shoots.

Kabuki was responsible for Gaga's make-up on the VMAs night when I first saw her smooching Kermit. He was assisted by another club-kid alumnus, a former drag queen and old RuPaul sidekick named Flloyd. (And yes, two *l*'s—originally it was Flloyydd.) If you've watched the *Party Monster* documentary, you will remember him as the one stumbling around the King and Queen of Manhattan pageant with his mouth pulled wide open with a bent out of shape wire clothes hanger. When Flloyd was booked to assist Kabuki on three days of making-up the latest queen of Manhattan, he remembered crying at seeing Kermit the Frog on the call sheet (a standard industry document that lists everyone involved on a project). The duo of ex–club kids spent a good three days with Gaga during the pre–"Bad Romance" days, during which Flloyd remembered a chaotic "who's in charge?" atmosphere within the retinue.

Flloyd spent about an hour alone with Gaga watching random YouTube videos and later wondered if he should have taken the liberty of showing her footage of his old club looks. But Flloyd had an almost knee-jerk aversion to self-promotion, one that Gaga and others totally lacked. Doing it for the Fame, remember?

After the night's "Paparazzi" performance, during which she dangled from the ceiling smeared in blood, Gaga rushed offstage so she could quickly change and pop back into the audience for an award presentation. "I took the blood off while Kabuki put more make-up on." What was she like after one of her most iconic performances? "She was distracted and busy like she was kind of the whole time, really. She was a little sweaty."

Blood and sweat weren't the only fluids in the night's mix. "Kabuki was upset that we weren't invited to the after-party" following the VMAs, Flloyd remembered, but he was intent on toasting the night by opening a small Jack Daniels bottle in the mini-bar of Gaga's suite. Ecstatic after days of hanging out with a rising pop queen, Flloyd was rewarded with a swig of urine left behind by a malicious hotel guest. "That was my post-Gaga celebration!" he said.

Fellow club-kid alum Desi Santiago is burly, bearded, and stylish, but like Kabuki possesses a warm smile and very gentle demeanor. His old club looks were by far the most ghoulish of the scene: spiked collar, a Jesus shirt with bleeding eyes, or black candles on his head, hot wax oozing down his face. It's not surprising that he ended up a "creative collaborator" for Gaga's Monster Ball tour, back when she was also trying to startle and frighten her audiences. His project partner was fellow club star and now famed designer Zaldy Goco, who also worked with Michael Jackson, Britney Spears, Gwen Stefani, and Cirque de Soleil.

Together Desi and Zaldy worked on Gaga's first big American tour, designing the golden Egyptian Anubis look, the black hair suit with wolf and owl faces, machine gun helmet, and red latex S&M outfits. Over lunch near his Chelsea studio, I asked Desi about his nightlife generation's influence on Gaga. He said, "Oh my god, I think it's completely influenced everything who she is. She's reiterating all these concepts that we were talking about. About being yourself. Be a fabulous nobody. Be amazing because you feel like amazing." Her then-stylist Nicola Formichetti too had "taken, drawn from the club kid culture." But for Desi, it was the unacknowledged context that mattered: "She's saying it within a certain aesthetic frame. She's creating certain looks that are coming from that generation."

Armed with design training from Parsons and the Fashion Institute of Technology, Zaldy's fashion finesse appealed to Michael Alig, Susanne Bartsch, and RuPaul, for whom he continues to design lavish *Drag Race* gowns. Zaldy told me that his club kid days were "not unlike what was happening when Gaga started being like, 'Let's all be freaks.' [. . .] It definitely has that similar feeling, although a little bit more streamlined." He quickly defended his past client's synthesizing savvy, however: "She's an original in her own right because you still have to pick and choose what those things are and how to put it all together into one package."

Amanda Lepore, a former club kid and now arguably the world's second most famous transsexual (after Caitlyn Jenner), also saw Gaga's extraction from her era. Sitting in her tiny Hotel 17 apartment, she remarked, "I think that [Gaga] emulated club kids basically, that was like a big thing with her looks and stuff and everything." But she rightly cited a trickle-down effect: Gaga's outré style made the rabid fans love and appreciate her forebears, which meant more bookings for Amanda and her clubland cohort. "They look up to us because we did it before her," Amanda explained. "Perhaps if she didn't come, we would be dated."

Amanda saw glimpses of herself in David LaChapelle's shoot for the *Rolling Stone* cover story, "The Rise of Lady Gaga." She observed, "David actually kind of made her look like me, with the frizzy hair and the body and everything." The mimicry didn't stop there. It continued in the looks for Gaga's Monster Ball tour. "Actually David said that she did one of my hair styles for her tour," Amanda cheerfully told me. "When she did that yellow hair, she said, '*Oh I've got Amanda Lepore hair.*'"

The influences were sonic as well as visual. Gaga's old DJ partner Brendan Sullivan explained the origin of their stage routine: "We took that from, not from hip hop, we took that from the drag scene, from the track acts, from Amanda Lepore singing 'Champagne' with all the backing vocals and drums perfect on the record and then her kind of singing over it. That's how we started with Gaga," having watched Amanda perform at Michael T's Motherfucker party.

Michael Alig himself saw the connection. Chatting with him in Ernie Glam's apartment, I wondered about the first Gaga image he saw while imprisoned. He quickly remembered a *New York* magazine photo of her in a shimmering disco ball outfit. "She did not look good," Michael said. "And I thought, 'Oh god, here's another sorry club kid rip-off to embarrass us around the world.'" Practically exasperated when we spoke in LA, James St. James told me, "There's no way that you can say that she's not taking other ideas that have been done before and passing them off as herself, very earnestly believing that she is the original."

But where the former Stef differs from her club kid forebears is that she very lucratively infected an entire mainstream generation with what the Limelight set mainly conjured for fringe audiences. As Justin told me back in LA, "She made it a thing in the music industry and in the entertainment industry as a whole where like being a little freaky is kind of cool."

When visiting my Columbia culture class, Brian Newman even suggested that Gaga's freak flag was an extremely savvy business ploy. He told my students about his own efforts to break through as a jazz star by organizing a wild burlesque show in TriBeCa and quite candidly explained that Gaga did the same thing but on a much grander scale. She used shock and awe to strategically break through the attention economy, a scheme that she can now finally put aside:

I feel like especially with Gaga, she's done less and less of that [shock] over the years. You know, in the beginning, meat

dresses and stuff like that, and giant eggs, but now you're seeing the substance. You're seeing what she had to do to break
through that BS that our society puts on everyone: "Oh we
want to see you do this, we want to see you do that"—to [now]
really be able to just pick and choose and do the things that
she wants to do, that makes her happy.

Desi and Zaldy worked with Gaga on fittings and rehearsals
right before "Bad Romance" came out, just as her star was really exploding. When she showed them clips from the video it gave them
some pause. "She's not part of that generation," meaning theirs, Desi
said, shrugging and shaking his head. "*Whatever, girl.*" Desi seemed
to fumble as he spoke, processing his feelings about The Lady right in
front of me at that restaurant. "Sometimes I think people feel like she
should give a little more homage," he said. "You should honor your
mentors a little bit. Things aren't created in a vacuum."

I wondered if Gaga was at all starstruck about working with
ex–club kids like Desi and Zaldy, knowing that she was now employing legends of a certain downtown demimonde to construct her
eleganza. "No. She had no idea who me or Zaldy was. Our history,"
Desi replied, "I doubt she knows the history."

Down the memory hole. I guess I can see what Penny was saying.

I thought of my meals with Desi, Kabuki, and the others while
I talked to Breedlove at his producer's apartment. He's an articulate
and laid-back guy who usually tries to genuinely be positive. He said,
"We lived to have a good time and then in the midst of the fun
something really cool happened, for one of us. And that person has
brought us along for the ride." I don't think Breedlove resents Gaga,
but it has to sting a little. To try and try, while your younger friend
achieved such desired but rare things. And meanwhile you pay your
rent by painting someone green over and over again, so that tourists
can watch and clap for a story created in 1900.

Breed was clearly wistful when he remembered being at one of

Gaga's sold-out arena concerts in London. Up on stage in front of thousands Gaga would start to casually chat with him and their old gang. "Oh, my friends are here," she happily remarked, as if bumping into them at Starbucks. She pointed to the packed arena and said to them, *"Look at what we did."*

Warhol illustrated a *Glamour* story titled "Success Is a Job in New York" and now the statement is often associated with him. I don't think many New Yorkers would fully agree, given how insanely expensive and exclusive the city has become. But if there is truth to it, for me Marla Weinhoff epitomizes the aphorism. She's a respected and sought-after set designer and as of the *Born This Way* era, the art director of the Haus of Gaga. Chatting in a park outside her studio in the West Village, she talked about her deep appreciation of the city. Alongside an apparent lack of bitterness and anxiety, this is a true marker of success: possessing the affluence to consume New York's best and detour around its worst.

At the time of our conversation Marla was one of the older and most experienced members of Gaga's team. Her training in cultural anthropology complemented incredible expertise in textile, interior, and set design. For Marla, culture is how tribes understand themselves, whether in a remote tropical habitat, the boutiques, schools, and cafés of the Upper East Side, or the hyper-ambitious downtown denizens that Marla and I chose to befriend.

Like other chats with Gaga's collaborators, speaking with Marla conjured for me images of the Haus as the Tasmanian Devil from *Looney Tunes*, the beast who spins around like a furious tornado, limbs flailing every which way. Busy, busy, busy, Gaga always is, her worker-bees said, as so many different elements of her operation have to somehow congeal: her voice and physical health, outfits, hair and make-up, choreography and dancers, stage design, band or orchestra. All coming together into a traveling circus of couture and chart-toppers.

And yet the level of creative freedom that the Haus enjoys is absolutely enviable for any artist: massive budgets, gorgeous venues, attention to the tiniest of details, audiences filled with wealthy and famous faces, and access to brilliant collaborators trained and mentored by the artistic giants of the twentieth century. But never enough time. Three days, a week maybe, to construct the looks and scenarios that will be dissected and devoured by the masses.

Part of Gaga's look is an ever-changing array of sunglasses, which act as a kind of shield for her, creating a protective layer of privacy for a face constantly sought out by cameras. To some it's unnerving. On Oprah Winfrey's cable network, in the middle of an interview question Oprah bestie Gayle King demanded, "Will you take your glasses off now so I can see your eyes, pretty please?" Gaga obliged like a scolded child, murmuring, "Yes, I will. I've been told."

My own love of shades derives from wanting to hide my very beady eyes and beak nose, although my glasses are of the five-dollar kind sold by Manhattan street vendors, not custom-made mini-artworks. So I had to find Kerin Rose Gold, the creator of some of Gaga's most distinctive glasses and accessories, who showed up for our chat at a Midtown café in her signature bright tangerine hair and a giant witch's hat, which she soon admitted was "ridiculous."

Although she's incredibly capable at what she does, Kerin's story also spoke to the power of both dense downtown social networks and just plain human decency. While working at Pat Field's, well known in its day for aloof and catty employees, Kerin once assisted a stylist pulling items for *L'Uomo Vogue*. A year went by until he emailed saying that he was now working with Nicola Formichetti and wanted to talk about her designs. That stylist turned out to be Brandon Maxwell, today Gaga's fashion director. He told Kerin, "I remember you—you were like one of the only people that was nice to me that day." He would go on to ask Kerin to design some of Gaga's most well-known ornamentations, including the spiked gloves she wore while chatting with Starlight and Darian in the HBO special, the shimmering ruby shoes for Gaga's *Wizard of Oz* homage on *Good Morning America*, a teacup embellished with pearls and ants (which she slurped on *60 Minutes*, totally baffling a giggling Anderson Cooper), the glasses with dangling lenses that she wore while sitting nude on a circuit board chair, and the black crystal dance boots she often wore during the early *ARTPOP* era. "I don't think she knows that I made the boots," Kerin added.

Like Marla, Kerin always faced a feverish time crunch. Brandon could ask, "Can you bedazzle a pair of shoes in twenty-four hours?" But the hectic work pace seemed to have paid off for the team. Since he took over as Gaga's fashion director from Nicola, he went on to start his own collection, now counting Michelle Obama, Jennifer Lopez, and Naomi Campbell as clients. Alongside business ties bloomed a close friendship between Kerin and Brandon. "He and I have actually become very, very close, like he's really a legitimate non-industry friend of mine," Kerin said. "Like, you know, we go out to dinner and talk about boys."

Though older than Kerin, another *ARTPOP* collaborator had a deep nightlife lineage. Rob Roth is another clubland success story, palling around with celeb friends Debbie Harry and Parker Posey and holding artist residencies where he created dark, haunting performance art. Through creative direction firm The Mill and in-demand fashion filmmaker Ruth Hogben, Rob was commissioned to create the *ARTPOP* app's ethereal Gaga-in-the-machine, a ghostly simulacrum called Petga that eats the "auras" of her fans.

Chatting near his Lower East Side home, Rob recalled a quick turnaround for the project, which he filmed at Milk Studios, right near his old clubland base of operations, the legendary venue Mother. Looking out from a Milk window and munching on a croissant from the catering table, Rob remembered feeling struck by the irony of the moment: "All the ideas that we were exploring then and pushing and sort of doing all these themes . . . I'm literally across the street doing it," now years later and for one of the planet's most famous women.

The Petga idea was entirely Gaga's, Rob said, "She had this idea of . . . this character ingesting these things." Rob's own vision of ghosts, veils, and sexy robots then conjured the actual Petga. He spent a long day filming Gaga at Milk and tracking her movements for the CGI animation: "All of Petga is her." After he and Ruth finished the film in London, he heard that The Lady's reaction was positive: "I know she loves, *loves* everything so that was good."

Rob didn't know if Gaga knew about his nightlife past but did mention their mutual friends, telling Gaga about working with Starlight—"Starlight did my make-up for my shows"—and knowing Darian through Miss Guy and Debbie Harry. Rob told me how happy he was to see Gaga bring his old pal Starlight on tour with her, seeing a mentor graciously repaid for her investment in a young starlet: "She helped her become this thing."

Back in the West Village park, Marla also drew a link from the days of her youth to later projects for Gaga. Her father managed a clothing store in Omaha, so the playthings of her childhood fantasies were fabrics, textiles, and handmade toys, like tiny mice made out of nuts. Decades later, she remembered, "I took a Super Soaker and made it into a swine for the iTunes Festival."

Marla herself might have disagreed with the Warholian "Success" aphorism when her first New York job in a windowless design office exposed her to mind-numbing drudgery alongside "people [who] were so mean." It was the famous *Midnight Cowboy* party scene populated by Factory stars that encouraged her to come to New York, although she felt unsure about how to break into the actual scene. Frequenting Area and Palladium and working at Tunnel doing decorative painting, Marla remembered seeing Warhol whenever she would go out, though never actually meeting him.

Her first job's misery pushed her to find work with architects and interior designers, eventually bringing her under the wing of mentor Robert Curry, who would be her bridge to celebrated photographer Richard Avedon. I watched Marla beam when remembering "Dick" tell Curry, "Marla's eye is as good as ours. It's different but it's just as good." She gradually moved into set design for print and fashion shoots, and transitioned from work with "mean" textile lemmings to the likes of Steven Meisel, Annie Leibovitz, and Nick Knight, who asked her to work on Gaga's interstellar Lilith gooey genesis video for "Born This Way," marking her move into the Haus.

When I asked about her most challenging projects, Marla mentioned the "Marry the Night" show at the Grammy nominations concert in 2011. Originally Marla delivered a very Studio 54 vibe, which Gaga didn't like, instead requesting "New York City rooftop, *Cats* meets Broadway meets the night and *Phantom of the Opera*." Gaga loved the results, telling Marla, "This is my favorite set ever, at the last minute!" Watch the performance. The detritus landscape through which Gaga danced was actual junk from Marla's workshop, all assembled in about a day's time.

Marla also fondly recalled doing the props for the canceled Born This Way Ball; the Born Brave bus installation for Gaga's foundation; the iHeart concert's motorcycle sculptures; and the White House Inaugural Ball for President Obama's staff, an unpaid gig for which Gaga requested a "spaceship piano" from Marla. Where does this all end up? Gaga's storage units in Los Angeles.

"Gaga and I get along very well," Marla told me. "I think I understand her artistically and respect her." The paramount guideline for Marla was always to keep the set design simple and secondary to Gaga's persona. Despite the time crunch, it's all just a question of coordination, asking choreographer Richy Jackson how many dancers he'll deploy and if they need a staircase, or asking stylist Brandon Maxwell what color she'll be wearing.

When Marla and I spoke it was the start of the *ARTPOP* era, before its mixed reviews and the turn toward a sanitized, whimsical jazz cycle, and then the country-esque *Joanne* pivot. Describing the future of her client's Fame, she cited a lyric from the "ARTPOP" track: "*It can be anything and it will be everything.*" Marla explained that she herself is always surprised by the twists and turns of Gaga's trajectory: "She can't stop the evolution."

When I first plunged into Gagaland, I discovered that I wasn't the only writer interested in her work. There was a small community of us at universities around the country. Some started blogs, others published edited volumes. Not long after my first Ladyland I came across an essay written by someone I'll call F, a grad student at NYU, where I would soon be starting a job (in a totally separate school). I messaged him about his work, inadvertently kicking off a truly bad romance. In hindsight I'm grateful for the heartache. If a love between F and me had worked out, weekends would have been spent in bed and brunches instead of prepping for a conversation with a nightlife bigwig or perusing photo archives. When the sun went down I might have gone to see him instead of chasing the downtown story.

My thoughts floated back to F on a November night in 2013, while I stood with a crowd of chic souls freezing on an East River pier. The shivering gathering eagerly anticipated turning up at the hottest ticket in town: Gaga's *ARTPOP* launch party. The day before we had been instructed by the Haus of Gaga, via email, to show up at a pier where we would "be ushered onto a 15 minute boat ride to an undisclosed location." The invitation had asked us to "arrive early to avoid disappointment," although I doubt that anything could have kept those rabidly eager fans from bursting into the East Coast's music party of the season.

Walking toward the pier that night I chuckled when I saw the winding worm of downtown notables, creative industry folks, and fans dressed in the customary barely there looks that you'll see at a Gaga concert. Leather jackets and no pants, seashells as brassieres, neon hairpieces, and huge platform shoes all adorned the mass congealed along the pier. Out from the waiting throng stood Darian Darling, wearing her fur coat and chatting with her usual groupies.

After we double air kissed, I looked over at a few nightlifers who I knew full well had insulted Gaga on social media. But resentments would not keep snide detractors from missing a party that *everyone* would be talking about the next morning, its fabulousness only amplified by its secrecy.

The nightlife people were fidgety, some standing to the side chain-smoking. One Gaga friend would later complain about waiting alongside the "riff raff." I admit that it was amusing to see those VIPs pulled out of their element in a temporary democratization of a nightlife moment. Most of them would normally breeze past velvet ropes and stroll down red carpets, posing and smiling for camera flashes. But on Gaga's big night, despite their finery, they had to wait on the pier like the normal Financial District commuters who used the ferries every day.

Eventually the line budged while a few uppity male models notorious for party crashing tried to cut in front of us. We gave our names to the gatekeeper, surrounded by hefty security guards, and received a bracelet. Boarding the ferry, I bumped into Rob Roth and his friend Nicholas Gorham, impeccably attired in black. We had all been on a panel the day before at a Museum of Arts and Design nightlife conference. Still hyped up about how lively and intense our panel on nightlife rituals had been, we gossiped about the other sessions. Whose were best attended? What notables showed up to which?

As the boat docked I could hear music pumping out of a large warehouse and ran into another Gaga friend, the always chic, always friendly Jocelyn McBride, already in full turn-up mode. At last we arrived to a bustle of photographers and platoons of security guards carefully eyeing the partygoers as they stepped onto shore. On line to check our coats, I said hi to Kerin Rose Gold, also excitedly dashing in.

Stepping inside the warehouse we were greeted by a massive Jeff Koons sculpture of a Sphinxian, bone-white Gaga gripping her breasts, a glistening blue orb between her legs, the same sculpture that appeared on the *ARTPOP* album cover. Lingering by the door, I watched wave after wave of guests enter the space. Upon meeting Gaga Sphinx the reactions were identical: mouths opened, bodies pivoted, cameras flashed. Selfies.

In line with the themes of Gaga's album cycle, the event was stylized as "artRave," trying to meld the highbrow art worlds and the sweaty, fist-pumping verve of rave and EDM subcultures. For the *ARTPOP* era, Gaga had explicitly committed herself to the visual punch of punk pink princesses and renaissance goddesses, buttressed by a new coalition of elite artists and tech entrepreneurs. Gaga loved hybridity and the mix of guests arriving at her party reflected the divergent worlds that her fame game was pulling together.

As I strolled around, F texted and asked if I was having a good time. I sent him a few photos of the breathing human sculptures adorning the scene while I walked toward the lavish open bar. Almost any drink was available, although I had a nine o'clock class the next morning and imposed a two-beer limit on myself. Within a couple of hours, though, most guests were wasted. I tweeted updates from time to time but mostly just absorbed the whole spectacle. How many times in your life can you order any drink, for free, surrounded by shiny neo-Pop sculptures while Tony Bennett strolls past you?

I congratulated Jeff Koons when he walked in, surrounded by gushing fans whom I really doubt would know about the millionaire artist were it not for his Gaga work. After bumping into Marla and Starlight, I spotted queen of the night Susanne Bartsch walking around with her assistant, fidgeting with her phone. Perfidia from the House of Field strolled around wearing massive red plumage. Eric Shiner, then director of the Andy Warhol Museum, arrived later, ready for a quick gossip session with me before diving into the party. *RuPaul's Drag Race* winner Jinkx Monsoon gently caressed an admiring boy, while photographers Inez and Vinoodh inspected the premises, largely unbothered by the attendees gradually descending into a stupor.

We all felt VIP, but as you quickly learned downtown, there were always even more VIP areas. Even at an event that evoked raves' populism, burly guards barred you from the really Up There VIP balcony overlooking the main area. Underneath the balcony was an exhibition space devoted to wild Gaga looks, including a kind of white wavy armor that spat out bubbles. Screens showed off her smartphone app and Petga, so we all took photos of Rob standing with his creation.

For her actual show, Gaga looked like a masked asylum escapee, and the first thing you noticed about her is that she is *tiny*, especially standing next to her muscular dancers. I stood with Rob and Nicholas front row, to the left of the Tatlin-esque wedding cake of a stage on which Gaga would sing her hits and dance barefoot. The reception to the album had been mixed, including criticisms of the album as an "artflop." But I wasn't thinking about this while watching her or as I slipped out after the concert. Boarding another boat, I spotted more than a few friends leaving totally wrecked, as in, two-people-need-to-hold-you-up wrecked. On the ferry ride back to Manhattan I imagined another version of the night, one where F might have been at the party with me, but mostly I wondered about how the hell my wasted friends could possibly survive fifteen rocky minutes on a heaving ferry boat.

As a professor I spend only a few hours with my students each week and yet ideally the semester-long experience will deepen their sense of the social world. Sometimes they're totally unready for a college classroom, other times they'll rally and work harder than they thought possible. And sometimes they possess an enormous spark of ability in them that shines so brilliantly. When it's there I always hope that they'll find the right people to feed it.

Maybe the grand downtown alliance between Gaga and Starlight was born that way. But notice how different they really are. Starlight launched a protégée into a pop mainstream that she loathed, preferring analog culture, classic vinyl, and extremely conceptual performance art. Eschewing the endless exhibitionism of most people's online identities, her social media footprint is minimal. For her, cultural production is about contemplation, obscure references, and independent thinking, not just recycling dated motifs or channeling hipster snark. In becoming Lady Starlight, Gaga's mentor transformed into a downtown legend who came to hate what New York itself became.

When I interviewed Starlight for a magazine story, we met up during her DJ gig at Darian Darling's Yotel brunch party. After exchanging double air kisses, I told her how very fit she looked, envying her totally fatless body. Chatting with Starlight while she DJed wasn't the ideal interview context but I did enjoy watching all of Darian's guests stop by and practically bow in respect. Our chat was routinely punctuated by these glowing greetings and genuflections, her loud laughter seasoning our conversation whenever she played her favorite songs. As Starlight bopped her head to "New York Groove," I asked about her creative process, about the bizarre solo numbers that would open Gaga's tour. "My goal in life is to get that thing from a thought in my head out into reality," she explained, "like purging, *like creative diarrhea is what I would say*." There was no grand theory of performance offered, aside from a hope that she'll leave fans "confused," that is, SHOOK.

Given the durational and highly conceptual nature of her work, I asked Starlight for her thoughts on Marina Abramović, arguably the godmother of contemporary performance art. Although Starlight spoke approvingly of her 2010 Museum of Modern Art retrospective, she replied, "On some level I don't like to look at other artists [. . .] It's really important to me that what I do is really pure and [. . .] it just comes from inside." Now she had *me* a little shook, given how much her disco child was described as an amalgam of past pop icons spliced together.

After so many downtown praised her sensibilities, I needed Starlight's take on her deep impact on them. She struggled a bit with what I realized was an unfair question, essentially: *Why do people think you're so awesome?* But she rallied, "None of them ever met anybody that thinks about things the way that I do. [. . .] There's always a sense of humor. It's just the way that I think. It's the same with Gaga, what I believe inspires her: the whole *'Just fuck it all. Do it.'* " Whenever we chatted, Starlight always spoke of Gaga with the utmost respect, praising the fan community she created and coming to grips with her mentee's shift from bar hopping to globe trotting.

Anyone would want to know the person who mentored The Lady herself, especially one with a rock moniker that explicitly invoked the radiance of the superstar. But it was almost painful to watch Starlight's tricky exchanges with fumbling fans. After our Yotel chat, I went to the bar to grab a mimosa, then noticed a little meatball of a fan waddle up to the DJ booth and start the usual awkward fan interaction with Starlight, who pleasantly reciprocated and showed real appreciation. But the fan just affixed herself right there, like some greasy barnacle, scrolling through her phone and gripping the booth while Starlight worked the turntables. A few friends mercifully tried to dislodge the clueless meatball, who eventually seemed to get bored and just wander away.

Oh Gaga, look what you've done . . .

Beyond that chat I tried several times to have a follow-up talk with Starlight, but between her travels and sudden spells of silence, we never spoke on the record again. But perhaps even more valuable was getting to know her while we worked together on a showcase of experimental performances. I worked with the brilliant undiscovered actress Jocelyn McBride on a successful one-night-only stage adaptation of Valerie Solanas's *SCUM Manifesto*. After a cute crowd of downtown kids came to see Joce perform at the Gershwin Hotel, the venue's booker offered me more nights. Starlight and her brother Jason were slated to open for Gaga's Born This Way tour until it was abruptly canceled due to her hip injury. When they were suddenly left without a tour calendar we decided to jumpstart a performance series, one that ultimately ran only three times but exposed me to the enormous difficulties of producing anything related to nightlife.

The weight of organizing and launching our show was left to me, since Jason is based near Albany and Starlight spent so much time traveling for gigs. So after teaching my classes I would jump on a subway and go meet with douchebag managers at their venues, negotiating bar guarantees, time slots, lighting and sound setups, ticket prices—things that I knew nothing about. Despite feeling totally out of my comfort zone, I tried my best to negotiate deals that worked for everyone involved, but nearly always fell short.

Collaborating with a beloved and extremely knowledgeable scene queen became one of my favorite night lessons. Still, I could see that her easy laughter seemed to mask a certain sadness, the mark of someone who had weathered a panic attack or two in her day. Her proximity to one of the world's most famous people was a source of pride but also seemed to weigh on her. Starlight was deeply preoccupied with her figure and resented fans' criticisms. And yet she's one of those people whose looks were always totally on point and careful mannerisms almost regal.

After our final showcase, I saw Starlight only once more: a quick catch-up outside Jerome's when we both happened to be wearing glitter eye shadow. Starlight looked flawless as usual but anxious to flee New York and settle in Germany. There her radiance would shine on British electronic musician Surgeon, playing their zany noise shows together around Europe. It proved impossible for me to reach her afterward, for reasons unknown to me.

During my Spill the Tea time, some students often wanted to know what I would ask Gaga if I could pose a single question. Originally my main curiosity was about whether or not she understood what she unleashed: the meatball clinging to Starlight; the gay boys flirting with Darian and Breedlove just to reach The Lady; the hordes of uppity wannabes for whom fame became a new hypermodern religion, who applauded Gaga's mantras about love and art but could actually be unbelievably shady toward each other.

But knowing how savvy Gaga is I realized that the better question is *how* she makes sense of what she unleashed. How did Chairman Mao feel when his fanatical Red Guards stormed the Chinese countryside? What sensations surged through Evita Perón when she stood on the balcony of the Casa Rosada, the chanting of her name echoing throughout the Plaza de Mayo?

It seems so silly that bits of a Gaga single during some reality show credits pushed me onto a downtown detour, far from pursuing a bland academic life. But despite moments of inconsistency, there's a valuable sociological component in her pop project: a promise of identity that's free, ambitious, exploratory, and endlessly renewable. As one of her manifestos declared, "We are nothing without our image. Without our projection. Without the spiritual hologram of who we perceive ourselves to be, or rather to become, in the future." The premise is simple. Instead of a Quixotic search for a version of your self that is unmistakably the authentic *you*, feel free to reshape your persona, transform as theatrically as you wish, tinkering with and exploring the boundaries of your persona. There is no holy grail of identity, guarded in some cave deep within your psyche. My own story speaks to the transformative power of this essential message.

Consider the most explicit statement of her premise, articulated in the first part of the so-called "Prelude Pathetique" of Gaga's "Marry the Night" video, a mysterious, stylized allegory of her break with Island Def Jam:

When I look back on my life, it's not that I don't want to see things exactly as they happened. It's just that I prefer to remember them in an artistic way. And truthfully the lie of it all is much more honest because I invented it.

Classic Gagaspeak about self-manufactured truths, deftly peddling a view of identity as infinitely revisable. But it's also remarkably like the world of *1984*, where the Ministry of Truth continually adjusts records of the past to suit the preferred reality of Big Brother, totally in line with Mother Monster's defense of reality's malleability. It's an attitude that Gaga used to catapult from grungy bars to the most A-list red carpets in the world. She crafted a mythos, cultivated allies in a variety of sectors old and new, and tossed inconvenient truths and people into a memory hole.

Aside from our brief moment at Harvard, I have never met Gaga. A contact in her management team once tried to arrange a meeting at the New Museum, but she was apparently delayed by another appointment. Another time I was told that she would stop by one of my performance showcase nights with Starlight, something that also didn't happen.

I'm still a fan, although we probably won't ever meet if she reads these pages. But it's the simple truth that I finished writing them with her album *Joanne* in my ears. Before its release I was skeptical. Invoking one of Pepper LaBeija's scenes from *Paris Is Burning*, I joked on Twitter that I was watching Gaga becoming a country singer right before my very eyes. Tinged with hints of Johnny Cash, Billy Joel, Sheryl Crow, and even Ace of Base, the only traces of Lower East Side Gaga in the honky-tonk record are a nod to Fulton Street and a call to "let's funk downtown."

Joanne made me think of my own father, who handed me a Simon and Garfunkel CD when I was a kid. But I listened to her voice— slightly raspy in her deep register, sometimes soft, always packing a big punch—and I was sold. When she shrieks or belts, I would get the same goose bumps as 2009. I have to hand it to her: from the pop-dance club queen to the high-concept performance artist to the jazzy old-school chanteuse—and now a bit of a Middle America country turn—no one else has modeled the malleability of identity in such a colossal and beautiful way.

But the promise that Jack Halberstam and others initially saw in a Gaga feminist revolution has largely faded. On the night of the 2016 presidential election, a tearful Gaga was totally in shock, staging an impromptu "protest" of the Trump victory by climbing onto a garbage truck in front of his Tower with a LOVE TRUMPS HATE sign. Surely the Haus of Gaga was already planning extravagant *Joanne*-meets-Jackie-O gowns for a Clinton inaugural ball. But in the practical reality of the brutal election, a politics gone gaga proved brittle, just like Margaret's old movements and the Chiapas rebellion. It was merely the exhaust from the sputtering motor of a megawatt Mother Monster machine born in a downtown of perfect delusions.

No genuine, lasting social progress will emerge from this or from more of her foundation's conferences, private benefits for the wealthiest among us, and endless hashtagging about kindness, love, and bravery. But protests and paparazzi, lace and lyrics, club kid wigs and campaign rally gigs, they all mesh together in Gaga's wild fame game.

It's said that Alexander the Great wept once there were no more lands left for him to conquer. Some researchers argue something rather different: after learning that there are infinite worlds in our universe, the Macedonian king who became pharaoh of Egypt and lord of Asia grew frustrated that it was so very difficult to finish conquering just one planet. Either version could apply to Stefani Germanotta.

After strutting through downtown scenes, then stomping through the music business, she turned her eye toward Hollywood, already grabbing a Golden Globe in a classic glamour look far removed from the days of meat dresses and teal hair. Appropriately, her debut in a leading role will be Bradley Cooper's rehash of *A Star Is*

Born, aligning the silver screen with her way Up There ambitions. As Gaga the Great continues her Warholian romp through our culture, I wonder who or what she'll toss into the memory hole next, and which new versions of herself she'll conjure for us. But if she does cry like Alexander, she'll save the tears for the stage.

2

UP THERE

Before the age of swiping and tapping, smashed screens and duckface selfies, we humans used plastic telephones wired into a corner of our homes. A loud ring filled your house, interrupting whatever you were doing, and then a scramble to answer. "I'll get iiit!" "Tell them I'm not home!" "*MAH-AHHHM*, it's for you!" And if you're a gossipy gabber like me, growing up you became accustomed to angry door knocks demanding that you get off the phone so someone else could use it. May these routine domestic screeches of postwar modernity rest in peace.

I hate telling my students this but I'm even old enough to remember my family owning a rotary phone. How clearly I remember our mustard-yellow model near the kitchen, and watching adults operate it so expertly. I must sound so ancient now, and you may suspect that these pages will end with me wrapped in a cozy shawl, playing pinochle with other retirees at Shady Pines, reminiscing about the obsolete machines of the past.

They won't end like that, but I do remember all the buzz attached to the advent of caller ID, which meant that we now had some clue about who was on the other end of that ringing line, a needed filter for social intrusions. I didn't have caller ID back in 1998, so when the phone rang on a school holiday, I was totally unprepared for the gravelly voice on the other end of the line.

"Victor, this is Monsignor O'Keefe."

My high school principal was snarling at me—he loved to talk with his teeth clenched—summoning me to his office, even on a holiday. I could picture the nostrils of his huge nose flaring as he gripped his phone. Proudly Irish, he was no doubt beet red too. *"Is something wrong?"* replied the coy little queen in me. "Victor, you KNOW what's wrong," he growled.

I definitely knew. That morning the regional newspaper had published a letter to the editor written by me. In the letter I criticized the pope's decision to beatify—bring closer to sainthood—our high school's namesake, the Croatian cardinal Aloysius Stepinac. I argued that he had actually collaborated with fascist puppets in Nazi-controlled Croatia, blessing and helping a pro-Hitler government responsible for monstrous atrocities. My school had been founded during the height of the Cold War by a fiercely conservative New York archbishop, so Stepinac's complicity was swept under the rug, tossed into a memory hole. Since the postwar Communist Tito government had jailed Cardinal Stepinac, the Vatican was trying to revise the past so that a friend to fascists was now proudly celebrated as a freedom fighter.

When I arrived at O'Keefe's office, his secretary somberly told me to wait a few moments. She always seemed rather browbeaten by him, a vain and hyper-ambitious member of a celibate tribe of bureaucrats who oversee rituals, budgets, and horny adolescent boys eager for father figures and guidance. I felt badly for her, especially since my own mother was a secretary at a Catholic school, working under a similarly pompous, petty, and domineering deacon.

The meeting in O'Keefe's ornate office began with dire pronouncements and grand accusations tossed at me. I had apparently shamed the school and myself. He reported that his phone had been ringing off the hook with calls from angry alumni demanding my heretical head on a platter. But I held my ground—clenching my fists so my hands wouldn't shake—arguing that I used my rights to free speech and offered reasonable points to support my case.

Gradually, I talked O'Keefe down and by the end he even muttered something about respecting me. I'm usually steady on my feet in high adrenaline moments but his mellowing had more to do with the feeble bravado of a bully, one accustomed to unearned deference. That day he learned that I wouldn't cower like his secretary or the doting pseudo-sons he "mentored," just as I learned that authority could tremble, including very minor figures who represented the divine authority of the world's oldest organization.

I left slightly shaken, yes, but determined. The next day of class was extremely weird. I was suddenly known, *looked at differently*. Even the teachers seemed a bit scared of me. Emboldened, as editor of *The Crusader* school newspaper, I kept on fighting battles with O'Keefe, publishing articles about contract negotiations with the teachers' union and always making sure that articles included quotations from O'Keefe's faculty rivals.

In the midst of my war I found an adult ally, a person who saw value in an extremely nerdy but brazen kid. Jeannie Stapleton-Smith was the kind of person whose intense personal energy could easily overwhelm you, but whose knowledge and boldness would impress you right away. Her son Andrew was a year behind me in high school and ultimately succeeded me as *Crusader* editor. Her older son Timmy, whom I never met, died of leukemia while at Stepinac and it clearly marked Jeannie, as it would any mother. But it also fanned a rebellious fire in her, one that mixed a fiercely feminist liberation theology into her staunch Irish Catholicism.

For a while Jeannie had been the school's development director until O'Keefe's cronies realized that she was no docile church lady fussing over bake sales. Jeannie was an independent thinker and savvy leader—respectful of the church hierarchy but no boot-licker—and so they shoved her out. In me she maybe saw someone else willing to stir up trouble, but one in need of guidance and maturity. I don't know if I could have endured four years at that school were it not for my chats and emails with a brave mentor like Jeannie, who died in February 2017. (In 2016, New York's archbishop removed O'Keefe from the ministry after allegations of pre-Stepinac pedophilia emerged.)

On the home front, I battled constantly with my mom, who fretted that I'd get thrown out of school for my troublemaking or never get into a decent college. I think that my dad knew how pointless it was to really fight me on the big things I wanted to do. At this point we were also in the middle of a years-long effort to become naturalized as American citizens. My mom anxiously believed that somehow the federal government would get wind of my picketing outside a nuclear power plant or my zealous pro-union editorials and toss the whole lot of us back to Mexico.

Anxious to break free of suburbia, I drove my friends crazy with my uppity rants and long-winded questions in class, although a few teachers encouraged me to rage on. While focused mostly on my silly protests with Margaret and my editorial rabble-rousing at school, I developed a deep, consuming crush on one classmate in particular, a fixation that gnawed my teenage mind as it went totally unfulfilled. He was the typically cocky, blue-eyed, all-American jock who played on varsity teams but for some reason liked talking to me about politics, music, and sex. Watching him play basketball shirtless during gym class was the height of ecstatic agony. This was the great heyday of AOL's Instant Messenger and I would spend hours chatting with him about basically anything he wanted. I seemed to be an easy respite from his sweaty dude world of sports, beer, and girls. We never really flirted or fooled around but every now and then, he would give me a ride home. For those ten minutes, sitting in the passenger seat next to him, listening to his music, I was the happiest boy in Westchester County.

Given my weak attempts to pass for straight, I was bullied by two truly awful kids that I grew to hate intensely. They even wanted to ham it up and made sure they had *everyone's* attention before initiating their torment of me. If you have experienced something similar, you might recognize that small but biting pain in your stomach each weekday morning before school. It started from the moment you woke up and increased as you approached campus. As you got closer you wished you didn't have to go, or you prayed that the people who loved humiliating you would be out sick that day or that overnight they had decided to move to some other town. On the worst days, you wished that they had choked on their cereal that morning or had been randomly abducted. Anything to make those awful moments stop.

And so I vividly remember being in homeroom on the second floor of the school as students drifted in. It sounds so stupidly melodramatic but I would actually lean on the windowsill and stare out at a road that fed into I-95, which could eventually deposit you in Manhattan. I'd watch the commuters' southbound cars and wish that they would somehow take me with them, whisk me away for a single day, an afternoon even. Years later, I would read James St. James's *Disco Bloodbath* describe a similar moment that he and Michael Alig must have had in school, projecting their youthful energy at their fabulous future New York selves.

But back then I didn't fantasize about downtown velvet ropes or being Up There. I just needed to be away—away from the boy I loved who didn't love me back, away from the ones that told everyone I was a faggot or a pussy, away from O'Keefe and his lackeys, away from parents who didn't understand me, away from everything. To paraphrase Dr. Hannibal Lecter, who understood illicit hunger and endless captivity, I could only dream of *getting out, getting anywhere, getting all the way to The NYC.*

To be quite honest, I don't think that I ever fully shed the pain of those years. Maybe no one can really erase the scars left by the high school mean girls who tell us we can't sit with them. But it would lead me to empathize with a man who maybe felt a little of what I felt growing up. Though insecure and shy, he fought convention and authority, making it all the way to The NYC and reshaping it as his silver kingdom.

"Is there really anything more to say on the subject of Andy Warhol?" This is how Grace Glueck begins her *New York Times* review of Bob Colacello's extremely juicy *Holy Terror* memoir way back in 1990. Imagine what she would say almost three decades later, when every single season there's a new exhibition, book, product, or film devoted to Warhol and his work. Even for someone like me who follows the petty intrigues of the scenes he left behind, this endless river of Warholia is truly impressive.

Calling him the "Great Posthumous Presence," in 2003 *Factory Made* author Steven Watson wrote, "It is as if Andy Warhol never went away. He was simply transformed into a tote bag, or a gender studies dissertation, or a reality TV show, or a thirty-seven-cent postage stamp." And it won't stop anytime soon. The Metropolitan Museum staged a highly criticized Warhol survey show in 2012, while the Whitney Museum is also planning a large retrospective in November 2018. And in 2016 it was announced that Jared Leto would star as Warhol himself in a film based on Victor Bockris's controversial biography.

Rebellion has its fruits, a lesson that Warhol learned decades before I did in O'Keefe's office. Despite an appalling lack of social graces, somehow this gangly, pale, and queer son of immigrants became one of history's most revolutionary artists, resisting the stale norms of both the art world and mainstream society. After his death in 1987 he left behind what's essentially his own art market, a massive body of paintings, portraits, lithographs, and drawings still being licensed and sold, not to mention the films that are in the process of being restored, digitized, and screened.

Warhol's Pop brand of downtown cool remains the lifeblood of New York swagger, from Kanye to Koons. Seeing Warhol's unmistakable imprint on our culture, some in downtown passionately detest him, seeing him as a thief, an unoriginal appropriator, or a manipulative, money-hungry corruptor of art. But even the haters must admit that Warhol was a man so prolific that decades after his death researchers are still hard at work on his incomplete catalogues raisonnés. His Pop portraits adorn the walls of financiers' townhouses and corporate boardrooms in the planet's great cities. Melding highbrow and lowbrow in a way that few have, the intensely insecure "swishy" man became, according to Arthur Danto, "artist laureate of the American soul." He left behind a global market of his works valued in the hundreds of millions, once presided over by a now disbanded Art Authentication Board.

The institutional legacy of Warholia lives on as well. His magazine *Interview* endures as a staple of New York's elite culture, spotlighting the great stars of the day, although now focused much more on celebrity culture to the exclusion of uptown high society. The Foundation for the Visual Arts bequeathed by Warhol's will remains a powerful entity, responsible for funding projects and research around the country. The Museum in his native Pittsburgh acts as a kind of keeper of the keys, housing archival pieces like his famous Time Capsules, a comprehensive collection of his works, and a staff of devoted experts and curators.

Warhol is also a reference point for downtown's creative classes, a way to establish common cause, an immediate synaptic firing that conjures images of fame hunger, fey mannerisms, urban chic, gorgeous friends, and fabulous parties. If *Sex and the City* is sometimes credited (or blamed, depending on your point of view) for unleashing an army of wannabe Carrie Bradshaws, then certainly Warhol too birthed an original strain of style south of Twenty-third Street. The shades, the leather jacket, the striped shirt, the skinny jeans, the boots, the slouch, the infinite documentation of everything can be traced back to him. As the art critic Jerry Saltz tweeted on the twenty-ninth anniversary of Warhol's death: "Andy is in the air we breathe; he is revolutionary because he changed the way the world looks and the way we look at the world."

Back in high school in Saganaw, Michigan, James St. James read Warhol's *POPism*, which he said changed his life. "You were reading it and you just kept thinking to yourself: there's a place for me out there. There are people who are like me and I'm not so alone," he told me. "So my goal was to come to New York and become a Warhol Superstar." Well-versed in celebrity culture and downtown stardom, James described the artist's unparalleled star wattage: "When he walked into the room every head swiveled. You got whiplash." Armed with his tape recorder and camera, Warhol became the center of attention as tipsy partygoers jostled for his attention. The key to Warhol's fame game? Few were able to straddle so many scenes and access so many different crowds.

Warhol's embrace of downtown outsiders like drag queens and trans performers blessed and upheld them as glamorous members of a new postmodern elite. Ex–club kid Kenny Kenny said, "People saw New York through the eyes of Andy. That's why New York was great for me." When Warhol died, the celebration of the misfit waned for a time. "We lost our mentor. We lost our guru." The Factory spirit would only return when Michael Alig's club kids attempted a restaging of the original Superstar scene. Kenny said, "[Michael] had created a place where the alternative people again had become the It people in New York."

F, my bad romance, was a devoted Warholite, one of those boys whose own style was obviously glommed off the original silver specter. This was a natural bridge to F being a huge fan of Gaga, who initially seemed to give musical expression to the Warholian aesthetic. Like the artist himself, F was "swishy" in his gestures, obsessed with the link between the visual and the abysmal, preoccupied by money, and raised near a big city by a doting Catholic mother. Seeing himself as a documenter of all things, including himself, F very consciously reperformed several Warhol photographs, like the photo booth head-cocked-to-the-side poses or the *Blowjob* film. He even interned at *Interview* for a while, relishing the sight of his name on the masthead and the office gossip he overheard. At sweltering gallery openings F and I met old Factory veterans, both of us thrilled by the shrinking of our degrees of separation from the long-gone Pop pope himself.

Like me, F went to a suburban Catholic high school, where he too was viciously bullied. Obsessed with Tim Burton's 1992 film *Batman Returns*, we bonded over our shared affinity for Michelle Pfeiffer's Catwoman, a defiant woman who is betrayed and killed repeatedly but nonetheless endures, ferociously defending her independence and identity. The high school abuse contributed to F later being flamboyantly open and effusive about his sexuality. Clearly overcompensating for his past torments, he wrapped up his twenty-something identity in gayness, policing the behavior of straight people when they would use words like "partner," which he defended as solely the province of queers.

Though hungry for the fame craved by Warhol and his devotees past and present, F was unwilling to really hustle for it. He wanted the pleasantries of a plush pop life but shied away from the schmoozing and quid pro quo finagling that it requires. Like Warhol, dealing with people and managing their competing interests could be too exhausting. F was like so many other basic young gays in the social media age: the online performance of a queer fabulousness was a lavish ordeal, while their real-life personas were often mousey and small.

The egos of today's gays often prefer worlds that are solely of their social type, afraid to truly mix it up like the Factory stars did. The self-segregation clashes with the cultural polyglots that Warhol needed to consolidate his empire. As former *Interview* editor Bob Colacello told me, "Andy loved to have a little entourage wherever he went, and so if you were working late, he would say, 'You want to come with me to this party or dinner?' and I think after a couple of times he saw that I could pretty much talk with anyone."

The aesthetic sensibility that Warhol bequeathed to young gay boys like F was easy; the hard part was the toughness, the will that let Warhol survive heartache, rejection, profound social insecurity, and a point-blank gunshot. The unevenness was by no means limited to F. I saw it in other young Warholites, the obsessed devotees of Michael Alig's club kids, the Gaga fans that scream YAS KWEEN! or the moody goth kids at The Box on Friday nights. The perfect delusions of fame, the yearning to be Up There was as intense among them as I imagine them being among the kids of yesteryear who yearned to make it into Studio 54 or the backroom at Max's Kansas City. If the cute and angsty youth of Jean-Luc Godard's Paris were the children of Marx and Coca-Cola, we in New York, hungry for glorious glamour and infinite attention, are very much the children of Warhol and Red Bull. *We learned it from watching him.*

F was in many ways the antithesis of that cocky jock I loved in high school. But there was something so enthralling about him, always smelling like leather and cigarettes, with eyes that had a little glint to them, like a cartoon character. We went to plenty of openings and parties together, drank way too much in East Village bars, and attended a truly fabulous Meatpacking District party that doled out tons of grade-A swag while Calvin Klein, Christopher Makos, and Lorenzo Martone milled around. When we visited Rob Pruitt's silver Warhol statue in Union Square at four in the morning, F promptly climbed it. At that point I was only beginning my physical and sartorial reboot. I had begun adding some muscle to my frame and fixing my skin problem but was still essentially that sad little man desperate to get into Ladyland.

Things changed one night in 2011 outside Jerome's, the day that the Gaga gang filmed their very Warholian promo for her appearance on MTV's Video Music Awards. We were watching Justin Tranter and Darian Darling strut into the packed bar when F put his head on my shoulder. I realized at that moment that I felt much more for him than just friendship. A couple of months later, we went to an exhibition that he was reviewing, although any moment not spent looking at the art I spent staring at him. Afterward we ended up at a Hell's Kitchen bar, where several drinks paved the way to the kiss that I had wanted for so long.

When I spilled my guts, telling him how much I liked him, he flipped out. F assumed that I first reached out to him because I wanted to fuck him, not because I genuinely respected his writing. We bickered on a dark Hell's Kitchen corner at one in the morning, putting on a totally ridiculous show for passersby. After going back inside the bar we were promptly asked to leave. Eventually we both calmed down and I took him to Thirty-fourth Street so he could catch a train home. We stood outside the Tick Tock Diner making out, hoping not to get bashed by drunk bros stumbling toward Penn Station. As I made my way home I stupidly thought that a real relationship with someone I deeply loved was about to start. I was wrong. By the time I saw him again, F had changed his mind about wanting anything more from me than a friendship.

I loved him in an adult way, I think, beyond infatuation. Our snarky sensibilities seemed to mesh so well, our reactions to people and places so much in sync. I felt understood by him. I knew his flaws and wanted to share mine with him. But to love someone with all your heart and discover that nothing you can ever do will make you good enough for them, well, that feeling damaged me in a deep way. I did what anyone else might have done. I curled up on my bed for a long cry, until my best friend Talal told me to cut it out so we could go out for a drink.

What followed were years of distance and rapprochements with F, a cycle that we both accepted as the tedious dysfunction of our relationship. It took me a long while to really get over him. My night outings offered the best therapy, alongside Talal's infinite patience while putting up with way too many sad laments about F. But the more I dove into downtown's games, the less wounded I felt. Aside from dealing with F, I was also reckoning with my own sexuality and feelings, something that I don't think Warhol ever fully did. His inability to make sense of his own desires meant that he died alone and frustrated, although really Up There.

Why were F and I so intensely drawn to Warhol? His works—bright and colorful Marilyns, Liz Taylors, electric chairs, flowers, car crashes, consumer products—definitely captivated us. But the most important element of Warhol's fame game was the social aura that he created, something that F and I would never experience in vivo. Images of the Factory conjured for us a sense of exclusivity, glamour, and a kind of outré fabulousness, filled with beautiful women emulating Hollywood stars, moody proto hipsters like Gerard Malanga, or hotties like Joe Dallesandro and Eric Emerson breaking male and female hearts alike.

Alongside F, M, and my oldest downtown pal, Thomas Kiedrowksi, author of *Andy Warhol's New York City*, we met some of these remnants of Warholia. As we studied and befriended a cult that fascinated us years before we even met each other, the pathos of his world gradually made more sense. F and I were Catholic, like the majority of the people discussed in these pages. As Bob Colacello observed, "There *was* something Catholic, something cabalistic and cultish, about the Factory and its Pope. Something, perhaps, that only those brought up in that magnificent, mysterious, and sometimes sick faith can really experience."

For a while, this cult would assemble on Warhol's August 6 birthday at the Flatiron District's Gershwin Hotel, becoming reunions for Factory veterans like Bibbe Hansen, Ivy Nicholson, and the late Billy Name, Taylor Mead and Ultra Violet. True to her disco name, Ultra would still wear her purple garments and accessories. Mead, a rather vaudevillian Factory jester, was hobbled by age but still managed to display his famously sly grin and fanciful twist of the hand. Warhol's friends were no longer just images or stories in books but living, breathing people that my friends and I got to know better, warts and all.

Some accuse Warhol of treating his friends like Kleenex: use and toss. But maybe Warhol's most complex relationships had impacts on him that he couldn't fully process. And although F might think that I flung him down a memory hole, he left a mark on me that was very hard to erase. During the summer of 2016 we briefly reconnected over vodka sodas at the Stonewall. I had to meet another friend in Brooklyn, so my time with F was limited. As we were getting up to leave, a song that I hadn't heard before blasted through the Stonewall's back room. Like "Bad Romance," all it took was a few seconds for the earworm to burrow its way into my brain. The song was Feder's "Goodbye," with Anne-Lyse Blanc singing about leaving someone you love far behind. F waited for the bartender to close out his tab. Standing behind him I almost leaned over and put my head on his shoulder but stopped. My fave new song pounding through the speakers suggested that I do otherwise.

Warhol was among the first artists to uphold a kind of lifestyle as art that is now firmly ingrained in us during the age of Instagram filters and Snapchat stories. Before Warhol, artists of renown like Pablo Picasso and Jackson Pollock were hallowed names in the art world, but few outside the elites could probably identify their faces in a crowd. Warhol morphed into more than a successful aesthete, becoming an emblem to adorn bags, mugs, and other overpriced museum tchotchkes. Himself a stargazer who fussed over stars ranging from Truman Capote to Marilyn Monroe, Warhol knew the substance of the shining iconicity he was pursuing.

His reach extends to the actual bodies of our common idols. Old Gaga pal Brendan Jay Sullivan recalled a moment of deep career flux for her while working for Interscope but not yet signed with the label. He recalled, "She told me she wanted to go and start over and get a nose job and be pretty and be a pop star. And the only way I could talk her out of it was I told her she needed to go to the Met and see this Warhol painting. It's called *Before and After*. And it's the image of a rhinoplasty. From then on I never heard anything else about cosmetic surgery and I heard only things about Warhol. I think maybe she connected to him in a new way."

Warhol's obsession with the surface appearance of things—the link between image and identity—was complicated. A Factory figure like the late Ultra Violet squeezed every last drop of fame from her proximity to Warhol, although her memoir offered a somber verdict: "This was a man who believed in nothing and had emotional involvements with no one, who was driven to find his identity in the mirror of the press, then came to believe that reality existed only in what was recorded, photographed, or transcribed." Through this fixation, he became the font of an aesthetic sensibility still coursing through our cultural sinews.

Warhol gave his coterie a downtown space where the likeminded fame monsters could dream big dreams of being Up There. As Jonas Mekas told Stephen Koch, "Andy admired all the stars, so to please all those sad desperate souls that came into the Factory, Andy called them 'Superstars.'" The disco names of Warhol's claqueurs became sexy sobriquets for the sidewalks that became their stages. He sanctified their unabashed hunger for fame. It became art.

And so the Factory's output was personas as well as paintings, a social scene alongside silk screens. The creation of his micro-star system evolved with Warhol always as the center of gravity. He fed their ambitions while they nurtured his aura. As René Ricard declared in the Jean Stein collection about Warhol's greatest Factory star, "Edie [Sedgwick] brought Andy out. She turned him on to the real world. He'd been in the demimonde. He was an *arriviste*. And Edie legitimized him, didn't she? He never went to those parties before she took him. He'd be the first to admit it."

While Steve Watson, Stephen Koch, Victor Bockris, and others have thoroughly researched the Superstars' lives, my goal here is to understand their place in downtown mythmaking. Joe Dallesandro biographer Michael Ferguson offered an apt summary:

> Andy Warhol was bestowing delusions of grandeur. His Superstars were a camp celebration of America's surrogate royalty, its Cult of Celebrity—which was infinitesimal compared to the grotesque worship we see today. Who was to say that his down-and-dirty, glam-trashy stars weren't precisely what he called them and no less worthy of their titles in superlative than those endowed by Hollywood?

Claiming the title of "superstar" meant calling themselves now what they hoped to become in the future, a mantra later amplified by Gaga's maxim about "the spiritual hologram of who we perceive ourselves to be." Club kid king Michael Alig understood the power of this preemptive performance when he crowned his boyfriend Keoki a "Superstar DJ." As Keoki told me, "Michael was like, 'You should call yourself Superstar DJ.' And I thought, 'Well that's kind of weird.' He was like, 'Why not? You just gotta say it and it'll be true.'"

The key to understanding the power of Warhol's downtown brand is this entourage of people feeding off his aura and in turn imbuing his public persona with their spark. Attentive to the heavenly stars' impact on us, ex–club kid Sophia Lamar observed, "[Warhol] was Leo. Sometimes in Leo with that personality [they] create that kingdom where they are king because outside that kingdom they are nobody. So he was a very talented and creative artist. And he created that kingdom, that small kingdom, where he manipulated people and played with them."

Today there's sometimes debate as to who really qualifies as a Warhol Superstar, a term whose origin Steven Watson locates around 1965, mainly in the Cinemaroc work of filmmaker Jack Smith, from whom Warhol also "borrowed" a great deal. In *Edie: American Girl*,

René Ricard claimed that the term was invented by Factory figure Chuck Wein and noted that he had only come upon the term once before in a 1930s fan magazine. However the moniker emerged, it reflected the crew's clear emulation of Hollywood stars like Marilyn Monroe, Liz Taylor, Lana Turner, Kim Novak, Hedy Lamarr, and others. It was both a reperformance of these American icons and a staging of what they wished to be: to break out of downtown and become true household names living luxe lives.

A popular listing exists on warholstars.org, a valuable resource for fans, scholars, and journalists. The site is run by Gary Comenas, an independent researcher in London who has meticulously documented key aspects of Warholia. Although his site lists three-dozen stars, here I mainly refer to the ones who haven't fallen down the memory hole and are still widely known and referenced in downtown New York today. Some of the most fabulous Factory stars, like Mary Woronov, International Velvet, and Viva, are no longer on the East Coast.

Warhol selected, but sometimes the Superstars recruited. The late Holly Woodlawn's anointing started when her pals Jackie Curtis and Candy Darling appeared in *Flesh* and invited her to a Factory party at 33 Union Square West to be presented to their hero patron. "He'll make us the three goddesses of the screen," they promised. When Holly and I spoke about this, she was adamant about her reluctance to be absorbed into a scene with which she'll forever be associated. She told me, "I never wanted to be [a Superstar], believe it or not, I did not want to be." At the party she remembered spotting Warhol wearing "the cheapest white yak hair wig I have ever seen in my life." He walked over. "You're so glamorous," Warhol declared. "I thought he was out of his mind," she sniffed.

There were really two generations of Superstars: a first group tied mainly to the Silver Factory and a subsequent cohort. Eventually both waves faded in lieu of a technocratic clique of male "kids" sporting suits instead of sequins.

The mostly male "kids" supervised the Factory's mutation into a corporation, thereby achieving the professionalization of Pop. As Pat Hackett wrote in her introduction to *The Andy Warhol Diaries*, when the Factory moved to 860 Broadway in 1974, Warhol asked the receptionists to stop answering the phone with the "too corny" Factory name. Their headquarters became known only as "the office." What was arguably the most famous artist's studio in the world was converted into Andy Warhol Enterprises, Inc. Some of the old Superstars still hung around but were no longer Warhol's close coterie. As Brigid Berlin told *Interview* in 1989, "It has become more of a business over the years—but there still is that sense of *family*."

One of the new "kids," Bob Colacello, made a clear distinction between the previous cohorts of "street kids," "speed freaks," or "disaffected heiresses" and his new group. He also recognized their resentment, telling me, "They all would be like very wary of us and [thinking] 'Who are these, kind of, suburban kids who went to Georgetown?'"

Premier downtown DJ Johnny Dynell has spun at the biggest clubs around and, alongside his partner Chi Chi Valenti, is responsible for the legendary Jackie 60 party. Moving down to the city from upstate New York, he soon met Warhol assistant Ronnie Cutrone, who took him to the Union Square Factory. "The first day there Andy did a drawing on my chest," Johnny remembered. "He drew like these pussies on my chest with a marker." But revenue was the name of the main game. "I remember thinking how business-like it was. It was all about advertisers," he said. Johnny would be invited to Factory lunches as "eye-candy," he admitted, but also befriended studio overseers like Paige Powell. Johnny's Jackie 60 party would later pay homage to Ronnie Cutrone and Gerard Malanga as "the first go-go boys in the world, ever," back when they were part of Warhol's Exploding Plastic Inevitable.

The new technocratic Factory regime was clear, with Vincent Fremont overseeing day-to-day business concerns, especially the all-important question for the Boss: did the checks come in? In appearance, theatricality was out, tailoring was in. "We dressed more conservatively," Vincent told me. "There was a dress code. Not that it was official, it was following Fred [Hughes]." Since many of them were in their twenties, frequenting parties supplied with sugar bowls filled with cocaine, Warhol assumed a paternal role for the new inner circle, rather than just the promoter figure he was for the Superstars. Vincent told me, "Andy was very protective of his kids. We were considered kids. He was very protective of us."

With this ambitious and business-savvy team behind him, Warhol roped in royalty, socialites, and A-list actors for new projects, especially portraiture commissions. The gritty downtown cool that birthed the Warhol aura had become lavishly packaged for an elite uptown crowd.

How could this empire of the fabulous emerge when the contradiction between Warhol's person and his persona seemed so huge? As Bob Colacello's *Holy Terror* recounted: "Andy was innocent *and* decadent, primitive *and* sophisticated, shy *and* pushy, the eternal outsider at the center of a series of self-created In crowds." His social nexus depended on the power of the mix, a swirl of sexualities, genders, races, classes, tastes, and affinities. Wealthy heiresses like Brigid Berlin and Edie Sedgwick were as necessary for the Factory fame game as Dumpster divers like Jackie Curtis or juvenile delinquents like Bibbe Hansen. Fascinations with Old Hollywood, Far East mysticism, the Kennedys' Camelot, and the Space Age boiled together in their midnight stew.

And sometimes *what* came from *where* gets really confused. When Gaga created a mermaid alter ego named Yüyi, she appeared on stage in a wheelchair. An enraged Bette Midler tweeted Gaga, claiming the mermaid-wheelchair routine as part of her act since 1980. The problem is that the late underground actor Paul Ambrose, who collaborated a great deal with Factory playwright Jackie Curtis, saw Midler as having appropriated the look from his Superstar friends. As he claimed in *Superstar in a Housedress*, "Somewhere along the line—and I'm not saying there's anything wrong with this—Bette Midler saw Candy Darling in a mermaid outfit, and me in a wheelchair, and ended up on stage a year later in a wheelchair wearing a mermaid outfit."

To Bob Colacello, all this repetition, synthesis, and self-referencing might not be surprising. He pointed to Warhol's fascination with seriality: multiple soup cans, Marilyns, electric chairs, faces, cows, lips, shadows, over and over again. "It was never like 'one of,'" Bob explained. "He was constantly undermining this concept of the original." All of his inheritors have followed suit. It shouldn't surprise us when people see a mixing of Abstract Expressionist elements, Jack Smith, and Marcel Duchamp in Warhol. Or a blending of Warhol, Leigh Bowery, and Dada in Michael Alig's club kids, or a churning of Warhol, Alig, Bowery, Bowie, and Madonna in Gaga.

Warholia celebrated the glorious artifice of a malleable identity, eager to cast away notions of a monolithic self hiding somewhere deep inside us. This freedom to explore various identities or eschew the burden of a single "authentic" one—to occupy and live in the interstitial—was paramount. As Jackie Curtis declared in *Superstar in a Housedress*: "Candy [Darling] and Holly [Woodlawn] take female hormones and talk about having sex-change operations. That is not for me at all, because my body is my body, and my sex is my sex, and my ambiguity is my ambiguity. And I cling to that, fervently."

This same fervor was apparent on a Midtown Manhattan sidewalk when I had brunch with Holly and her manager Robert Coddington. Like her friend Jackie, throughout her career Holly celebrated ambiguity, defying gender labels and even language itself. Anyone who attended one of her events during her last years can recall the guttural noises, gurgles, and guffaws that replaced more than a few words of her sentences. Still, back in 2014, she was flamboyant yet relaxed in her wheelchair, cheerfully greeting our waiter with a "Bonjour!" and thanking him with a "Grazie!" During the meal I repeatedly burst out laughing at her sassy impressions, but was also slightly shocked at seeing her out of look. Dressed in the kind of dark suit and pale blue dress shirt that your dull uncle from the suburbs might wear, she ordered scrambled eggs with home fries and toast, an espresso, and a glass of Chardonnay. She was coquettish on that sunny morning, telling me, "You're cute but you're not . . . *wait till you see my boyfriend.*"

Holly went out west in 1990, joining fellow Superstars like Joe Dallesandro and Mary Woronov. She returned to New York over two decades later for a Baruch College show that was understood to be her final performance in the city. (Our conversation was her final New York interview.) At Baruch, when journalist Michael Musto asked about her preferred gender label, she made sure that her farewell show would be remembered. For the first time in forty years of performance, Holly pulled off her wig on stage and tossed it away, an elegant rejection of the encumbrance of gender markers and the great freedom that her ambiguous identity gave her.

It wasn't a planned moment. She simply felt exhausted by a lifetime of questions about being trans or doing drag or what label she preferred. Musto's insistence that she account for her identity became the last straw. Though feeling cornered by Musto, Holly had a choice: answer his way or the Superstar way. "And my way was, 'OK, you want tranny. *Boom. Here,*'" Holly explained, deciding to toss aside the blond wig. Her mood soured while she recalled the on-stage encounter: "Don't fuck with me, honey." She then pivoted back to her classic humor, rhetorically addressing the always snarky, has-been commentator. "Oh please, Michael, give me a break," she said. "Here, put this wig on. Let's see how you look in a blond."

Warhol's early Factory nickname of Drella spliced Dracula and Cinderella, blending pauper-to-princess fairy-tale glamour with a ghoulish aristocrat who sucked out his victims' vitality. It was a perfectly apt name, given Warhol's obsession with escaping poverty—leading to a hoarder complex—and his desire to slurp out of those around him what he lacked: beauty, confidence, refinement. Also fitting was the way that Mary Woronov's memoir labeled him: "He even looked like a vampire: white, empty, waiting to be filled, incapable of satisfaction. He was the white worm—always hungry, always cold, never still, always twisting."

Naming something implies the power to label, to designate a self. Members of Warhol's tribe saw his attempts to bestow a Factory moniker on them as an imposition of identity. Woronov resisted attempts by Warhol to call her "Mary Might," becoming "a name I instinctively fought and refused to answer to, knowing that somehow it was a plot to steal my soul." Just as Jesus Christ consorted with social dregs and upheld them when repentant, so did Warhol with his outcasts: blessing, reshaping, and rebranding them.

But so much has been written about how Warhol's conniving ways contributed to very dark consequences for those around him: the drug-related deaths of Edie Sedgwick, Jackie Curtis, and Eric Emerson, the disappearances of Ingrid Superstar and Danny Williams, the suicides of Freddie Herko and Andrea Feldman, and even the circumstances of Warhol's own death in 1987. What was Warhol's ultimate responsibility in all of this?

Warhol sometimes oversaw a process of consciously replacing players in his fame game. Once they had become too uppity, or rejected him in some way, down the memory hole they were thrown. Far from the shy innocent that Warhol worshippers elevate, he wielded a carrot and stick in a calculating Machiavellian way. Bob Colacello remembered Warhol as "cunning" and "manipulative" (while also speculating that he might have had Asperger syndrome). When word got out that Bob intended to publish a memoir, for example, Warhol had his lieutenant Fred Hughes call Bob's agent Mort Janklow and ask that Bob's book be dropped in exchange for representing Warhol's diaries.

Far from a magical downtown family, belonging at the Factory meant endless rivalry. Ultra's memoir, for example, described her battles with Viva, "As soon as I see her, I know that she will be my chief competitor for Superstardom. She has the same reaction, for we constantly upstage one another." According to Steven Watson, titles like "Queen of Underground Movies," "Girl of the Year," and "Miss Pop" were capriciously bestowed on whichever It Girl's name was emblazoned on Warhol's marquee at a given moment. Watson wrote, "In Warhol's version of stardom, beauty and glamour were inextricably linked with its demise." To uphold The Star, to put her on a silver pedestal, is to foresee and even wish to see her downfall. We all saw this impulse performed rather bloodily on a Radio City Music Hall stage in 2009.

Another example involved Ingrid von Schefflin, who was rechristened as Ingrid Superstar as part of a catty scheme to show Edie that she had been replaced as Warhol's supreme scene queen. René Ricard explained to Victor Bockris how the Warhol group found this young woman: "They had noticed: 'Doesn't this girl look like an ugly Edie? Let's really teach Edie a lesson. Let's make a movie with her and tell Edie she's the big new star.' They cut her hair like Edie's. They made her up like Edie.'" This plot reflected their sexy Superstar sadism, a clear kick in the gut to someone, an active way to signal that there was always a memory hole precariously nearby.

Like any hierarchy, loyalty was key in determining a liege's favorites. Bob explained that Warhol's preferred Superstars were Joe Dallesandro and Candy Darling. Fondly remembering Candy as "adorable and very vulnerable," Bob told me, "she never debanded. Holly Woodlawn and Jackie Curtis would get very angry and come to the Factory and scream [that] they were going to call Valerie Solanas and Andy would get terrified and go lock himself in the editing room with Joe Dallesandro standing guard."

For Holly, this may have been a reaction to working around Factory and show-biz people who manipulated and wrangled the Florida runaway turned underground film star. "And [people] thought, 'Oh, oh, we can use this person a little.' So I let them use me," she explained to me in between sips of her brunch Chardonnay. "And by letting them do that, I learned a lot."

"I never felt used," insisted make-up icon Jane Forth, who toured Europe as a Warhol film star and earned a Factory paycheck for office work. Possessing a natural savvy, she understood that there was a revolving door for Warhol's arm candy. She told me, "Your involvement with Andy could be short-lived so don't expect anything more than what it is, if you choose to get involved with him. I knew that there could be a time that your time was up." Instead of waiting to get tossed down a memory hole, she chose to step back: "I didn't want to be one of the angry, used people. I had the control within myself not to be that."

Hers was a benign view far removed from others' accusations of a vampiric sadism, or the doting apologists who believe that he was just too emotionally fragile to be capable of real human destruction. Did he owe anyone a pass from oblivion? Warhol understood the problem of being blamed for the failures of his followers. In *POPism*, he wrote, "They had star quality but no star ego—they didn't know how to push themselves. They were too gifted to lead 'regular lives,' but they were also too unsure of themselves to ever become real professionals." Someone like Warhol orbiter and ballet dancer Freddie Herko did push himself—or rather dance himself—out through a window, a flamboyant finale to grand ambitions fueled by amphetamines and access to Warhol.

The male Factory "kids" would all bicker among themselves too, the alpha impulses of artsy nerds emerging for the voyeuristic enjoyment of their Boss. Enmity lingers today. At Lincoln Center, M and I once heard Paul Morrissey spit out the most vicious denunciations of Warhol, claiming that he is credited for work that is largely Morrissey's. Despite profiting financially from his Factory work, the bitter venom of this withered curmudgeon was rare even by downtown standards, where whispers of jealousy and resentment at a party can be found as easily as a bump of coke. Not even Morrissey's old protégé backed him up. As Joe Dallesandro told me, "But back in the day, it was all about that, 'You have to think of it as an art film, Joe, because these movies will be shown in museums forever and ever because it's Andy Warhol.' [For Paul] to go and make this extreme switch to not want have anything [to do with Warhol] is completely opposite of what it was all about when we were doing them."

Warhol and Morrissey, Joe's patrons, worked to maintain a grip on their heart throb film star and actively tried to close doors, the very opposite of what mentors should do. "Well, they said stupid things about me back then. Paul was into telling people that he didn't believe I could do a script," Joe recalled. "And Andy would say stupid shit like, 'I think he's a drug addict.' That's not the best thing to say . . . And then they go around telling people they're very supportive of me finding new work. That wasn't the truth." Some earnestness, some feeling peeked through Joe's raspy voice, feeling the bite of things that famous men said to hold him back. "And Paul was my mentor. I trusted in him a great deal . . . We're not *good* friends but we're friends to this day."

During Holly Woodlawn's Baruch show, Morrissey was her other on-stage interlocutor, alongside Musto. They had previously agreed to just say "AW" when touching on the silver specter hovering in that auditorium. Gradually, she persuaded Morrissey to relent in his petty attitudes toward a past from which he benefitted. She recalled, "And then little by little, I said, 'It's Andy, you know. You got your twenty-six million out of it. What do you care?'" He agreed. If anyone should be upset, it should have been her. *Trash* made millions. Holly got $125.

I have nicknames and monikers for most friends and several colleagues. When I spent a year in Mexico after college it turned out that my grandfather had the exact penchant. So it's genetic, I suppose. These days I usually introduce myself as *Vic*, but most people still say *Victor*. F called me simply *V*, while *Vicky* was somehow settled upon by a few, including Jacquie, the custodial staff member on my NYU office floor. Many downtown personas adopt a disco name as a way to shed their previous self and inhabit a new identity, although plenty, like Michael Alig and Susanne Bartsch, just use their birth name.

I loved the fact that the man who made the Silver Factory silver took as his disco name simply *Name*, a poke-in-the eye to the whole reinvention convention, to the human need to point, designate, and label. I needed to meet him, so I hopped on New York's suburban commuter line and rode it all the way up the Hudson River to its terminus in Poughkeepsie. The ride is absolutely gorgeous and I really suggest you do it sometime. While I basically grew up on another train line that ran from Westchester into Manhattan, I had taken the Hudson Line only once before—to meet with two West Point officers way back during my military research days.

When I got out of the cab I saw a shabby gray house with a dark enclosed porch and unkempt yard. Frankly, it didn't look lived in. Did I get the wrong address? I started to look through the notes on my phone when a head popped out of a second floor window. There was Billy Name (Linich), wearing big shades, over the years his hair displaced from on top of his head to a long scraggly mass on his chin. A big chunky ring on virtually every finger, he shook my hand and welcomed me into a tidy home filled with crystals, statuettes, and objects revealing that his interest in accessing the mystical still endured.

He seemed weary, slowed by a stroke in 2010, and not especially eager to be interviewed. I would actually expect this after a lifetime of being asked about the space that he created and the Superstars he palled around with. Although Billy got a little impatient with my questions at times, I could tell that he was really trying to muster some passion about questions of creativity, community, and freedom.

Like so many others, including me, growing up Billy was bored by the stifling inhibitions of suburbia. Unlike me, he was popular, even becoming president of his senior class. "But it was all rote to me," he explained. "It was all filling out the roles like a movie script." He did come out during his final year of high school, reminding me that this was 1957, long before the pop celebration of queer culture that exists today. To be "gay" didn't even fully exist in the vernacular.

In the early 1960s, Billy found refuge in the magical realm of "the Village," a joyful little land centered on a noisy Washington Square Park crammed with guitars and bongo drums. Settling into dense Greenwich Village social networks, he fell in with a group of artists where he finally belonged. "All the people that you could hang around with were just like you," Billy said. "They were escaping from somewhere to New York and being new in New York and experiencing the freedom and just being thrilled with life."

He ran around with Nick Cernovich, Robert Heide, Ray Johnson, and La Monte Young, learning from them, attending happenings, collaborating on projects. Heide, a playwright, was one of the first Warhol pals I met, way back in 2010 at a Gershwin Hotel party. It was my peak Gandhi phase, about six months before the first Ladyland outing. I don't know which was shinier at the time: my wireframe glasses or my shaved dome. But what was true then and now is that Heide loves to chat about his camaraderie with Warhol and Edie. Billy remembered other, more carnal encounters with Heide. "Well, I always tease him about how he brought me up to his apartment one day to see his etchings and he ended up fucking me," Billy told me, bursting out laughing. "I mean, it was easy for me to be hoodwinked in my younger days because I was so naïve."

The collaborations, happenings, mentorships, and fucks with the likes of Heide all prepared Billy for a moment that seared him into downtown history: making Warhol's Factory silver. He said, "It was my favorite project, I think, because I started from a gray, ugly space and I built it into a beautiful crystal palace. It was this great Silver Factory and I did it alone also." It was the perfect backdrop for the

Superstar rivalries that Warhol unleashed. Attuned to the energies that can surge through cultural spaces, he could sense the growing verve of their little upstart family as more and more reporters and celebrities sought them out. Outside of the Factory it all became clear to Billy: "We could sense our power because when we would go places people would just move aside for us."

He finally left the scene in 1970. After ten years of total saturation in Factory life, Billy remembered, "I was silver inside and outside." Living as a shut-in within the Factory's dark room ended with an abrupt exit. He only scrawled an odd little note, which Warhol used to end his *POPism* memoir: "I am not here anymore but I am fine." Why did he leave? The Factory, he thought, was no longer "an avant-garde art emporium" of filming, painting, and taping. Paul Morrissey and Fred Hughes had triggered the displacement of art by money, making it "more of a crass thing."

Billy veered off on a few tangents about modern gay identities and numerology before showing me around his apartment, including a closet stuffed with Warhol books featuring his photographs. After thanking and leaving Billy, I walked down to the Hudson River and sat on the shore for a while. It was too beautiful, a perfectly quiet and peaceful spot that I haven't returned to since, sadly enough. Curiously, about an hour north of Billy's home is the small, picturesque town of Hudson, New York, which has turned out to be quite a Superstar enclave. Gerard Malanga, Bibbe Hansen, Jane Forth, and Donna Jordan all live there now. Viva's daughter Gaby Hoffman, a successful actress on Amazon's *Transparent*, spends time there too.

Bibbe, the youngest of the Superstars, met Warhol fresh out of a juvenile delinquency facility in 1964, while still a young girl under her father's care. She soon ended up at the Factory shooting films with Edie Sedgwick. Aside from being Fluxus pioneer Al Hansen's daughter and Grammy winner Beck's mother, today she's a wonderfully provocative artist in her own right, taking gruesome photos of wounds and stitching through them with string, or composing spacey digital constructions via Second Life. She even has a drag alter ego, a short African American gentleman named Cleofus Guenvere. Her live reperformance of her father's *Elegy for the Fluxus Dead*, set to the desperate melancholia of "Can't Help Falling in Love," will give you goose bumps. Back in Poughkeepsie, Bibbe's old Factory pal Billy mentioned her great public presence, "She's always positive and beneficent in how she talks about things. She speaks well about things."

When I first spoke with Bibbe, she recalled being involved in some kind of artistic practice from the very beginning of her life, especially an obsession with making birdhouses, or using a local cemetery as a space for childhood performances of Billie Holiday songs. "I had to have an audience," Bibbe explained. She'd later make downtown New York her stage, diving into community theater, Judson Church's experimental dance scene, and happenings involving her father or avant-garde film pioneer Jonas Mekas. Bibbe constantly collaborated with other creatives, old and young alike. What was the allure? "Community. I think that's something people really long for," she said. "My favorite work has always been collaborative."

Despite an adolescence marked by stints in juvenile detention halls, having a known artist like Al Hansen as her father facilitated meeting Warhol at a restaurant. At the time, she and her father struggled financially while the wealth and fame of friends like Warhol grew steadily. During their meal, Warhol looked over and plainly asked the teenage girl, "And what do you do?" Subsequently pulled into the Factory scene meant friendships with a big sister figure like Sedgwick. Like so much else in their world, angst was aestheticized, so Bibbe's juvy times inspired Warhol's *Prison*. She starred in the film alongside Sedgwick but few have seen the film, queued for restoration in the coming years.

Now a devoted den mother to young New York culture makers, Bibbe will vigorously push you to do better work and cut through pointless drama in your life. She loves mixing it up with young people, patiently listening to their anxieties, watching them ham it up in social settings, or closely examining their art. Bibbe has graciously visited my classes at Columbia and NYU, always leaving the students inspired and energetic. During our first chat she mentioned all the kids who reach out to her about Fluxus, Sedgwick, and Warhol. What were they looking for? "What they're reaching for is art," Bibbe said. "Art is calling them. Art is, as my father said, pulling them by the elbow and dragging them into the arena, and saying, *'You need to be here now.'*"

I visited Bibbe's lovely Hudson home in 2014 after a summer of working with Michael Alig caused what felt like a mini nervous breakdown. In her kitchen we talked and laughed for days while her husband Sean Carrillo cooked up amazing meals. Over the years I've benefited enormously from her gentle guidance, especially when she has shown me some much needed tough love after I overreacted to a few situations. Her insistence on the need to constantly refine one's creative practice is key and I really try to apply some of her lessons. It's all about work, growth, and discipline, a process of steady improvement that avoids yielding to our base instincts.

Although I wear shades in my photos to hide my eyes and nose, Bibbe always wears Ray-Bans, even indoors, due to a rare eye condition. Behind those dark lenses she is studying you, carefully reading your gestures and discerning your motives. If you meet her, it might be unnerving, but roll with it.

At the Warhol parties at the Gershwin Hotel, Bibbe and Ultra Violet were mainstays, often photographed together, the youngest Superstar and the most, well, colorful. Known for her signature purple looks, Ultra stayed true to her Factory persona until her final days, despite never quite finding her way Up There.

On one of the first intensely humid days of 2014, I hopped on a bus headed toward the famous Frank Campbell funeral home on the Upper East Side. Ultra had succumbed to cancer a few days earlier. Twitter lit up with nods to a woman who led a wild maelstrom of a life, even by Factory standards. After fleeing her Catholic boarding school in France, Ultra arrived in New York in 1953 and quickly established ties to European royalty, avant-garde artists, and Manhattan high society, eventually finding her way into dinners with Maria Callas, Aristotle Onassis, Yoko Ono, and John Lennon, and collaborations with Salvador Dalí, who first introduced her to Warhol.

I was working as Michael Alig's assistant at the time, so I messaged him about Ultra's death. In Michael's own romantic reading of her passing, he said that Ultra had "gone to that great final booking way up in the sky." Doing a pretty solid impression of the French-born muse, Michael remembered Ultra asking him, "Can you fit me into your schedule? I'd like to come to the club." The Warhol generation asking its inheritors for jobs.

Campbell's had been the mourning site for Judy Garland, Greta Garbo, Jacqueline Kennedy Onassis, and Heath Ledger, so Ultra would have felt proud of her A-list setting. An open casket wake is never an easy moment, especially for a woman so known for her beauty. The turnout for Ultra's wake was a curious mix. Old representatives of Warholia like Ivy Nicholson and Penny Arcade meandered through the room, alongside Ultra's well-groomed French family members. I chatted with artist Conrad Ventur and another woman who recalled dropping acid with Ultra in another time, when both stayed out all night and tried to stumble into a nine-to-five job.

My first encounter with Ultra was in the men's restroom of the Chelsea building that housed her studio. Thomas Kiedrowski and I visited together in order to jointly interview her for *New York Art Beat*. Head still bald, I wore a canary yellow polo shirt, baggy brown pants, and another pair of plain loafers. I was serving 1970s yellow and brown professorial realness. I used the men's room before our chat and on my way out I saw too tiny legs clad in purple stockings peeking out from underneath a stall. I froze. Had I accidently walked into the women's room? Nope, she just decided to use the nearest bathroom, regardless of its gender assignment. I rushed out.

At that point, Ultra was teetering on the edge of a memory hole.

Her place in the Factory lineage is muddled (Bob Colacello calls Ultra's time in the scene "ultra-brief".) Still, she appeared in some remarkable photos, including the 1968 cover of a *New York Times Magazine* story titled "The Return of Andy Warhol." She was dressed in one of her purple-accented blouses, alongside Warhol and her rival Viva, who vigorously disparaged her memoir *Famous for 15 Minutes*. Other scholars have also criticized its historical record, but as a reflection of how Ultra saw the Factory fame game in hindsight, it was truly fascinating. She described their pursuit as follows: "The whole game is people: meeting them, getting them involved, asking them for money, pulling them into our orbit, being invited to their parties and events. Every new person is a new possibility, a link in an ever-lengthening chain, an ever-climbing ladder."

Her Chelsea studio was adorned with works featuring Mickey Mouse and Michelangelo, revolvers and circuit boards, mirrors and neon lights, and, of course, photos of her. It was one of my first and most bizarre downtown conversations. The works were obviously Warholian in their seriality and color schemes, and I wondered why she was so drawn to the iconic Disney mouse. Ultra quickly snapped, "I am not drawn to Mickey Mouse. If you can read the title, I am drawn to Michelangelo. Why? Because he was a genius, because I do not neglect what went on in the past. What I like are the wings. This is an angel. Can't you see? This character is flying. This is not Mickey Mouse. I used to paint a lot of angels. It's really not Mickey."

It was an odd, abrasive tactic, somewhat like O'Keefe's attempted scolding back in his office, but Thomas and I held our ground. After a while Ultra relaxed and became honest about her hustle, which didn't seem to have paid off as she hoped it would. "I was showing my work in Basel for the first time in my life. My conclusion from being there was, 'Wow, this is the temple of worship, and how can I enter the temple of worship?'" She laughed at her own ambition, now as naked as she was in some of the photos around us. "But yet, keeping a certain integrity. If I look into my mirror, I have to like myself.

Anyway, so it's quite a dilemma," she said knowingly. *"And you have to play the game, you have to cheat and lie and flirt."*

As we discussed art's present and future, Ultra began posing questions and answering them herself: "What's the American dream?" she asked us. "The dollar sign, the glamour, the fame, the flowers, the first man walking on the moon, that's the crowning of the American dream, extraordinary. What's great about Warhol—and nobody sees it that way, they say 'Oh, he has pretty color'—he also did the reversal of the dream: the disasters, dream and disasters, those are probably his greatest paintings."

After our interview Thomas and I had dinner with Ultra, Robert Heide, and his partner, the actor John Gilman. After munching on gnocchi, I asked her to sign my copy of her memoir. Looking tired after an afternoon of memory churning with us, Ultra politely asked what she should write. Slightly surprised by her question, I replied that she should write whatever she liked. A blasé, cheeky Warholian to the last, she scribbled, in purple, "For Victor Corona 'Whatever you like' Ultra Violet 2010."

At a Loews hotel on Park Avenue, I waited to meet Joe Dallesandro, a man whose youthful self was so beautiful that men and women alike react intensely to seeing his body, inevitably bared in most of his films. His Paul Morrissey–directed trilogy (*Flesh*, *Trash*, *Heat*) is an exceptional record of American culture. My favorite is *Trash*, a hilarious reckoning with addiction, sex, status, and the welfare state in 1970. Two other Superstars give wonderful performances. Holly Woodlawn's comedic genius shone through as Joe's scammer roommate, while Jane Forth played a bored housewife that Joe tries to rob. I have screened *Trash* in class only once, when Holly suggested that I do it. It didn't go over well, partly because it's so tough for many to look past extremely explicit male and female nudity and connect with Morrissey's absurdist portrait.

Joe now works as a building manager in LA but in 2016 was flown to New York to reunite with Jane Birkin, namesake of the famous Hermès bag, for a Lincoln Center screening of Serge Gainsbourg's *Je t'aime moi non plus*. Although I hadn't yet seen the movie when I met Joe, I knew what to expect. To prepare for our chat I sat through some of his films, both Morrissey directed and European made. They're somber and dull variations on the same sexual theme: the low, grumpy murmurs of a disgruntled but hot nobody, inevitably coveted by the gorgeous women around him. As his smitten biographer Michael Ferguson wrote, "The drag queens and the other Superstars were interesting, quirky, witty, even fun, but they were also on some level threatening. Joe, on the other hand, inspired fantasy, engagement, dreams of an afternoon fuck."

Joe is a testament to the power of beauty that Justin Tranter mentioned, a power that I never wielded during my night outings. Like Warhol, I lacked what those around me seemed to exude so effortlessly. But pitfalls accompany beauty's power. When you have the kind of looks and physique that fling open downtown's doors, what happens to discipline, craft, and work?

Back in the Loews lobby, Joe emerged from the elevator wearing a plaid shirt, a Versace scarf, and a long dark coat. Hair slicked back, he bore the square-jawed visage of an older Charlie Sheen and an easy smile on his face, although it was maybe more of a curl of the lip. And despite being grouchy and easily distracted, Joe was polite in a gentle, old-school kind of way, maybe a humble acknowledgement of the fact that all these years later, he still mattered enough to get flown to New York and set up on Park Avenue.

I wanted to know what this legend of underground film missed about his old downtown haunts. "Uh, nothing. Nothing. Don't miss New York at all," he murmured, in a deep voice made gravelly by age and cigarettes. I mentioned that his *Trash* poster hung at The Box and he shrugged it off. When I asked about what he was looking forward to seeing or doing, he replied, "I don't get excited about anything anymore. Nothing excites me anymore." Not even his reunion with Jane Birkin at Lincoln Center? "No, no. I'm just old."

Joe was in a hurry to get to other appointments. And his LA duties still pulled on him: an employee named José called during our conversation looking for work around Joe's building. The next day, I arrived at Lincoln Center a half hour before the screening to find a long line already assembled. I cut ahead by dashing over to Bibbe Hansen and her husband Sean, who were chatting up the photographer Dustin Pittman. We all sat in the front row, debriefing on the latest gossip while waiting for the film to start. The dreadful film was dubbed over, so not even the classic Joe murmurs came through.

The film's essential premise was that Joe's gay character loved Birkin's delusional tomboy gamine, who believed that offering herself anally to him could satisfy their queer coupling. It was the kind of film that I loved in college but now find tedious. There was little glamour or potency to it, just wallowing in confusion and loss.

But the event was sold out. As soon as the movie ended, the crowd stirred in preparation for the Q&A. When Bibbe's husband got up to find the bathroom, the Village People's cowboy, Randy Jones, took his seat, giving Bibbe a tight hello hug. During the Q&A, Joe sat hunched over, not even removing his coat. Birkin, though, was extremely articulate and earnest, still somehow almost innocent after decades of a storied life. It was another very surreal moment that the old Gandhi-in-khakis Vic couldn't have imagined: sitting in a Lincoln Center theater next to a Village Person and a Warhol Superstar, listening to the aged version of one of the most beautiful men ever filmed and the namesake of the most sought-after luxury item in the world.

Afterward a wave of downtown denizens surged to the front to greet Joe and be photographed with him. Looking through the photos the next day I marveled at how fans were so overjoyed to see Joe and how totally over it he seemed. The staid face was classic Joe, but over the next few days he was gushing all over Twitter.

The fame game will always excite its players, even if New York no longer does.

Joe's *Trash* co-star Holly Woodlawn also fled New York. As she lamented, "It lost its flavor, it lost everything. New York City was gone." And she was lonely, wondering where her friends were. In LA she found "a little village" of other downtown refugees, like the star of Warhol's theatrical foray *Pork*, Cherry Vanilla. During our chat her manager stepped in to ask if AIDS-related deaths of her friends contributed to her exit. She cut him off: "I wish people would really stop talking about diseases. *We left because we were bored.*"

Keep in mind how hard Holly, Joe, and others worked to get to New York and stay here. She wasn't ashamed about her time hustling on the street after fleeing Florida, an escape famously chronicled by Lou Reed in "Walk on the Wild Side." She remembered "doing what you had to do to survive," adding coyly, "Some of it was fun." But she refused to romanticize her wild street days: "You had to basically sell your body, your soul, whatever, you know, to survive. And I did."

Although the skyline is a little more jagged and rents way more expensive, before Holly left the city for the final time, we were reminded of New York's constants during our brunch kiki. Down the block a mentally ill person started wildly shrieking and cursing, denouncing some antagonist seen only by him. We give the typical New Yorker reaction: look over to assess the threat level, shrug, go back to our eggs and toast. Holly deadpanned, "Well, we're back in New York."

Cancer of the brain and liver claimed Holly in 2015, but even in death, scandal flourished. Penny Arcade swooped in to start a memorial fund in her honor, pulling in over $60,000, alongside Robert Starr, a supposed friend of Holly. A few critics, like Gary Comenas of warholstars.org, demanded transparency and accountability in the funds and wondered why they weren't used to make sure that Holly's final days were as comfortable as possible. Joe Dallesandro noted that when he visited Holly for the first time, she had no cell phone and was wearing dirty pajamas. "When I went to visit Holly, I just thought things were real harsh in where she was staying." He brought her some chocolate, a favorite treat, and was surprised to see that she hadn't eaten any in years. "She gobbled them up," Joe remembered. "I had to wipe her face and everything because she had chocolate all over, that's how fast she was trying to eat it." Joe resented being kept from calling or visiting his old Factory friend.

A perfect contrast to a Lincoln Center theater crowded with chic film stars and their artsy, black-clad fans is just thirty blocks south: the loathsome Penn Station, a Midtown transit hub that connects various subway lines to Amtrak and commuter rails to New Jersey and Long Island. Rather infamously, its gilded, temple-like predecessor was demolished and replaced with a garish underground basin, surely unloved by even the most fanatical of modernists. The contrast drawn by the Yale art historian Vincent Scully is apt: "One entered the city like a god; one scuttles in now like a rat."

I remembered Scully's words back in February 2012 while standing not far from a group of National Guardsmen toting massive rifles at their sides. Watching staircases disgorge endless streams of passengers with mussed hair, bulky packages, and grumpy children, I deliberately scanned each woman's face so I didn't miss Jane Forth, another of Joe's *Trash* co-stars. Despite being among the most beautiful of the Superstars, she fled fame, crisscrossing the country and eventually relocating to Hudson, New York, just like Bibbe Hansen.

Jane escaped from the acting profession that so many Factory folks wanted to storm. For a time she was married to Oliver Wood, cinematographer for films like *Sister Act 2*, the Bourne trilogy, and *Fantastic Four*. She explained, "I did find myself becoming self-conscious due to the lack of desire," instead finding a love for work in make-up and special effects. She moved behind the scenes, becoming a union make-up artist for films, TV commercials, and music videos and working with Pat Benatar, Barry Manilow, and Julio Iglesias.

I wasn't sure what to expect while waiting for her in Penn Station, but recognized her immediately. Her pale copper eyes sparkled with the same luster that must have enchanted Warhol and Joe. Jane's now grayed hair was pulled into an up-do and her skin retained its flawless porcelain quality. After I enthusiastically greeted her, we rushed out to find a taxi, leaving the gaudy subterranean space behind.

On that cold winter day I was writing a profile of Jane to be accompanied by photos shot by downtown veteran and make-up artist Veronica Ibarra, who had modeled much of her own visual identity after Jane's iconic look: mostly shaved eyebrows, slicked hair pulled tightly behind the head, rouged cheeks, and vibrant eye shadow. Veronica is also known for taking famous early photos of Gaga and Starlight. Back during her days as "Veronica Vain," she donned denim vests, studded belts, and garters to host Lower East Side parties alongside Starlight, Lüc Carl, and Anna Copa Cabanna (according to Breedlove, she also had a fling with Lüc). Since Veronica and I obsessed over Jane's hilariously memorable *Trash* scene opposite Joe, we decided to find and invite her to Manhattan.

Our shoot with Jane tied together multiple downtown generations, from the Factory to the club kids to Gaga and back again. Kabuki Starshine, the Limelight veteran who worked with Gaga on the VMAs "Paparazzi" night, wore kneepads while painstakingly painting Jane's face for hours. Darian Darling, wrapped in a leopard-print dress and fur coat, showed up to meet Jane and, of course, be photographed with her. Darian told me weeks later that she texted her photo with Jane to Gaga, reporting, "She was very jealous about it."

Veronica and others in the Gaga gang always saw themselves as Factory inheritors. Darian remembered a wasted Fourth of July rooftop night with her friends: "Veronica turns to me and she's like, 'We're the new Factory, we're totally like the new Warhol Factory.

It's true, like no one knows it yet but people are gonna know it.'"
During my chat with Jane, I asked about the artists she followed. She
quickly gushed about Darian's pal, explaining, "I think that Lady
Gaga is one of the most gifted performers and musicians around. I
adore Lady Gaga [. . .] She's like living art." Wondering how Gaga
might react, I mentioned this to Darian, who quietly murmured, "*She
would be so tickled.*"

In *Trash*, a teenage Jane and her co-stars spun out an absurdist
scene that wonderfully critiqued attitudes toward marriage, class,
drugs, and violence. As a bored bourgeois homemaker, Jane essentially asked Joe, playing a junkie thief, to rape her. The moment was
interrupted by the arrival of her dapper spouse. It all ended with
Jane's shrieking hysterics as a naked Joe overdosed on heroin right
in front of her and the husband—a disturbing escalation that she
said was not expected. Jane stole the scene with her alabaster skin
and mysteriously coy demeanor in the face of a home invasion. She
was a last minute replacement for Patti D'Arbanville and didn't even
bother with specialized costuming. As she told me, "That's how I
looked every day."

Jane described the film to me as "a series of what we would term
as 'trashy events,'" avoiding any deep reading into themes. "That was
the beauty of Andy's and Paul's films, that they weren't overthought,"
she said. Aside from insisting on not being nude, "None of it was
predetermined," Jane said. "There was a rough outline for the film.
Even when I got there that day, I didn't really know even what the
outline was going to be."

Unlike other Superstars, Jane was more embedded into Factory
life, earning a paycheck doing office work alongside Joe. For a while
she believed that other Factory people were toying with her when
they claimed that a man named Billy Name lived in the back closet.
Jane later toured Europe with Warhol, Joe, and Paul Morrissey to
promote *Trash*, enjoying swanky hotels, sightseeing, and having
Morrissey as a "tutoring" guide taking them to old churches. Jane

lived near Joe in the East Village, where they would cook dinner together and have play dates with their children.

She remembered getting phone calls from Warhol at two or three in the morning, asking if she was watching the same classic movie as him. She usually was. A second-wave Superstar like Jane could enjoy the spoils of Warhol's fame, spending summer weekends in Southampton with him, Jed Johnson, Peter Brant, and Fred Hughes. On Sunday mornings, Warhol would sit under a giant tree and read *The New York Times*. Hughes would play Gershwin's *Rhapsody in Blue* and the group would at times venture into town to buy rhubarb pies, lobster salad, and fresh berries. She adds, "I would always buy my Yoo-hoos. I loved Yoo-hoo." Jane's soft tone changed as she told me all this, sounding blissfully lost in remembering a time that was "so normal and peaceful and tranquil."

At a fun group dinner following Veronica's shoot, other Jane fans joined us, including supermodel Andreja Pejic, Anna Copa Cabanna, Breedlove, Jocelyn McBride, and Niki M'nray. I practically skipped home after witnessing the fabulous assembly of downtown superstars: the make-up of one of Warhol's favorite Factory figures carefully applied by a past star of the club kids' Limelight scene, and photographed by a formerly "Vain" fixture of the Starlight and Gaga gang. I picked the venue for the convergence: the restaurant Almond in the Flatiron District, which I would again suggest two years later for Michael Alig's post-prison welcome home dinner.

If you're a nosy voyeur like me, there are costs and benefits to where you sit at a speakers' panel. If you're up close, the panelists can't help but make eye contact with you, so if you want to chat afterward, your visage already exists in their mind. You get to study them up close, watching how they fidget or grimace if a question bothers them. See if the hems of their pants are slightly frayed and how wrinkled their jacket might be. Note how the skin of the truly successful or wildly famous often glows a little, the product of a life with a few less worries than the rest of us.

But if you're sitting in the back, you can see who shows up, and after all, *you go to see who goes.* The fun is in watching the parade of who arrives with whom, how they look and, oh, look at what they're wearing. If it's someone you'd like to meet or kiki with, you might end up sitting with them. But you can glean so much from the people-watching, gaging the demographics of the audience, especially how young it is. This is especially important at a Factory-related event because if the youth component is strong, then you really know that Warhol's shadow will stretch far into the future.

At a late 2015 panel at the Strand launching Brigid Berlin's book of Polaroids, I decided to sit up front. Check it out on YouTube: that's me in the corner. But in the spotlight are four Factory pillars, including Brigid herself, she who was both uptown Hearst heiress and downtown Duchess, the B to Andy's A, the only Superstar to remain with Warhol until the very end, right up to his burial on a Pennsylvania hillside. She has struggled with her weight for virtually her entire life as a plump, rather eccentric black sheep of Manhattan high society. Confined to a wheelchair at the event, she seemed buoyed by the other three friends and panelists, fellow Superstar of the silver era Gerard Malanga, and well-off Factory "kids" Vincent Fremont and Bob Colacello. I needed to be up there.

In 1989, shortly before the Museum of Modern Art's Warhol retrospective, *Interview* put the old Boss on the cover and published updates on the Factory stars, including Brigid. One instance perfectly depicted her lavish sense of excess. Through an inheritance from a family friend, she rented a house on Fire Island and truly lived the high life. "*I was very, very grand,*" she told executive editor Kevin Sussums. "I'd hire private seaplanes to take me into New York to pick up my mail. On the return I'd ask the pilot to circle very low over my house so I could drop emerald cuff links and other kinds of jewelry into the pool so my husband could dive for them." From these ludicrous heights, she dove into the downtown depths of underground subcultures, her Factory name becoming Brigid Polk "because I was poking amphetamines," she told *Interview*.

Sadly, one of Brigid's friends told me that the daughter of the overseer of the Hearst media empire (one that Warhol coveted) had become a recluse and couldn't give coherent interviews, mostly due to her health. Gerard's manager also declined my request to chat with him. But at the panel I watched them all be their characters, as their utterances drew plenty of laughs from an audience that included F, Thomas Kiedrowski, Bibbe Hansen, Robert Heide, and John Waters, whom I finally met that night. The smattering of young people was small. But I didn't get the full visual swipe. Why? Exactly. Because I was sitting up front.

As committed Republicans, Brigid and Bob Colacello were quick to attack the Clintons. Brigid talked about watching a filibuster at one in the morning on Fox News: "It's more like an Andy Warhol movie than anything Andy ever did." The other two were more centrist: the poet Gerard, an early recruit who at times bitterly resented the Warholian shadow he lives in, and millionaire Vincent, the person who has perhaps profited the most from proximity to the Pop sun.

Vincent and Bob are living Warhol's lifelong dream of being Up There, a comfortable existence consumed by a hectic itinerary that sizzles with boldface names. When Bob and I spoke in his cozy Upper East Side apartment, not far from the palatial Ralph Lauren boutique, I sampled a realm of elite rituals taking place in homes like his, or out in the Hamptons or the Hollywood Hills. It's a world of endless questions: which upstart artist sits with which collector at which charity lunch or gala, who is staying at whose guesthouse, who is dating, divorcing, or suing whom, and, oh, but is there time to stop by and see so-and-so after dessert?

Bob casually mentioned a recent dinner party for philanthropist Mercedes Bass hosted by a great questioner of the twentieth century, Barbara Walters. Apparently she likes to have everyone sitting around her A-list table weigh in on big, heavy issues like affirmative action or one's belief in a god. Oh, and Henry Kissinger stopped by too.

As I sunk into Bob's big, comfy couch, he explained that he just returned from a West Coast trip that included the grand opening of The Broad, a speaking gig at LACMA, and a Republican primary debate at the Reagan Library (he supported Marco Rubio). Bob is now a senior advisor to Vito Schnabel, delivering his ties to older curators and collectors to the son of art world giant Julian Schnabel. Bob is truly a social and generational nexus, having bonded with downtown drama queens and then moved on to interview royals like Charles, Prince of Wales, and his wife, the Duchess of Cornwall, alongside members of the continental nobility. His move on up to the East Side avoided the pitfalls of exposé journalism, for the most part anyway. Dewi Sukarno, widow of the late Indonesian dictator, once sued him and Ivana Trump called his *Vanity Fair* cover profile of her a "hatchet job."

How did a man molded in the Catholic sensibilities of suburban Italian enclaves—just like F—live unrestrained by any heavy identity and instead prove that you can go uptown and Up There if you play the downtown game well?

While an undergrad at Georgetown, Bob expected to be a diplomat, or a businessman like his father, but the Vietnam War and a brief moment in radical politics pushed him away from government service. His campus rebellion passed on Molotov cocktails in favor of fifty-cent bologna sandwiches that Bob and his comrades would fling at a nearby police academy in the middle of the night. In addition to hurling deli meats at The Man, he fell in love with French and Italian films and saw Warhol's *Chelsea Girls*, falling down a rabbit hole that led right back to New York. Enrolling in Columbia's MFA film program, Bob quickly discovered that he was better at writing film reviews than operating cameras. *Village Voice* film critic Andrew Sarris taught at Columbia, collecting the best of his students' reviews and publishing them. Paul Morrissey called Bob after Warhol read a review of his, a phone chat that led to Bob being hired at Warhol's new magazine *Interview* as managing editor and art director.

Bob told me that his ability to build rapport with diverse social circles came largely from having outgoing parents who were salespeople and classically "gregarious" Italian Americans. He also mentioned his early recognition of life's total absurdity, informed by reading Kafka, Camus, Sartre, Baudelaire, and Genet. At one point, he seemed ready for a tangent: "I guess maybe being gay without even knowing it then had something . . ." He trailed off, avoiding further talk of his sexuality. Vodka also helped with intimidating social characters, although he considered himself lucky enough to have escaped what he called a "staircase to oblivion" consisting of Stoli vodka and cocaine. Sip and snort, repeated throughout the night at clubs like Les Jardins, Studio 54, Area, and Nell's.

Working for a man accused of stealing ideas from all and sundry, Bob himself knew what it meant to have a great thought and watch someone else run away with it. Evita Perón has always been a heroine of mine, so when I read Bob's *Holy Terror* account of developing a story with Candy Darling playing Evita, I fangurled. "Yeah, and I learned my lesson," Bob told me. "Never give a show biz person your treatment." Paul Morrissey had asked him to develop a film vehicle for Candy and Joe Dallesandro. The love of geopolitics nurtured during his Georgetown days flared up during dinners with Diana Vreeland, who told him stories about Evita importing entire couture collections to Buenos Aires. Bob wrote a song and a treatment, with Candy as Evita, Ernest Borgnine as Juan Perón, and Joe as Evita's younger brother.

Through Warhol, they had drinks with legendary entertainment impresario Robert Stigwood. Morrissey suggested that the treatment be given to Stigwood so they could perhaps pull together a co-production of Bob's sketch. "And instead they just somehow gave it to Andrew Lloyd Webber," Bob explained. "I assume that's how . . .

It *could be* that he simultaneously came up with the idea," he added, his tone brimming with skepticism.

Bob sounded a little morose maybe, but not bitter. He left the Factory with the foundations of a glorious career, although he and others struggled with their proximity to Warhol. Bob remembered desperately wanting to dissociate from the Factory, but was told how impossible it was: "I remember Brigid Berlin saying to me, 'Bob, you know, that's like a futile effort. Don't you know once you're connected with Andy you never can be disconnected from Andy?'"

Back at the Strand panel, he sat next to another of the "kids" who managed Warhol's empire. Vincent Fremont lives right around the corner from my NYU office, so I would occasionally run into him before he became CEO of ARTnews Ltd. (now Art Media Holdings, owned by Peter Brant, who owns *Interview* as well). Despite lacking formal schooling, Vincent managed major art world publications like *ARTnews* and *Art in America* (he stepped down as CEO in March 2017), owns a Hamptons estate, and lives not far from the Union Square Factory sites.

Over lunch at a nearby Pain Quotidien, Vincent was courteous, gracious, and so refined in his Up There habitus. He announced that the following week he would be out almost every night for dinner parties, benefits, and art openings. He mentioned needing to winterize his home out in Bridgehampton. Recent outings? Oh, his friend Tracey Emin being honored by Elton John's AIDS Foundation. But he missed his usual Halloween outing: the annual themed bash at the West Village townhouse of Allison Sarofim and Stuart Parr, written up in *Vogue* and attended by Naomi Campbell, Donna Karan, and Demi Moore, among other glitterati.

When I saw him at the opening of Brigid's Polaroids exhibition not long before our lunch, my eyes and forehead were covered in glitter make-up and face jewels in preparation for a night at The Box, so I was slightly worried that this well-coiffed millionaire—the former Vice President of Andy Warhol Enterprises, Inc.—would dismiss me as some ragtag fag loony. I mellowed once he talked about a long-haired youthful version of himself in a rock band, trying psychedelics and smoking pot in high school. Like Bob, the first Manhattan nightclub that Vincent mentioned was Les Jardins, especially the night that actor Helmut Berger chased him around the club, yelling, "You're my type! A schoolboy! You're my type!" He deadpanned, "I had to keep moving. If you didn't move, he was going to pounce."

Vincent was reared in the peculiarities of the art world out in California, thanks to parents who were artists and acquaintances of William Copley and Man Ray. He landed in New York after his band drove cross-country, and thanks to a friend who already made contact with the Factory, quickly found Warhol and came under his tutelage. Image mattered. Vincent's consciously crafted "LA rock 'n' roll androgynous look" led him into the legendary back room at Max's Kansas City, coming across Brigid, René Ricard, and Candy Darling. Although he remained close to Brigid, he recognized the pathos of the Hearst heiress, including a drinking problem, overeating, and an inability to really apply herself to any grand, long-term endeavor. "Brigid scared people," he explained. "But Brigid in those days was on speed. The only person I know on speed that could gain weight rather than lose weight: she had more time to eat."

By January 1971, he was hired at the Factory, which he referred to as "the studio" throughout our chat. He amassed responsibilities by being willing to throw himself at any task given to him, working full days for only sixty-five dollars a week. He lacked the entitlement of some of the young wannabes I know, being perfectly comfortable with sweeping floors or doing smaller tasks, even holding the boom mic during the filming of Paul Morrissey's *Trash*. He exuded gratitude for the toughness of the upward climb: "New York gave you an opportunity to become your own person."

Warhol's death in 1987 set off seismic waves among art world heavies eager to find ways to cash in on the massive Warhol estate.

The friendship among Brigid, Bob, and Vincent survived that time, while others, like Pat Hackett and Paul Morrissey, pulled away. As we talked about the aftermath, Vincent's mood lowered a bit. "You really do learn who your friends are," he explained rather somberly. "Reality sets in. Greed sets in. The masks fall off. And then you see what you're up against."

Vincent became the exclusive sales agent for Warhol's estate and eventually the powerful Foundation that Warhol's will created. Occupying this role from 1991 to 2010, Vincent quickly amassed an impressive fortune through commissions. Despite the wealth he made, as we finished lunch, Vincent became slightly wistful. "I'm in a weird state," he said. "Once the Foundation got rid of me because they gave the rest of the art to Christie's, then your phone stops ringing. I knew that would happen eventually, when you don't have something people want." Somehow being Up There—the A-list friends, the fancy homes, projects with Brigid and Deborah Kass, and a memoir in the works—weren't enough for the former rock dude from Cali who became leader of two of the biggest art operations in recent New York history. My lunch with Vincent ended on a stern note, and I wasn't entirely sure how to respond. "So I'm kind of like the old man off Union Square, reminiscing," Vincent said. "That's a sorry state of affairs." I walked him to the corner of Eleventh and Broadway, said goodbye, and went off to buy more glitter.

What would Warhol say about the scene and people he left behind? Why does he still grab headlines and dominate art markets from the grave, remaining a currency in the fame game? Jane Forth pointed to how his enigmatic persona stimulated a need in people to find out more about him. "There was always a part of him that you felt was a secret and I feel like this carries on even like after his death, like to this day people still can't get enough of him," Jane said. "And I don't think he knew the real power he held within himself." Ambiguity feeds the hunt for answers, which might be a fool's errand in the case of an artist obsessed with surface meanings.

During a long drive through endless winter grayness to visit Michael Alig in prison, former Limelight and Tunnel director Steve Lewis eagerly rolled up his sleeve to show me the tattoo of Warhol's signature on his arm. The nightlife godfather often asked his staff, "'What would this club be like if Andy walked in? What would he think?' Every single night of the week, 'What would he think?' *That was the measure*." This is why so many downtown still dwell in the mystique of Warhol's silver kingdom, from F to M, from the DJ with a Warhol sticker on her laptop to my cute neighbor with the Campbell's soup can shirt: Warhol became the measure.

Steve remembered one of the many clubs he operated, The World, being in serious disrepair due to the owners stealing from each other, resulting in plumbing problems and broken sound systems. One night, Warhol strolled in and Steve walked over to apologize for the shabbiness. Warhol's response put Steve at ease: "Any place that's too neat or too clean can't be any fun."

What did awkward Andy enjoy about the maddening pulse of clubland? "I think Andy liked the speed of it all," Steve explained, "the visual attack that nightlife is." Naturally, Warhol became absorbed into the very spectacle itself. Who went to see and be seen by Warhol? "The failures, the successes, the almosts, the wannabes," Steve said, a tidy typology that could easily be plopped onto nightlife today.

Another measure was where the old Superstars' shadows fell on later downtown scenes. Michael Alig's first brush with Warholia was as a sixteen-year-old seeing a fabulous Edie Sedgwick *Ciao! Manhattan* shirt. Ever the horror movie aficionado, Michael would later see the *Frankenstein* and *Dracula* films starring Joe Dallesandro. He fondly remembered two personal interactions with Warhol: once handing him an invitation to Danceteria, and later hanging out in his dressing room at Tunnel, shortly before he died. Bringing him cranberry juice and making small talk, the Party Monster told me, "I was very intimidated."

Edie Sedgwick inspired club kid legend Richie Rich: "Even in my club kid days in the nineties I used to like do my hair and make-up like her, as a boy, but androgynous. She just had that effervescence [and] energy of running around living life." But after Warhol's death in 1987, his Factory stars would ask their leader's presumed inheritor for jobs. Michael Alig remembered booking gigs with Ultra Violet, Benjamin Liu, and Holly Woodlawn, even while the Party Monster and his followers were laying claim to the Superstar mantle. "In the beginning it was all supposed to be a satire," Michael said. "Although we looked up to the Warhol stars, we were also kind of rolling our eyes at this point at the tragic Ultra Violet and Penny Arcade."

Michael even recreated the Factory in jail. He paid fellow inmates to work on different elements of his paintings, just like Warhol's studio assistants helped him in his artistic assembly line at the Factory. Michael told me, "People would come by and look in and they'd see this person painting a background, this person doing a blow-up, this person doing the shading, and they'd be like, 'This is like a factory of art.'"

Joey Arias, the gender-bending downtown chanteuse, befriended Benjamin Liu and eventually Warhol himself upon calling to set up a movie date with Liu. Intoning Warhol perfectly, Joey remembered the Pop artist's reaction to their introduction: "Oh wow, you're famous." Warhol then essentially invited himself along to the movie date, first meeting at Serendipity 3 for some ice cream. When I asked Joey what surprised him the most about their friendship, he replied, "How much fun he was," easily engaging in banter about fame, sex, and nightlife hotspots, or cooking up schemes to get men to pull down their pants.

Miss Guy, a downtown DJ and bestie to Debbie Harry, Boy George, and others, did Warhol's make-up not long before his death. "He was out so much in those days," Guy remembered. "You saw him everywhere at night, at clubs." Today, having known Warhol becomes a calling card, the ultimate name to drop while schmoozing. You might suddenly be worth knowing because you knew the silver specter himself. Sophia Lamar, the acerbic ex–club kid and now beloved downtown elder, mocked pathetic attempts to curry favor. She remembered people telling her, "I used to party with Andy Warhol," to which she would reply, "Yeah, Andy Warhol was Andy Warhol. You are who? What was your name, sir?"

However their leader's legacy might be judged, the Superstars and "kids" of Warholia show us how precarious downtown's fame game can be. There are no guarantees of happiness or passes from the memory hole. The pursuit of fame won't silence simmering insecurities or make the sad thoughts go away. It couldn't help Warhol find real joy in all his silver kingdom and it certainly couldn't make F love me. Fame won't deliver a fulfilling identity that keeps you from ending your days embittered, accompanied only by reminiscences. It can't make human connection easier. If anything, we see how fame can twist and distort it. And when you're so famous, beautiful, rich, or connected that the doors of this world are flung open for you, there's a risk of never developing the core part of yourself that only you can master and offer. Honing a devotion to the art that is solely yours to make is the best way to survive that rarified Up There air.

3

THE DEATH OF
THE PARTY

Yale or Europe. When college application season came around, that was the extremist promise I made to my dismayed parents and guidance counselor, as they rolled their eyes and shook their heads at me. After my mom and I took a train up to New Haven for a campus visit, I applied early decision and vowed that if I didn't get in, I'd move to Europe for a year, maybe stay with my cousin in Switzerland for a while, or backpack around and work in a kitchen like Orwell did.

I wanted Yale because it seemed like I could be happy there, like I could *finally* be part of a space where I belonged. It was also typical of me trying to have my cake and eat it too. On one hand I felt really attached to my lefty activist friends and didn't want to leave that scene behind. But I also wanted some distance and separation, a chance to reboot my life and become someone new. A school that was a two-hour train ride away, in another state, seemed like a fair compromise. The gambit panned out: a big white envelope arrived in the mail and

I started thinking about a fresh start in New Haven, having zero clue about what to expect.

Although my parents didn't finish college, they constantly stirred in my brother and me a love of reading and the arts, while my grade school teachers really drilled rules of grammar and punctuation into their students. Jeannie and my English teachers in high school put up with my insane ideas and patiently taught me so much about thinking, writing, fighting, and living. All of this laid the foundation for the pages you're reading. But none of this was enough to prepare me for an adjustment to Yale. And so the first two years of college were extremely tough.

College is intended to be a time for hopelessly horny and distracted young people to somehow acquire knowledge, friends, and a new sense of self. It's also about losing things, like your virginity or the backward beliefs of your upbringing. All of this happened to me but first I learned what it meant to truly flail and despair, looking up at the gray New Haven sky and wondering if I had come this far only to break apart in the middle of Old Campus. To what extent could I, or anyone, hope to truly transform, to escape from their origins?

Even among other Latin students at Yale, I was the minority, since most students claiming a Mexican heritage were from either California or Texas and born in the United States. It seemed so odd to them that I was from a New York suburb, especially a town called *White* Plains. Yale pulled Puerto Rican, Dominican, or mixed students from the area, but Mexicans? Not so much, at least then. The campus Chicano group was little more than a hookup center and drinking/420 club, but having my youthful obsessions molded by people like Jeannie and Margaret, I wanted to really dive in and fuck things up. When I started working on projects with city politicians or union members more than with their group, they shooed me away as a "coconut." Brown on the outside, white on the inside—get it? Never mind that unlike many of those proud Chicanos and their lofty talk of *la raza*, I actually spoke Spanish, was born in Mexico, and had been in this country illegally.

I didn't tell anyone about the illegal part, though. I had other secrets to keep, like my attraction to men. A lingering Catholicism and my parents' traditional mind-set contributed to an agonizing confusion. An encounter with a boy wouldn't happen until the summer after my sophomore year and as soon as it was over I quickly tried to toss the fumbling moment into the nearest memory hole. I considered the hookup an aberration because I still felt attracted to women, even dating a brilliantly entrepreneurial woman for almost two years. Nevertheless I soon became the sorry butt of ongoing Tom Cruise jokes, a campus closet queen stubbornly armed with feeble excuses whenever questions about my sex life popped up.

Overall I couldn't find a stable footing early on in college, instead feeling branded by my brown Otherness, working class background, and queer uncertainties. Thankfully, a few close friends and I quickly became a little oddball clique, the work-study brown kids who worked in the dining halls or libraries. Then and now, I identified with others who lived at the margins, even as we created our own social hierarchies and policed belongings. Resenting the privilege of Yale's affluent white kids, we teased them for their blandness and social awkwardness instead of finding some common cause. We were all wrestling with the same questions after all: dealing with suitemates' disgusting habits, plowing through endless piles of schoolwork, trying to make the most of our four years there, chasing intimacies and maybe even loves.

Back in high school even the hunky jocks tended to come from middle class families and boasted no great pedigrees. But Yale was a different story. The "legacy" kids were scions of wealthy bloodlines, although they would roll into class in basketball shorts and flip-flops. Plenty of their family members had gone to Yale or other Ivies, which had probably offered them admission too. Their parents owned several homes, managed Fortune 500 companies, or had way-up-high government gigs. Freshman year, in the suite next to mine lived a boy whose parents often played tennis with the University President. Jordana Brewster of *Fast and Furious* fame lived across the courtyard and the Crown Princess of Sweden was taking classes there too. President Bush's daughter Barbara and I were in the same residential college and we once watched a movie in the same theater, after which she and her friends all piled into a huge Secret Service SUV.

I did not belong there. At least that's how I felt, at first.

The elitism of the institution wasn't all bad. Growing up I was a HUGE fan of *My So-Called Life*, the short-lived but intensely worshiped drama of a young girl's teenage yearnings. The stars of the series, Claire Danes and Jared Leto, survived the show's collapse to become A-list celebrities. Danes attended Yale while I was there, so imagine the gleeful fangurling look on my freshman face when I walked right by her on College Street one morning, making straight on eye contact with my beloved Angela Chase biting into a bagel.

And one afternoon—oh my god—hungry after practicing my French at the language lab, I stopped by the massive Commons dining hall. The lunch rush was over, so I had the sandwich bar all to myself. I piled bread and cheese onto a plate. But when I looked up from my tray, Danes turned the corner, just steps away from me, and walked over to pick up who knows what. We again made eye contact, I froze, and dropped my sandwich. Bits of lettuce and cheese scattered around me as Danes went about her business.

But could I have ever hung out with her? No. I couldn't even jive with the progeny of the one-percent who sat next to me in class each day. They just had a certain ease with each other, the result of growing up within dense social networks that stretched from Manhattan charity galas to European capitals, from the Hamptons to Aspen and all the big-money zip codes in California. Multiple generations of their families had been to Ivy schools and knew all about the secret societies, school fight songs, commencement rituals, and so on. Their ability to access the requisite Yalie identity was just a question of activation and performance.

I believed that I was smart enough to be there, but I also soon realized that I was surrounded by some supremely intelligent people. Feeling overwrought in my classes, I tried to keep up with the work but eventually fell behind. Working in the dining halls didn't help, since I was literally washing the dishes that my classmates had just eaten their dinners on. But student kitchen workers were part of the unions' bargaining unit and this identity as a union member added some grounding, community, and pocket change to my life.

The other students always appeared to be so at ease. It seemed like being smart or hardworking wasn't enough. I lacked what Pierre Bourdieu called a habitus, the set of attitudes and dispositions ingrained within you over a long period of time, marking you as a member of a class. You're socialized in distinct modes of dress, diction, posture, and consumption, gradually learning the rules of certain elite settings. By the time you're at Yale, it's almost muscle memory to you: marshaling intimate knowledge of scholarly references, following the cues and norms of classroom discussions, casually socializing with the most affluent kids there. The best Manhattan prep schools model their classes according to Ivy academic standards, including the vigorous seminar discussions that characterize Yale pedagogy. The students arrive in New Haven already comfortable with the energy and etiquette of intellectual sparring and with managing a schedule where you can read and write for hours on end and complete impossible amounts of work.

It's this habitus that was vital. And exactly what I was missing at the time. The mastery of that Ivy sensibility is what ultimately sets apart curious and entrepreneurial high achievers and those who can't focus on something for three minutes without fumbling for their phones. The challenges of discerning and learning the correct habitus would continue when I started grad school at Columbia, worked for the Army, and made my way downtown.

I know. I have a real masochistic streak that pushes me to repeatedly sniff around places where I don't belong. But by the time I started my Army work, I was older and had a stronger sense of self, plus some sociological training. During the first few years of college, though, there was so little to cling on to. My parents did their best but couldn't possibly know how to help me, and my brother Joel, who went to Yale after I graduated, had an even tougher time but persevered. (He graduated and even met a wonderful girl there to whom he's now engaged.)

My unchic friends and I found outlets in the usual things that college kids do. But had we been in school in Manhattan during the late 1980s or early 1990s we might have come under the sway of someone who promised to make the pain of Otherness vanish. Someone who could gleefully open the gates to a magical world of fun, belonging, sex, and release. Someone like Michael Alig, a pied piper of the night who like me had high school dreams of *getting out, getting anywhere.* His modus operandi wasn't to learn the rules of the game but to break them, since Michael has always seen himself as existing beyond the boundaries that constrain the rest of us. His boyish boldness and good looks made up for what he lacked in downtown habitus. But his killer smile and tremendous charisma ultimately dragged several people into the abyss, including himself. Addiction, death, dismemberment, and delusion are now the legacy of the Club Kid Killer for whom I would end up working.

With his team of frenemies in tow, Michael achieved what media savvy creatives can't do today: the creation of a well-funded collective that dominated four major Manhattan clubs, appeared on mainstream TV talk shows, published a magazine, threw wild outdoor parties, and convened "Style Summits," pageants, and national tours. And all *without* social media, nifty apps, and iPhones. Their madcap events drew Björk, Jared Leto, Marilyn Manson, and Chloë Sevigny, long before they were famous. Many of today's nostalgic wannabes are intensely inspired by the looks, lexicon, and even the invitations that serve as flags of the club kids' self-celebration. What explains this influence? Maybe Astro Erle summed up their mind-set best: "We're geniuses but we're freaks but we're outlaws."

Their moment ended in 1996, when along with Robert "Freeze" Riggs, Michael did the unthinkable: the killing of a fellow downtown kid—a drug dealer known for wearing angel wings—and the dismemberment of his decomposing corpse using knives bought at Macy's. The killing of Andre "Angel" Melendez led to a manslaughter charge and sixteen years of prison for Michael. In the *Party Monster* documentary released a couple of years after the crime, James St. James declared, "If you've got a hunchback, you know, throw a little glitter on it, honey, and go out and dance," an early be-yourself, it-gets-better mantra later reprised by Gaga, RuPaul, and other pop personas. But no amount of glitter, or even time and penance, can erase the stain of having cleaved apart a human person. Nothing Michael can ever do will shove Angel's killing down a memory hole.

I can't imagine what it must be like for Angel's family to have their relative's memory endure as a supporting character, a big winged human prop, in the sparkly saga of Michael Alig. And to have Wilson Cruz—little Ricky from *My So-Called Life*!—play the role in a feature film starring Macaulay Culkin and Seth Green. Or to see young male performers audition for the role of Angel in musical adaptations of the story, or dress up like him for Halloween. As James put it in *Disco Bloodbath*, Angel aspired to be a "Club Kid Superstar Drug Dealer," a pathetic ambition but a motivator nonetheless. As dreadful as Angel might have been, I bet his peers relished spitting on him: the unattractive, poor spic faggot who could never match up to all those pretty clear-eyed white boys prancing around in their underwear. Sound familiar? Maybe he even had someone like F break his heart before Michael and Freeze smashed in his head. Angel sold drugs to bypass the velvet rope. I sold sociology.

•

To work on a book about a notorious nightlife figure and get texts from that person as you're writing is an odd thing. But odd is an apt label for the summer after Michael's release from prison, when I worked as his assistant. Over the course of thirteen prison visits and tons of letters, I had developed a solid researcher's rapport and personal understanding with him, at least I thought I had. I volunteered for the unpaid role because I had a light summer teaching load and wanted to see up close what his reintegration into free life would be like. As I told a friend who had dressed up as Michael for a party or two, working with the convicted felon was one of the most fascinating, hilarious, and exhausting experiences of my life. Eventually I walked away from his pathological presence, baffled as to why the State of New York would release him.

My duties included cataloguing the over two hundred paintings he created while imprisoned, a long process that meant sorting, naming, photographing, pricing, and organizing images of them into a file that could be sent to gallerists and buyers. I also scheduled his interviews and meetings, processed invoices for him, and even styled him for photo shoots by the likes of Francesco Carrozzini, who at that point had just started dating Lana Del Rey. It was the oddest possible scenario for the old Gandhi Vic: packing up make-up brushes and hairspray, or matching up shirts and pants in order to doll up the aging Party Monster.

I also taught Michael how to copy and paste on his computer and debated everything from the nature of mental illness to the minutiae of hair care how-to's. After scheduling press interviews, I would make sure he knew how to get there, sending along detailed subway directions. And with so many interview requests coming in from all over the world, we discussed the merits of each of them. Was it some random wannabe blogger asking for a two-hour conversation so they could ask the same fucking questions that ALL previous interviewers had asked him? Or *GQ* or *Details*?

Together we rode rollercoasters, had margaritas with my mom, saw the Whitney's Jeff Koons retrospective, and went shopping at Pat Field's boutique. I sat in CNN's green room at the Time Warner Center while he was interviewed live on air, relieved that we had made it on time. Years of solitary confinement destroyed his ability to process the passing of time, Michael said, so he was always obscenely late to appointments. Always.

By the time I stopped contact with him in 2015, I concluded that there were at least four personas within Michael. Each of them in some way enabled both his accomplishments and his crime.

THE THINKER. The most pleasant Michael, by far. This one is fluent in German and can intelligently discuss postmodern satire, obscure members of the Warhol Factory, the CEOs he most admires, the coming of the singularity, and ways to resurrect Detroit as a cultural mecca. While at a restaurant or gallery he will immediately conjure up ideas for a fabulous event: what should happen in which corner and what you can hang from where. Fun stuff. This version usually appeared during quiet one-on-one moments or dinner parties at the homes of his most accomplished friends, including teachers, entrepreneurs, and creatives. He's eager to hear others' opinions, though still often sarcastic and irreverent. And he inevitably finds a way to pull the conversation back toward him. People meet this one and are relieved or excited to do business with him, not realizing there are other Michaels.

The Thinker originally aspired to build a national community devoted to cultural innovation. An old friend of Michael's, Artie Hach, won an Emmy for his styling work on *Sex and the City* alongside Patricia Field and is now collaborating on Michael's fashion line. Chatting in his artsy Upper East Side apartment, he located the apogee of Michael's reign in the opening of Peter Gatien's Club USA in Times Square. The club kids had traveled to major cities in a hunt for the country's coolest citizens. "One person from each city was picked and they were flown in to New York for the opening of USA. You know, *that's fabulous.*"

THE ADDICT. A man preoccupied by the satiation of physical impulses, whether a blowjob, a bag of sugary candy, or worse. This Michael is hooked on hookup apps and is obsessed with the salacious, showing XXX videos on his phone to whatever gay man happens to be nearby. The one pulled toward the abuse of heroin, special K, Klonopin, Xanax, and a laundry list of other drugs to which he became enslaved. The Michael that apparently used drugs soon after his release and lied to me about it for months. A man who is running extremely late to a meeting with potential collaborators but will still stop to buy Sour Patch Kids and Starbursts that he'll then offer to the appalled people he kept waiting. I kid you not.

Ernie Glam lived with the Party Monster both pre- and post-prison, and collaborated with him on fashion designs, *Project X* magazine, and other efforts. When I asked Ernie about Michael's allure, he told me, "[Michael] has like this desire to get his way even if it might hurt other people." As club-kid roommates, they both developed drug habits. Crystal meth was used, trays of ketamine or cocaine passed around. Michael became so messy that he would always lose his keys. The Addict's solution? To break the lock to their home so he wouldn't need keys at all.

Artie visited Michael at Rikers Island not long after Angel's killing. He remembered, "And he actually asked us to smuggle him drugs and he told me how to do it. You put a bump under a stamp. So when you mail him a letter you put a bump of K [ketamine] under the stamp." Artie refrained from fulfilling the favor.

THE CHILD. The boy who failed to develop the ability to process pleasure like most adults: to want something, have it, feel joy, and move on to other concerns. This is a partying little punk Peter Pan who throws tantrums. Literally tantrums, as in folding his arms and refusing to move, like a kid in first grade, screaming, "I hate you,

Victor!" This Michael was particularly problematic when he had his eight o'clock parole curfew and I was forced to pull him from a fun party. And have you ever been on the subway when little kids get on talking really loudly? Then mom or dad will step in to shush the kid, right? That was Michael and I when we rode the subway after his release. I had to teach a fifty-year-old man what a "subway voice" was.

When he decided to rebrand himself as an artist he was totally uninterested in learning the rules of the art world. I advised that he plan out gallery walks the way my art students do or visit the studios of other painters. Instead he assumed the role of a clueless brat, whining to anyone who would listen about how badly he wanted a gallery show. But being the Child does not imply cute innocence. Kabuki Starshine saw Michael as a reckless prankster and the "number one mess on the planet." Comparing him to Alex DeLarge, he remembered a night of revelry and rampage, when he saw Michael "smash an ATM machine in a bank, like beat it with his fists and break it."

THE MANIPULATOR. The version that incessantly tries to cajole, entice, and use those around him via sob stories and actual sobbing. Like Gaga, the one who can let the emotions flow on cue. The one who promises heaven in a handbasket but genuinely enjoys tormenting others. It starts with casual teasing, the kind that I actually enjoy partaking in myself. But he doesn't know when to stop. You see the sinister twinkle in his eye and that mischievous grin that appeared the first time I met him in prison. A version of him aided and abetted by the Child and the Addict, easily overpowering the Thinker. This Michael knows full well that something is mean or cruel but will laugh anyway. He relishes blowing up someone's spot in the most flamboyant way possible. James St. James, Lollipop, and other ex–club kids know this one all too well.

Lollipop's short clubland tenure of only about a year was enough to be pulled into Michael's employ, making clothes and seeing his manipulative sadism up close. As Lollipop explained, "He loved to pit people against each other, kind of just to watch what would happen." And yet one of Michael's portraits hung behind me as we talked in Lollipop's apartment. She remained loyal to him throughout his prison term. Why? "Really because of him creating this world, I am who I am today." The ex–club kid Walt Paper is similarly honest about his old leader while still professing affection, "He's a very good liar. He always has been and he knows exactly how to play people. So like, I love him but I know him as well."

Working as Michael's assistant let me see up close the source of his cult's power: *his utter lack of any sense of limits.* For better or for worse, he possessed virtually no reasonable appreciation of boundaries on his conduct. Yes, he has a deep knowledge of cultural history, one that spans Grand-Guignol to Leigh Bowery to Mauricio Cattelan. This could be seen as a kind of limitation or grounding, if he recognized himself as part of a broader artistic lineage, an extended transhistorical continuum. Instead, it somehow becomes a license to act as he pleases. When it comes to Michael, I learned what Cady Heron did in *Mean Girls*: the limit does not exist!

"Michael took it to a limit beyond the limit," ex–Limelight collaborator Steve Lewis said. "The limit comes when it's no longer educational: it's snobbery, when it's not accepting of new blood, it's a hierarchy for power purposes. And that's what happened to Michael." Seduced by status and drugs, Michael only cared about his inner circle's habits being satiated.

I gradually phased out of the assistant role after five months or so. Although I felt totally drained, there *was* a particular trigger. After chatting with Lollipop, I warned Michael about stirring up drama between my friends and me. Sure enough, around the time of his first exhibition in June 2015, Michael the Manipulator did *exactly* that. The last straw. I was so done.

Like Warhol and Gaga, Michael's biography has its own set of narrative building blocks well known to most people who give a damn about him and his antics. The *Party Monster* documentary (1998), the infamous *Disco Bloodbath* book by James St. James (later retitled *Party Monster*), the feature film (2003), the *Glory Daze* documentary (2015), and a planned sequel to the documentary continue to spread his dark mythos to wannabes and misfits today.

Michael grew up in Indiana under the care of doting mother Elke, whose eccentricities are seen in other works about her "little boy." Elke and I have never met in person, but while Michael was in prison we spoke often over the phone, off the record. Our chats led to what I thought might be an actual friendship, although I knew full well that she primarily saw me as a conduit to her son, both while in prison and right after he left. The "Hi, Victor, how are you?" was very quickly followed by a "Have you heard from Michael?" Make no mistake. Despite always complaining about her health problems, Elke can be conniving. *He learned it from watching her.*

During our phone kikis, Elke would talk freely about her past, raising Michael and her other son David, a divorce from their father, and her own family in Germany. Elke would also at least make the effort to ask about my personal life, joking about finding me a husband, what I should do with my hair, and so on. She even gave me a name in case I ever tried drag: EUREKA BOOZE. Get it? Early on, Elke and I agreed that whatever was said between us about Michael would remain between us. In November 2014 she broke that agreement and we have not spoken since then.

Throughout the time that I knew Michael I heard and saw plenty of his fans fawn over him. Suburban straight women with families and dogs—picture-perfect examples of mainstream hypermodern domesticity—lovingly purchased all his keychains, magnets, wristbands, and other kitschy wares as soon as they were available. They had obsessively consumed Michael's mystique via press interviews, *Disco Bloodbath*, the films, and all the club kids' rowdy appearances on the *Geraldo*, *Donahue*, or *Joan Rivers* shows.

One of the fans converted via the talk shows was Indiana native and recovering addict Lindsey Bise, who now runs the "Official Club Kids and More" Instagram account with over eight thousand followers. The wacky kids parading around on the talk show stages gave Lindsey an identity. As she remembered, "I was the one wearing like club kid attire through school, so I was the weird one. I was the one that like people made fun of because I was wearing things that I had seen from the club kids and dyeing my hair different colors and all of that stuff."

Over the phone, Lindsey told me about attending college for a bit until she "got into the party scene too much." She battled a five- to six-year-long addiction with heroin and OxyContin until finally detoxing when authorities threatened to take away her son.

Lindsey created the Instagram account simply because her obsessive collection of so many old club kid images on her phone had maxed out her storage capacity. She just needed a place to archive them, not expecting anyone else to ever see them. Why did she save the club kid looks in the first place? "What they did was art." Still, she had no actual connection to the reality of the scene itself, either then or now. During our chat in 2015, she explained, "I've never been to New York. I've just really been obsessed with it from afar."

On social media, Lindsey quickly became one of Michael's most vocal defenders after his release. She finally met him when he visited Indiana and noticed the same thing that I did when first seeing Michael: how short he is. "I guess because in my mind he's such a larger-than-life figure I was real surprised that he's not as tall as what I thought he would be," she told me, giggling. Like so many other moms, Michael drew out the caretaker in Lindsey: "I'm a mom for one thing, but I just had this sense of like, I wanted to protect him, and I want to take care of him."

Sitting on a tall stool in a crowded Starbucks near his Upper West Side rehab center, little Michael let out a loud burp before starting an on-the-record chat about his upbringing. Like others, he felt responsible for his parents' fighting and eventual divorce. His sexuality was a key driver of the conflict. "My mom and dad had been fighting over whether or not I should be allowed to play with dolls and my mom said I should and my father said I shouldn't, that it would make me a sissy," he said. Nevertheless Elke got him a dollhouse, which he would hide from his father. At school, Michael would get into trouble for picking his nose and wiping his finger on someone, or recounting the gory horror movie scenes that he has always loved so obsessively.

Although he originally intended to go to Purdue with his boyfriend, their breakup pushed Michael to apply to Columbia, NYU, Cornell, and Fordham. Only the last of these accepted him and offered him a scholarship, so off he went to the Bronx. It didn't last, given the powerful pull of a pulsating club scene just a train ride away, brimming with all those cavorting cute boys.

In months of working, drinking, and traipsing around the city with Michael, I rarely heard him speak with the utterly wistful fondness and yearning that he reserved for the old Forty-second Street cinemas and the triple-run horror movies they featured. He vividly recalled dragging boyfriend Keoki to watch the *It's Alive* trilogy, *Trap Them and Kill Them*, *Make Them Die Slowly*, and *Cannibal Holocaust* in the grimy theaters of the old gritty Times Square that so many people fear or miss. These were places so dangerous and disgusting, Michael said, that he couldn't go to the bathroom by himself, needing to venture through decrepit hallways where lurkers smoked angel dust or got blowjobs. Maybe seeing that I was appalled not so much by the scene he described but by his intense longing for it, he explained to me, "That kind of thing keeps New York so edgy that the rich, normal people are afraid to come here, so it belonged to us."

His old club kid compatriot Christopher Comp sympathized. Now a Pittsburgh resident and office worker, he only visits the city maybe two or three times a year. He told me, "It's a fabulous place. However, there isn't the same street culture and I don't mean just the crime, although to be honest with you, when Mayor Dinkins was mayor, I liked the, kind of, scariness of the crime. Maybe I wouldn't like it as much now, as an adult."

Miss Guy, a longtime scenester and hit DJ, was critical of what his downtown domain has become. "Nobody ever went to Ludlow Street in the late eighties unless you lived there or you were going to buy drugs." Today, he said, the East Village and Lower East Side are dominated by "frat boys and bitches in heels that are too high for them to walk in." Lollipop also noticed the new supremacy of a safely conformist style devoid of edgy danger. She sniffed at current bourgeois fashion blogs: "I mean, *Man Repeller*, wow, cool, you're wearing overalls again."

Jojo Americo, another nightlife veteran and former Patricia Field employee, remembered the horror of his neighborhood after riding his skateboard home one night. Calling his mother, he told her, "My roommate's a heroin addict and there's blood splattered all over the floor and I saw this woman running down the street with a knife coming out of her head in a nightgown. I kind of want to move!" Another time, street kids attacked Jojo and his friends, wielding baseball bats with razor blades mounted on the ends. His friend emerged slashed and with a broken arm. "I ran fast," Jojo recalled. "I was like, 'I'm not dying tonight. I gotta go.'"

During this gritty Gotham era, starting at the bottom of the clubland social ladder and without mastery of the right nightlife habitus, Michael faced an initiation. In *Disco Bloodbath*, James recalled his own role in trying to keep out his future partner-in-fabulousness: "There are a million stories of how we all tortured him, ran from him, and tried desperately to thwart him. When he was a busboy at Area, I might throw drinks and ashtrays on the ground and scream 'Busboy!' just to make him grovel. When he started throwing parties at Danceteria, we wouldn't be caught dead gracing them with our social presence."

Undoubtedly it's James St. James who can claim credit for having infused the club kid story into pop culture via *Disco Bloodbath*, although there are probably days when he regrets having done so. As others have observed, Michael and James are maybe the archetypal frenemies, bitchy rivals but also inextricable fragments of each other's lives. They seem to understand each other in a very real way. To feel truly understood by another human being is a rare thing, no?

When I first reached out about a chat, James was initially reluctant to dive into more endless chatter about Michael. Meeting in the beautifully ornate lobby of the Roosevelt Hotel in Hollywood, James rushed in, waving his hands wildly, on a lunch break from his job blogging for World of Wonder, the entertainment company founded by downtown scenesters Fenton Bailey and Randy Barbato. Meet James and you'll quickly notice a crisp elegance to his voice and a cheerful quality to his giggle. It'll put you at ease. He suggested ordering desserts, so we munched on chocolate and caramel confections as he dished.

James moved to New York to study theater at NYU, but like Michael, quickly got caught up in downtown thrills. The mid-1980s were dominated by the club Area, which attracted the cool set upheld by *Details*, the bible and chronicler of the It crowd. Soon enough *Newsweek* baptized James as a hot new "celebutante," getting tossed up into a fabulous new urban elite. Michael Musto showed James the ropes and for two or three years they went to parties together. As James remembered, "For an eighteen-year-old kid to have his introduction to New York under Michael Musto's tutelage, it was an amazing thing." Still, ex–Limelight director Steve Lewis insisted that James never ended up becoming a true curator of the night. "James never attended a meeting about what the night was going to be. He was a mess," Steve told me on a club patio. "His value as a host is that he got fucked up and flitted around and did outrageous things."

Fleeing to LA was not enough to escape incessant club kid talk, and James admitted that he would be asked about Michael forever. He told me, "I would go to the grocery store and I'd be standing on line at 7-11 and somebody'd be like, 'Tell me about Michael Alig...'"

During our chat James was candid about being an aging clubland star and his need to fight off the bitterness encroaching on his thoughts. So knowledgeable about cultural history, and extremely funny, I could have talked to James all afternoon, but he needed to return to World of Wonder desk duty. After I mentioned to him that I would again be visiting Michael in prison, he was quick to assure me, *"But Michael and I don't have any problems."*

Reigning nightlife queen Susanne Bartsch told me that she was the one who fatefully introduced Michael to king of clubs Peter Gatien, since he originally wanted her to throw parties at Limelight. She was reluctant, but did do a couple of events because she owed him: Gatien had been a financial backer of her legendary boutique at one point. "I never viewed myself as a club kid, by the way," Susanne clarified to me, eager to distance herself from Michael. "I think I was more from the Leigh Bowery school. Leigh Bowery was not a club kid." Then and now, both Susanne and Michael lay claim to the same clubland forebear, a shared god of the night.

It was revered nightlife doorman Kenny Kenny who first told Michael about Bowery, the second person, after Warhol, who is considered the scene's greatest inspiration. As James corroborated in Anthony Haden-Guest's *The Last Party*, "Leigh was the Club Kid god. He was the one who outdid everybody. He grossed out all of us."

Growing up in a tiny Irish town, Kenny immediately felt excluded due to his effeminacy. A woman in a nearby candy shop would say, to his face, "Oh it's such a shame! You would have made such a beautiful girl." His parents were part of the problem, thinking that there was something wrong with him. Today, the dramatic flair of his lavish sartorial sensibility, plus his Irish accent, make him, like his old collaborator Susanne, a person who is often imitated. But he does some really excellent impressions too, including Michael's manic Americanisms.

Kenny's style became a life raft while stuck in his town. "It was saying, 'I'm not ashamed. I'm not going to become invisible. You're not going to have complete power over me.'" At art school, he found a new freedom that prepared him for London, where he fell in with the Leigh Bowery set. After shopping his fashion collection around town, he begged Bowery collaborator Rachel Auburn for a job. "I dropped off my portfolio and Leigh looked at my drawings, and Leigh said, 'You should hire him,'" Kenny told me, thereby solidifying his status in the bitchy, camp, over-the-top London scene that birthed Susanne and inspired Michael.

Calling Michael a "funny, evil little brat," Kenny nonetheless acknowledged him as the giver of his disco name. Doing a spot-on imitation, Kenny remembered Michael saying, "You have to get a club kid name! I want you to do a party!" Back in London he was just Ken, but was later told that he was more of a *Kenny*. Michael thought he couldn't be *just* Kenny, so he added another Kenny and voilà.

After hearing about Bowery, Michael and Rudolf Piper promptly paid the London scene queen two thousand dollars to show up at Tunnel. "He was just like this magical creature," Michael remembered. "I mean, he wasn't even human. He was like this superhero club kid, but more." Kenny pointed out Michael's homage to Bowery, telling journalist Frank Owens, "Michael made cheap copies of Leigh's clothes and did bad copies of Leigh's makeup. It's pathetic to rip somebody off that obviously. But Leigh didn't mind. When he came over and saw the club kids for the first time, he thought it was genius."

Michael wasn't entirely deferential to Bowery in person, according to nightlife crooner Joey Arias. He told me about finding Bowery on the verge of tears after Michael put him in a tiny Limelight room instead of the main stage. As Joey remembered, Bowery told him, "Joey, I don't understand it. They flew me all the way from London to perform in this corner? I feel like I want to walk out of here. I'm really kind of upset with Michael right now. He's been so good to me. Is this a joke or something?" Soon Michael arrived and commanded Leigh, "OK, bitch, get on that stage and do your thing!" Joey then "slapped the shit out of him," causing the young downtown prince to flee from his offense of the club kid god.

Michael himself admitted to a falling out with Bowery over a bid to design the restrooms at Club USA. Bowery demanded ten thousand dollars up front before even submitting ideas, a proposal that offended club kingpin Gatien, who wondered what would happen if the ideas weren't to his liking. A suspicious Bowery assumed that the club would use his ideas without paying, so they arrived at an impasse that was never resolved.

Despite mangled relationships with disco deities, it was the stunning success of Michael's Disco 2000 party that really made his name. So where did the idea for the iconic Limelight party come from? Reacting to my curiosity about what TV shows Michael watched as a kid, he mentioned old school classics like *Bewitched* and *I Dream of Genie*. He added, "In fact, *Gilligan's Island* was my influence for Disco 2000 because you had seven people on this island—seven completely different people—and when I was first booking Disco 2000 I was booking seven completely different events in all different parts of the club: you know, an S&M leather ball, and a party for a model, and a party for a fashion designer, and a party for Hare Krishnas, whatever, so you would get that weird mix."

So there it is. One of the most beloved parties in New York's nightlife history was inspired by a corny TV sitcom. Only in this town could the Child's fascination become a famed, lucrative, crazy carnival in a corner church.

But some blame Michael for nearly destroying downtown. Perfidia, the House of Field drag queen, proudly declared that the Fields were their own social circle apart from the club kids, whom he likened to the Charles Manson Family. As for Michael, he said, "I'm just not interested. I mean, I made up my mind and I forgive him but I don't want anything to do with him, personally." Perfidia remembered Michael's infamous penchant for having others drink his urine, especially via his "ecstasy punch." He said, "It probably had everything in it: some pee, some ecstasy." Armen Ra, another House of Field stalwart, told me, "I'm personally alarmed that he has become a role model for demented teenagers because he murdered somebody."

Artie Hach fondly recalled his front row seat to Michael's rise and fall and all the antics in between. "Like, he had a cute aura about him," Artie said. He also remembered Michael and other club kids once being late to catching a flight somewhere. "So Michael called in a bomb threat to the airport and it worked," he told me, giggling. "They held the plane and everyone got on the plane." Michael would also occasionally try to shut down competing clubs by calling the fire department. But even during those heady days, Michael understood the fleeting nature of his clubland reign. He remembered sitting with James and others in a limo that would ferry them to all of their parties. In between sips of champagne and bumps of coke, Michael remembered telling one of them "to remember this day because this cannot last."

Wielding even less of a downtown habitus than Michael initially did, Angel Melendez burrowed his way into clubland's status hierarchy by proffering substances that people desperately craved. In his book, James offered a common view: "Dingy old white wings, that were always knocking off my wig or spilling my drink. Oh, he was such a nightmare." Ex–club kid Lila Wolfe told me that although Angel was originally a pier queen, even then, "he was always a pariah," a "weird, low-energy, kind of glommer-on-er, like kind of negative, and want something from you at all times." Lila, who otherwise talked of the healing and positive energy that she could provide as a chiropractor, spoke with biting candor about Angel. "Nobody liked him, ever, ever," she made clear. "Poor thing and stuff, but something happened. He wasn't right in the head, man. He was just a fucking creep."

But there will always be fucking creeps in nightlife or at your job or school or anywhere. They don't deserve to be chopped up like a chicken and used as furniture. One of the more cringeworthy scenes in Ramon Fernandez's *Glory Daze* film is the moment when Astro Erle claimed that Michael used a box containing Angel's lifeless body as a coffee table. Astro told me the same thing. According to him, Michael began wearing dead Angel's platform shoes, and coyly asked, "Who's missing, Astro?" "And Angel was in the box," Astro explained. "And I'd be like, '*What is that stench? Something stinks.* You need to clean your apartment, Michael.'"

It's also an overlooked irony that one of Angel's former lovers agreed to host Michael following his release. Ernie Glam, Michael's longtime clubland collaborator and past roommate, had sex with Angel a few times. "I lived with the killer and slept with the victim," he said.

Love, sex, glamour, and murder collided in the heart of Michael Alig. Aside from Angel, the worst casualty of Michael's story is perhaps Keoki, a bad romance that nonetheless inspires young gay couples today. Their meeting is a key feature of the *Party Monster* saga as told in print and on screen. Keoki thinking he was straight, Michael cruising him, fleeing their cab ride without paying, Michael trying to mold him into a "Superstar DJ," and so on. There was definitely a spark there. They moved in together after knowing each other only two weeks, paying $170 in rent, beginning a relationship that would endure for seven years.

When photos of them together appeared after Michael's release, many fans enthusiastically cheered their reunion. After failed club efforts in Houston and Los Angeles, Keoki later returned to New York to throw parties with Michael at the Lower East Side club Rumpus Room. But Keoki battles addiction to this day and left New York in early 2017 to start rehab. It's sad to see young boys want to emulate what they think is a fairy tale of gay love, not realizing the enormous price that each has paid for their fame hunger.

My kiki with Keoki happened over the phone, after we met at

Sébastien Ra's Le Souk party. We would be reunited much later at Michael's art show opening at the Lower East Side gallery Castle Fitzjohns. A native of Hawaii, he told me about being drawn to music early on but intensely wanted to escape to New York, which he initially found to be "overwhelming as hell." Gay bars and multiple sexual encounters with men provided his own downtown education.

Michael, however, was his first great infatuation, an obsession that led to his career as a DJ. "Whatever it took to be near him—that's really why I became a DJ, I think," he told me. "I never really said that in any interview—this is the first time I'll ever really admit it—but that's why I became a DJ. I wanted to be near him, so I was like, I'll do anything to be near him."

But while sitting in prison a year before his release, Michael dismissed the great love of his life, presumably feeling hurt about their distance, and lashed out. In a May 28, 2013, letter to me, he bitched about Keoki: "youd think by now he would have grown up a little! hes almost fifty years old for kripe's sake! he should be grateful that anyone even still cares about his old ass! seriously, what has he even done lately to make anyone care about him? has he released any cds or anything? i swear to god i don't know how that guy even supports himself"

During our phone chat, Keoki sounded enormously conflicted about his relationship with Michael. For a while, he would DJ events thrown in homage to *Party Monster* and had dinner with Macaulay Culkin and Seth Green a couple of times in order to help them in preparing for their film roles. He avoids those parties now, explaining, "I've never been able to sit through the whole film. I just—even thinking about it now—I get a lump in my throat and I just feel really like nauseous."

Months before, while sipping wine with ex–club kids Richie Rich and Astro Erle, I mentioned my initial difficulties in trying to reach Keoki, so Astro called and left a message in the bizarre disco dialect that Michael developed: "Hey Keok-la-da-doo, skroodskrod-skrood! Um, hi. Call me back." Totally off-topic, Astro later pointed to me and told Richie, "Doesn't he look like Keoki?" Very generously, Richie replied, "He's way hotter than Keoki." They both professed love for him, but still, Richie reflected, "I just wish Keoki would have kept his shit together more."

It was a sentiment that recurred throughout my chats with other club kids. Lollipop told me, "He got this like terrible reputation of not showing up." On one night, Lollipop and Ernie Glam went to one of Keoki's upstate gigs. "We went up to Poughkeepsie," she said. "They had flown him in for this party of this sushi lounge place. Literally no one was there. It was sad." His DJ collaborator and rave pioneer Scotto also told me about Keoki showing up hours late to a Webster Hall main stage show. Keoki's lateness problem was consistent. "He's always late for some reason," Scotto said. "It doesn't matter what it is. But at the end of the day, if you're late to your job at 7-11 you get fucking fired."

In a way, Michael and I finally met when we did because of Lady Gaga. In early 2012, Ramon Fernandez, the director of the *Glory Daze* film, asked me for an interview after reading my essays situating Michael in a lineage of pop provocation between Warhol and Gaga. I had written about Gaga's Warholian model of pop performance art and the shadow that her Fame casts over nightlife scenes. Someone mailed my essays to Michael, who passed them on to Ramon.

After taping my interview, I wrote to Michael and we started an exchange via mail. Initially, his letters were earnestly appreciative and filled with fascinating commentaries on culture, past and present. In his very first letter, dated January 25, 2012, he immediately described the crux of his fame game as a restaging of a Warholian past. He wrote, "The club kids were merely an updated rehash of the Factory! But rather than take + redo an idea verbatim, I like to see the club kids as a continuation, an *updated* continuation, of something that had come before."

When I first visited Michael at Elmira Correctional Facility in 2012, I felt uneasy about being in a place filled with men considered worthy of long-term separation from society. By this point my transition away from my Gandhi phase was well underway. In order to fill out, I started lifting weights, chugging protein shakes, and running the six-mile loop around Central Park. I stopped shaving my head and lightened my hair to blond during the school year or straight up red or blue while on break. And heaven forbid I ever show up at clubs serving a yellow and brown professor look, so friends suggested picking up tighter, darker clothes at places like TopShop or H&M. This identity reboot unfolded in a tentative and staccato way, and when I showed up at Elmira I was still really anxious about how Michael and his jailers would treat me.

But after a total of thirteen prison visits with Michael, the visitation ritual became habitual. I inserted countless quarters into vending machines for popcorn and coffee and learned to just faintly smile at guards whenever they made snide comments about "the Party Monster's guests." Walks through metal detectors and encaged pathways adorned with glistening razorwire became normal features of a day spent in the upstate nothingness of rural New York.

My visits with Michael, usually alongside his editor Esther Haynes or ex–Limelight director Steve Lewis, were always intense and exhausting exchanges. Although plenty of sociology courses include Michel Foucault's work on the history of the prison system, few scholars actually visit an institution. For obvious reasons, you can't bring phones or cameras so a handful of Polaroid portraits, each costing two dollars (paid in quarters), serve as records of those days.

Elmira's garish beige visiting room for its General Population resembled a small cafeteria, although one entered through two locked doors. Inside it seemed that evergreen was the new black, not orange, since most of the inmates wore baggy uniforms of that hue, making them look like brawny janitors. They hung out with wives, girlfriends, pastors, or children, eagerly devouring junk food bought at vending machines. Into this thoroughly tattooed crowd would eventually pop in a short man with a childlike bounce in his step, wearing pants that were several sizes too big for him. He wore the kind of gold-frame glasses that I had to wear in elementary school in the late 1980s, around the time that this Indiana native began his rise to national fame as the king of New York's club kids.

During my first prison visit I arrived with Esther and my friend M, who was then auditing my summer culture class at Columbia. At that point Michael was locked up in the Special Housing Unit, or SHU, a separate wing near the back of the prison complex, after he was apparently caught with marijuana. This meant solitary confinement for him, a nightmarish time of mind-bending captivity. But in contrast to the General Population's noisy and crowded visiting room, being in the SHU also meant that we could chat with him in our own quiet little gray room, complete with its own security screening process, vending machines, bathrooms, and attending guard. Even in prison, Michael Alig was in a VIP room.

While waiting for the guards to bring in Michael, we started inserting quarters into the vending machine. I noticed a mousetrap tucked into the corner. After I pressed a button for some Skittles, I turned around and there he was: pale, gaunt, twitching, and hyper, eager for friendly contact during his brief respite from solitary. He had to sit down right away per the guard's orders, then put out his hand and said, "Hi, I'm Michael." Like Lindsey Bise, the thought that immediately crossed my mind was disbelief that someone so short could have caused so much damn trouble.

Michael got right to business, asking Esther if she had done this and that, and what did she think about his latest memoir chapter. Starving, he quickly devoured the bags of candy, chips, and chocolates that we had procured for him, eating so manically that he was practically gulping air after a while, leading to a fit of hiccups and burping as he talked. Esther seemed accustomed to this. M and I looked on in quiet shock.

After his frantic meal and business talk with Esther, Michael relaxed and started asking me questions. As soon as I mentioned that M, an attractive young boy, was technically my student for the summer, I saw, for the first time, *the smile*. That dimpled, mischievous grin for which Michael is known, accompanied by an evil twinkle in his eyes and that obnoxious giggle. *Hu-huh, hu-huh*. The one you see and hear repeatedly in *The Shockumentary*. And then innuendo about my relationship with M.

And so a small truth hit me: *it's still him*. For better or for worse, it's the Party Monster, the clubland prince who could kiss you one moment, piss on you the next. And he's still holding court, playing his games, but now caged behind bars instead of dancing on a bar, surrounded by the most awful men in the state instead of the most fabulous people downtown.

My subsequent chats with Michael focused heavily on his memoir and paintings, a long-term relationship with another inmate named Mike, fan letters he received from around the world, and post-release moneymaking schemes. Our conversations bounced from old clubland stories to the Manhattan real estate market, from celebrity scandals to which of his old friends now looked terrible. We discussed his role in Angel's death on only a couple of occasions. Michael was nearing the completion of a punishment imposed on him by the people of the State of New York and like any other inmate who completed his sentence, Michael was claiming the right to reboot his life, this time as a writer and artist in twenty-first-century New York, as Michael the Thinker.

During our first few meetings in prison, the thoroughly self-absorbed Michael rarely asked about me, despite immediately plunging into very personal stories about his bodily functions, emotional state, and sex life behind bars. But over the course of visits and letters, he became more open and less formal. He started teasing me about my hair and mannerisms and asking me about my fitness regimen. Since my fellow visitor was usually straight, he would gleefully turn to me for extremely detailed boy talk about the hotness of his fellow felons.

I had also mailed him my articles about Gaga friends who continued to be active in nightlife after Mother Monster's ascent into the pop firmament. During the summer of 2013, he had heard speculation about Gaga being "over" and the expectations around *ARTPOP*, to which he responded with excited approval of her "Applause" single. From behind prison bars Michael followed the new album's rollout, enthusiastically complimenting her flying dress and effusively tweeting via Esther, "Gaga is the female pop-star reincarnation of Leigh Bowery!" Recognizing an obvious connection to his movement's style, Michael was thrilled when the September 2012 *Vogue* cover story about Gaga mentioned the club kids as an inspiration for her (the article was written by Jonathan Van Meter, who previously profiled Michael for the magazine *New York*).

On several trips up with Steve, Michael asked me to transfer his paintings to Esther, so for days I lived with original Aligs in my Manhattan apartment. His most impressive pieces included a Hitchcock *Birds* tableau with blue Twitter logos assailing a man instead of crows, a cheeky interpretation of a cultural moment totally driven by what can be instagrammed, tweeted, and snapchatted. But remember that Michael crafted this commentary on canvas while incarcerated, having never used the Internet or social media or held a smartphone, much less carefully compared Instagram filters or managed friend requests.

Eventually, he'd learn it all. More or less. It was in March 2014 that the New York State Department of Corrections and Community Supervision, in its infinite wisdom, decided to let the Party Monster out of captivity. Once the news was made official on the Corrections website I sent out messages to Michael's loyalists. About a week before his release, Steve Lewis and I went up to Mid-State Correctional and I told him that he had been a trending topic on Twitter. "That's great," he replied. "What does that mean?"

After his May 5 release date was posted and dubbed #cincodeMichael by Twitter fans, a steady flow of texts, emails, and phone calls started flowing in. People who hadn't bothered to write or visit him in years suddenly wanted to throw a party for him or somehow use him to hock whatever shitty clothing line they made. And they were suddenly blowing up *my* phone. Multiple visits with the Club Kid Killer meant that I somehow mattered in downtown's eyes. Alongside Esther and Steve, during those early days after his release was announced, I was a member of his "Small Council," like the royal advisors of the Red Keep in *Game of Thrones*. It was a formation that didn't last long, as Michael was quickly pulled in a hundred different directions by people who wanted him as a "business partner" or arm candy for an Instagram.

Ramon Fernandez and Lisa Brubaker wanted to shoot his first day out of prison for their *Glory Daze* film, as did World of Wonder for a sequel to *The Shockumentary*, so the productions needed a site for a welcome home dinner. I suggested the Almond restaurant near the Flatiron Building, where I had organized the gathering for Warhol star Jane Forth.

On the fifth of May, I walked out of the subway with a knot in my stomach that confirmed the totally bizarre tenor of his release day. Ernie Glam, James St. James, and I waited near Almond's front door for Michael's van to arrive. As the cameras converged around the van, he bumbled out and ran like a giddy little school kid into James's arms. The dinner inside was beyond weird: munching on a salad while the film crews' huge cameras and lights hovered near my shoulder, all while sitting next to James, who had a merry kiki with Michael as if zero time had elapsed since their skrinkle-skroddle days. Michael was nervous but excited, and for a New York minute it seemed like he could actually pull off an unprecedented downtown comeback.

Instead, within three months, he was cruising apps for sex, was said to be using drugs again, and had resorted to hocking gimmicky keychains and magnets online. As in refrigerator magnets! Dashed were his Small Council's hopes for a humble, quiet life as a writer, artist, and repentant Thinker. Kitsch trumped *kunst*. There was even an online AligMart, riffing on Warhol's Andy-Mart, his own ill-fated spin on the Automat.

Since I had just screened *The Shockumentary* in my culture class, I spilled the Michael tea to my students, who seemed fascinated by all the pop drama. One student later asked me if we were secretly dating. The answer was a clear and total NO and I can report that Michael and I have never even kissed, much less had any kind of sex.

I probably won't be able to ever confirm this, but in all likelihood my proximity to Michael after his release cost me my faculty job at the Fashion Institute of Technology, which, funny enough, several club kids attended. During most semesters I use the club kid story as a case study in my Introductory Sociology classes, a way to expose the students to questions of identity, status, subculture, deviance, nostalgia, and a gritty old New York that no longer exists. Almost always, it's a home run. Students who never raise their hands suddenly have so many questions about the scene and its abundant pathos.

With the end of the spring 2014 semester coinciding with Michael's release from prison, my students were really interested in his attempts at re-acclimation. Since Michael had been calling me from prison, I had the inmate phone system's number saved as a "favorite" on my iPhone so I'd get the call even if I put the phone on "Do Not Disturb." I told him when I'd be in class so that he wouldn't bother calling at that time. But one afternoon he did, and the phone rang in the middle of my FIT lecture. I asked the class if they wanted to talk to him and they eagerly agreed, asking the caged Party Monster on speaker phone whether or not he knew how much the subway now cost. (He didn't.)

One FIT student was so inspired that she designed an entire collection inspired by club kid aesthetics, so I invited her to that World of Wonder / *Glory Daze* Almond dinner for Michael on the day of his release. That was it. I had zero intention of inviting a felon convicted of manslaughter, fresh out of prison and completely overwhelmed by the sights and sounds of twenty-first-century New York, to my sociology classroom.

But about a week and a half after the release, a *New York Times* profile of Michael quoted me and mentioned my book. I woke up delighted to be quoted in the newspaper of record for the first time. When I got out of the shower, though, there were several voicemails on my phone demanding that I call my boss, the chair of the social sciences department. A congratulatory greeting? Nope. A student from a previous semester's class—not the one that Michael called into—complained to the administration, claiming that I intended to bring a killer to class.

Apparently I was the talk of the school's administrators, and someone in the vice president's office asked that I be investigated. "Investigate away!" I told my chair, who had conducted my peer review and knew that I was a strong and effective instructor. I was told who the aggrieved student was and I remembered the person being pleasant but distracted and not very capable. When nothing came of the "investigation" and I was given teaching assignments for the fall, I assumed that I was in the clear. The classes were pulled from me, however, over minor bureaucratic reasons, a cowardly way for them to ease out an adjunct with zero job security.

Others also got skewered for supporting Michael. Nightlife star Kayvon Zand pissed off his scornful peers by sponsoring an event paying homage to *Party Monster* two days after Michael's release. His own experience with exclusion led him to feel some sympathy for Michael's plight. Although at first Michael appreciated Kayvon's extended hand in solidarity, his fondness for petty mockery—Michael the Child—led him to insult Kayvon on his YouTube show *The Pee-ew*, causing grave offense to someone who went out of his way to welcome him back to clubland.

Like so many, Kayvon soon saw Michael's true colors and abandoned any expectations of decency and humility. Today, he sees the value of Michael's story as a cautionary tale to young people, especially addicts. Kayvon expressed disappointment at Michael's skewed values: "Now it feels like his priority is really about making a comeback and being famous." Considerably younger than Michael, Kayvon was astute enough to realize the flimsiness of the fool's errand that still preoccupied Michael the Addict. "Getting on Netflix and stuff—is that gonna make him happy with his life?" Kayvon asked. "I don't think so. Because it's another drug. *Fame is a drug. Attention is a drug.*"

That summer, being Michael Alig's assistant sometimes felt like working for *Mean Girls*'s Cady Heron, who as a product of her parents' African research trips and homeschooling, had to be educated in the most basic social rules when she was suddenly plopped into a Midwestern high school. Upon Michael's release, a friend had given him an old cell phone and at first, after each call, he would turn the phone off, not realizing that you're supposed to leave the damn device on. A friend showed Michael how to forward an email—and explained what that meant—or I'd show him how to search his Gmail account for a file that I had already sent him three times. And it was sometimes hard for me to suppress a giggle when he would grip, jab, and poke a smartphone too hard, lacking the kind of techie muscle memory that most now grow up with.

Twitter, of course, he took to right away, an easy fix to feed his fame hunger. While I was his assistant, his following hovered around thirty-two thousand and I managed his account on my iPhone, sometimes tweeting and posting photos for him. This meant that my phone got a steady stream of notifications from fans, manically begging him to follow them or showing off fabulous school outfits worn in homage to their favorite club kids.

Michael would sometimes forward emails from hot young boys living in the middle of nowhere who fawned all over him, or long messages from wacky quacks pitching ideas for truly stupid get-rich-quick schemes. I remember the desperate pleas from a tragic duo calling itself "The Fabulous Wonder Twins." They begged Michael to tweet what has to be the WORST song and music video that I have heard in my nearly four decades on this planet. After the trickle of blood from my ears finally stopped, I told Michael that he just *had* to refuse their request. Blame me as his bitchy assistant if he wanted, but to endorse pablum for the sake of popularity would diminish his brand value.

Silly me! He would end up doing that all on his own.

For our work sessions I'd sometimes meet up with him outside his rehab clinic not far from Columbia, watching a steady stream of patients meander out. My Terminator robo-vision was fully activated, but now scanning a decidedly non-fabulous crowd. Fascinated, I watched Michael's fellow patients, like the older woman who slowly walked out the front door in what seemed like pajamas, stopped in the middle of the sidewalk, and silently stared at me, mouth open, before shuffling off toward Broadway. Then the unshaven, gradually paunchy Club Kid Killer would bounce out behind her wearing wrinkled clothes—usually either too tight or too big—that his devoted legions of fans had sent him.

We also had a lot of fun. Our email exchanges were playfully silly, always gossipy, teasing but never flirty. Michael often called me "miss thing" or his "groovy guru" in the midst of obsessing over his social media followings and the sales of his paintings. He loved comparing me to Dame Maggie Smith's imperious and flamboyant teacher character in *The Prime of Miss Jean Brodie*, and after I watched the movie I could kind of see why.

At Yotel in Midtown I organized a little gathering so that my curious former students could meet Michael and in between periods of sobbing he of course fell in love with one of the boys from my gender class at Hofstra. Warhol star Bibbe Hansen stopped by the afternoon assembly, as did Gaga's friends Breedlove and Jocelyn McBride. Months later I threw a small birthday party for Michael and Jason Martin, Lady Starlight's brother, at my apartment. More old students came, as did Ernie Glam and his husband David, plus nightlife stars like The Box's headliner, Rose Wood, who gave Michael a box of condoms made out of condoms. Michael left both events very drunk, but happy to be fêted and surrounded by the smart, pretty people who embraced him. He actually seemed grateful toward me.

At an all-you-can-eat seafood buffet in Midtown, I also watched Michael reconnect with old clubland pals like Jennytalia, Pebbles, Karlin Supersonic, Desi Monster, Walt Paper, Ernie Glam, Christopher Comp, and David Alphabet. Gray flecked their hair and the lines on their face ran much deeper than the Limelight days. Disco names, club garb, and party invites seemed very far away. Still, they had survived and there seemed to be a genuine love and appreciation for their aging family of the night. Jenny, now a mom and respected Lower East Side mentor, shared a tearful moment with Michael, recognizing how far they had both come.

Michael rubbed old friends like Kenny Kenny the wrong way. When they met face-to-face after Michael posted a Facebook photo that Kenny didn't like, a confrontation ensued. Kenny remembered saying, "You know, Michael, you came out of jail and you went straight ahead to just, 'Be famous.' And everybody was expecting a phone call—especially the people that had written to you or had worked with you—to say, 'Hi, can we do coffee?' This is the more human thing to do." Apparently, Michael replied by admitting to Kenny, "I really think there's something wrong with me."

Before Michael's release there were times when I doubted that New York's prison system would ever let him out alive, particularly the night that he called, crying hysterically, after prison guards tossed him around like a ragdoll. Never before, and never since, have I heard anyone weep so manically, with such unfiltered fear at the possibility that he was living his last night alive. To hear Michael cry like that and to feel that my own actions in those moments could determine his fate made my steely sociological mask break open. My voice cracked and I felt frozen at the sheer helplessness of the situation. I pulled it together and called his editor Esther, who knew how to handle the prison officials.

His letters would often recount the severity of prison life that you and I will probably never understand firsthand. In a June 19, 2013, letter, he wrote, "you just cant imagine what it feels like in here . to be surrounded constantly by people who are scheming, out for something, wanting to trick you, fakely [sic] befriending you in order to gain your trust so they can rob or hurt you later in some way . . . it REALLY gets to you at some point ..you begin to lost [sic] faith in all people even though i realize, intellectually that people out THERE arent like this . . . well, i dunno."

What must have been the awful bleakness of those prison nights crept into my mind months later while riding the subway with Michael, watching him peer around the train looking for hot boys, just like he would in Elmira's visiting room. "Victor, Victor, look! What about him?" I would stare at Michael and shake my head, thinking back to that ragdoll night, when I ended the phone call wondering if it would be the last time I ever spoke to him. But standing next to Michael in the subway he had no way of knowing about the recollection in my head. He just pouted and cried out, "Oh, Victor, what now?!"

Michael's not-so-subtle cruising of boys was a fixture of any outing with him. At first I assumed that this was a natural consequence of a gay man being caged for sixteen years or even a possible sex addiction. But then I noticed that behind his lustful performances was a deeper obsession with appearance, affection, and attention. Michael was nothing if not consistent in his boundless narcissism: his goal was actually to solicit the attention in return, to get the boy to look back, to be *wanted* by the boy. If sex and affection followed, so be it, but the sport of it all—the "cruise"—held the most allure for

Michael, who as a man hovering around fifty, feared that any future partner would want him merely for his infamous past.

Joe Polsonetti is the only person that I know who refers to the ex–club kid king as "Mike." After a prison correspondence, the Massachusetts native became Michael's first serious post-release boyfriend, although their long-distance relationship caused tensions from the very beginning of their odd couple pairing. Thoroughly tattooed, the second thing you notice when meeting Joe is his charmingly thick Boston accent, where a word like *yours* is endearingly rendered as *yaws*.

When Michael called me to ask about a certain bar where he wanted to take Joe during his first visit, by chance I was just a few blocks away with my mom. Meeting up at Yotel, Joe was slightly nervous, but sweet and open, freely talking about making a living through phone sex and webcam chats with men. After a few drinks, our funny little quartet decided to move to another one of my fave Hell's Kitchen spots, Don Patron. There we were, strolling along Forty-second Street, my sixty-something Mexican mom chatting with a phone sex operator about the gages in his ears, while I caught up on gossip and PR stuff with the Club Kid Killer.

Joe and I got along at first, but we did have a few spats. I initially saw him as an out-of-town interloper and a distraction to the projects that Michael the Thinker and I were trying to launch. But he proved to be one of the most kindhearted people that I have met in the last few years. Joe doesn't care about guest lists or fabulous parties or book deals. All he really wants, I think, is companionship and close friends in whom he can confide. When I developed a post-F crush that again broke my heart, Joe was there to console me, calling me from Boston to make sure that I was OK. I'll always be grateful for that.

From his earliest kindergarten days, Joe knew that he was gay, feeling different from other boys. To stave off his queerness, his mom would buy him preppy clothes from Sears, which a young Joe promptly tossed away. He later found a sartorial channel for rebellion via a goth identity, but under the pressure of bullying, anxiety, and depression, dropped out of school at the age of sixteen. When he finally came out as gay at the age of twenty, he dove into nightlife and drugs, snorting coke in the bathrooms of Boston clubs like Machine and Club Café. Drinking made him tired and overheated, Joe told me, but drugs have always appealed to him. At only eleven years old, he started smoking weed and did his first hit of acid.

A year after Joe came out, he watched the *Party Monster* feature film and documentary, loving the heavy use of drugs in the films. When he saw an article about Michael being released from prison, he wrote a letter and inserted a few photos of himself, like so many of Michael's young admirers did. Their exchange became more intimate and Joe was excited to hear that Michael wanted him to visit New York after his release. What was Joe's first impression of Michael? "Very handsome," he remembered. "He didn't look a day over like forty."

They did seem to genuinely care for each other, but I don't know if their relationship could have lasted. The Party Monster frantically rushing around with reporters, old downtown friends, and crazed fans, and still trying to squeeze in time for Joe's calls or infrequent Boston trips?

To make it all worse, Joe remembered, Michael was abusing Suboxone and cocaine when they were together. As Joe told me about accompanying Michael to Harlem to score coke from a drug house, I felt disgusted, especially since I wrote an article for *BlackBook* saying that as long as Michael stayed clean, "he can count on me like family." It turned out that the Addict was lying to me—his assistant, his ally, his friend—the whole fucking time.

In the course of one cocaine run, Joe recalled being gypped by a group of men who took their forty dollars and sold them some other powder. They were finally able to score an eight-ball but didn't have enough to pay up. Michael's solution? Ride with the dealer back to Ernie's apartment in the Bronx, and then pay for the dealer's cab ride back to Harlem. When the transaction was completed, the relieved couple set out to enjoy their successfully procured prize. Joe remembered hugging him tightly. Later, "I was sniffing lines and he was smoking it—smoking crack."

But Joe later realized that Michael went into his wallet and took out $140, leaving him without funds to get back home. Out of the magnificent goodness of Michael's heart, Joe was given money for a Chinatown bus back to Boston and some subway fare. Their relationship fizzled from there on out, Joe said, feeling that his bond with Michael had become more about being "drug running partners" than boyfriends, with Joe needing to counsel him on how to beat drug tests. So much for New York State's parole and rehab programs.

One night, Joe, Michael, and I were all at Ernie's apartment while he and his husband David were away for a few days. I was cataloguing Michael's paintings and going through my to-discuss list with him, while Joe worked on some sketches for other painting projects. Since Ernie and David live so far up in the Bronx, I was invited to just crash on the couch for a night.

We were drinking, of course. (Michael's favorite rib: "Victor never says no to a drink.") A few glasses of rosé in, one of Michael's zany antics got more than a little weird: the Party Monster pretending to malevolently wield a knife and threaten to stab me. Remember, NO LIMITS. Michael loves to push people's buttons, so he did actually come at me with the knife. A little prick of my sternum. Drunk and relishing my shocked reaction, he started cackling maniacally. The sight of it all was just too much. The old king of the club kids, fresh out of prison, standing right there in his boxer shorts and a fan-made Disco 3000 T-shirt, clutching a kitchen knife and finding the act of stabbing his assistant just totally hilarious.

Joe tried to help me. "I thought that it was maybe like a joke between like, you know, just two friends or whatever," Joe remembered.

"And I remember getting up, saying like, 'Get that away from him!'" My phone was right there and I snapped a few photos. I couldn't help it. Maybe part of me expected something like that to happen all along.

I knew that Michael was trying to be funny but I was also really unnerved. It's just not normal. I tried to laugh it off as we decided to turn in. They went off to his bedroom and I curled up on the couch. No way would I be able to fall asleep. I thought of all the pranks that Michael the Child would find totally funny. Pissing on me while I slept or putting his bare ass next to my face. Something stupid that he would record on his phone and then tweet out to the world.

So I waited until the sun came up a few hours later and I quietly slipped out. I got home and went to sleep, waking up mid-afternoon to a flurry of texts and voicemails from Michael, Joe, and his editor Esther, who all assumed that I had been brutally savaged in the early Bronx dawn.

Although it was mostly just playing around, imagine one of your friends pretending to stab you while holding a knife and laughing insanely. Oh, and he just happened to have been recently released from state prison for MANSLAUGHTER. And not just the act of killing but dismemberment too. In no way was it acceptable.

Years later, Joe is still in Boston and we've kept in touch. We sometimes chat about what became of Michael but mostly we talk about the usual things that friends chat about: cute boys we met, what movies we saw, our families. During our on-the-record chat, though, I asked him what he would say to one of the many clueless fans still pining for his old boyfriend's attention on Twitter or at his Rumpus Room party. "He's not a very good person to associate yourself with," Joe spat out.

Joe and I managed to overcome our initial standoffs, but he and Ernie's husband David Maurici hated each other completely. A total clash of identities on every possible register. David, always helpful and courteous, found a fulfilling career working in a Chelsea doctor's office primarily serving gay men. The practice isn't far from G Lounge, the gay bar where he first met Ernie. During their first few months of dating, David had no idea that Ernest Garcia had a nightlife past as Ernie Glam. It was only at a birthday party where Ernie and friends were looking through the late Alexis DiBiasio's photos that he learned about his boyfriend's club kid past.

When Ernie floated the possibility of hosting Michael postprison, David refused. Ernie imposed the decision, but eventually David settled into an indispensably helpful role with Michael, becoming for him what he couldn't be for Ernie. "When you live with somebody for ten years, like I live with Ernie, he's very self-sufficient," David told me. "He doesn't need anybody helping him do anything." Michael's arrival gave David a project. "He became my *gayby* [gay baby], so meaning that like, he needed me to help him do things. It was nice to be needed by somebody for certain things, because when you're in a relationship with somebody and they don't need you for anything really, like, sometimes maybe you feel neglected."

But David assumed something beyond the role of roommate and caregiver. They began falling asleep together in bed. Cuddling and massaging ensued. It seemed to others and me that David was growing a little too attached while also having to watch Michael date Joe and hook up with other men, some of them procured via apps. "Michael wasn't allowed to have sexual partners in the room, but he did," David remembered. He insisted to me that their friendship was platonic, and moreover, David told me, "He smelled." Despite David's total denial of a sexual relationship, I would at times get calls from Michael worrying about the unwanted advances and possessiveness of his roommate.

Michael brought excitement to the Garcia-Maurici household and, as Joe said and David confirmed, drugs. Together, David told me, they shared Michael's prescription for Gabapentin, as well as morphine, Suboxone, heroin, ketamine, and crystal meth. High on molly and drunk on liquor, David and Michael were thrown out of

John Blair's party at Stage 48 after Michael vomited. "I did see crack pipes in his room," David corroborated, "and I saw broken crack pipes on his floor . . ."

I asked David how his relationship with Michael finally unraveled. His reply was a convoluted chain of last straws, beginning in early 2016. I tried to follow along as David unfurled a strange story about a nightmarish New Year's party, a cocaine dealer, a fake "hostage taking" in the Bronx, a sexual fetish involving cigarettes, a stolen iPhone, video denunciations, Facebook shaming, and secret plans to end their YouTube series *The Pee-ew*. "[Michael] was atrocious during the filming of *The Pee-ew*," David remembered. "He treated me like shit when we filmed *The Pee-ew* at Love Gun and told Ernie not to pay me any money for my hard work that I did."

It's amazing to see the long string of people who became so close to Michael before fleeing him. Men like Joe and David loved and cared for him in ways that I never did. But I was able to process my frustrations with Michael through these pages, by speaking with his old club kid friends, or contextualizing him in downtown history during my sociology lectures. Guys like Joe and David had to reckon with it all on their own while somehow finding a way to move on.

Marcia Resnick's book about "New York City bad boys" and an accompanying photograph exhibition at the Howl! gallery showcased her fleshy, emotive portraits of legends like Jean-Michel Basquiat, John Belushi, William S. Burroughs, Divine, Mick Jagger, Klaus Nomi, Iggy Pop, Johnny Rotten, and Andy Warhol. Marcia met these downtown icons through her nightlife outings, which were both fun and functional. "I documented the Mudd Club but mostly it was a vehicle so that I could get people to come to my studio, you know, so I could meet people," as she told me during a walk-through of her exhibition.

I spoke with Marcia about her fascination with the figure of the downtown "bad boy" and how nightlife offered a fertile place for recruiting these subjects. But what was it like to photograph the biggest bad boy of the '90s, responsible for the worst possible thing that a human being can do? A year and a half before our walk-through, Marcia had photographed Michael, a shoot for which I styled his hair and did his make-up. I haven't talked to him since the summer of 2015, but the photo he uses as his profile pic on Twitter is still Marcia's portrait. "I enjoyed the fact that he was so worried about his laugh lines showing and his looks," Marcia said, chuckling about all his guffawing during the shoot at her apartment.

But now consider this. What if this bad boy's bloody crime was all somehow subconsciously intentional, derived from that whisper in the limo about his fabulous moment eventually ending? Kenny posited this theory, "Susanne [Bartsch] said he was worried about it all falling apart, that it's not going to last forever and that's why he did drugs. And I think Michael actually mentioned that to me himself—that he self-destructed because he knew it couldn't last forever." If true, it's absolutely horrifying that so much harm was inflicted because a brat from Indiana needed to knock down his house of cards before it collapsed on its own.

Steve Lewis told me that he started pulling away from Michael even before the crime. "I abandoned him because he had abandoned himself. He had abandoned our religion," he said. A similar disillusionment happened with me. The promise of a reformed aesthete contributing to cultural innovation faded in favor of the disheveled, narcissistic Addict. Toward the end of our work together, being around Michael would trigger in me a feeling that I hadn't experienced before: a desperate sensation of *please get me away from this ASAP*. Every interaction was so draining, so brimming with crisis and drama, weeping and whining.

And yet Michael is wildly imaginative and a lot of fun. He does some really great impressions. His imitations of me are spot-on. You don't become the most famous party thrower in the world by being a mousey wallflower. But I don't know where he'll end up. By the time you read this he may be dead, back in prison, or surrounded by a fresh circle of sycophants. Or he might actually be a sober, thriving entrepreneur. It seems unlikely. The Child, Addict, and Manipulator are now in full control.

Whatever you might conclude about Michael, definitely credit him with being honest about his hunger for fame. During our Starbucks chat, I asked him why, among a crowd with names like Starshine, Monster, Astro, and Sacred, he never adopted a disco name. Casually, he replied, "I was really interested in becoming known and I wanted the kids in my high school to see that I had become successful in spite of their not believing in me." It's understandable, and I think that we all have an urge to give our haters a middle finger if we make it Up There. But we see what happens when a person truly believes that the limit does not exist. To blindly pursue a downtown crown without any real devotion to a creative craft or a broader ideal will only lead to an empty, maddening life.

I don't know if people can ever truly escape their origins. Although I made it through Yale and Columbia and became a professor, I still sometimes feel a lack of the collegial habitus. This discomfort partly pushed me to seek out other ways of living via my downtown outings. There I found a way to gradually become a person that I liked, that I felt comfortable *being*.

To be honest, I feel sorry for the fans that blindly love Michael. They're seeking out the same things I did: an identity, a fulfilling way to live. But they weren't there to see his clubland empire rise and fall, nor was I. Frank Owens phrased it well in describing what Angel's death should have made clear: "The truth about the club kids and their thrill seeking—that violence is inherent in carnival—had become grotesquely apparent." But to his fans, it's not apparent. They'll gleefully put on the golden jock straps or assless unitards, paint on colorful dots or evil-looking eyebrows, teeter around in giant plat-

Rose Wood, 2015. (*Photograph by Christel Mitchell*)

Rose Wood, 2015. (*Photograph by Christel Mitchell*)

Anna and Kayvon Zand at The Box.
(*Photograph by the author*)

Raven O in The Box's dressing room, 2015.
(*Photograph by the author*)

Suzie Hart and Kayvon and Anna Zand
speaking to my NYU class, 2015.
(*Photograph by the author*)

Michael Alig after trying to stab me at
Ernie Glam's apartment, 2014.
(*Photograph by the author*)

Jocelyn McBride and Breedlove at a St. Jerome's photo shoot, 2015. (*Photograph by the author*)

Snoop Dogg at The Box's Fashion Week party, 2015. (*Photograph by the author*)

Steve Lewis and Michael Alig at Elmira Correctional Facility, 2013.
(*Photograph purchased by the author at Elmira Correctional Facility*)

Ernie Glam.

(Courtesy of the Alexis DiBiasio Collection and Ernie Glam)

James St. James at Bloodfeast.

(Courtesy of the Alexis DiBiasio Collection and Ernie Glam)

Kenny Kenny and Armen Ra.

(Courtesy of the Alexis DiBiasio Collection and Ernie Glam)

Keoki and Perfidia.
(*Courtesy of the Alexis DiBiasio Collection and Ernie Glam*)

Kenny Kenny.
(*Courtesy of the Alexis DiBiasio Collection and Ernie Glam*)

Michael Alig at Bloodfeast.
(*Courtesy of the Alexis DiBiasio Collection and Ernie Glam*)

Mr. Pearl and Susanne Bartsch.
(*Courtesy of the Alexis DiBiasio Collection
and Ernie Glam*)

Pebbles and Christopher Amazing.
(*Courtesy of the Alexis DiBiasio Collection
and Ernie Glam*)

Perfidia and Ernie Glam.
(*Courtesy of the Alexis DiBiasio Collection
and Ernie Glam*)

RuPaul and a leatherman.
(*Courtesy of the Alexis DiBiasio Collection and Ernie Glam*)

Susanne Bartsch, RuPaul, and a clubgoer.
(*Courtesy of the Alexis DiBiasio Collection and Ernie Glam*)

Dancers at The Roxy.
(Courtesy of the Alexis DiBiasio Collection and Ernie Glam)

Lady Gaga at Motherfucker, 2007.
(Photograph by Geraldine Visco)

The Jeff Koons Gaga sculpture at her *ARTPOP* launch party, 2013.
(Photograph by the author)

forms and be as purposefully obnoxious as possible. *They learned it from watching him.*

Others were susceptible to this theater but eventually grew up. James St. James understood the costs of Michael's mania by the end of *Disco Bloodbath*: "[Michael's] example taught me what I thought I would never find in myself: that to endure you must live within society's structure, and work with it, and join in the rest of the world." Even after sixteen years of incarceration I don't think Michael learned this lesson. It's appalling and—as a taxpayer, a little frustrating—that after a long prison sentence he is still essentially the same man, one without self-control or humility, stuck in a mind-set that delivered a frenzied fandom but certainly not happiness or health.

I was drawn to Michael's pathology because of the fascinating sociological riddle that he represented, and because I knew all too well how it felt to be the outsider. But I also mistakenly believed that he could be fixed, that the Thinker's redemption could be a bright, shining example of downtown's possibilities for reinvention. Now I just hope. If only Michael can truly rein in his addictions. If only these pages can help someone see the massive dangers that delusion and drugs bring. If only they can point someone away from an obsession with Michael's cheap grabs for fame. If only they can contribute to some bit of real justice for the Angel he killed.

4

THE KIDS ARE
ALL RIGHT

On big election days, you'll find me staying up all night watching the flashy spectacle on CNN: the BREAKING NEWS alerts crawling across the screen and the bright red and blue maps that the anchors poke and swipe live on air. And of course the stern pronouncements of the people's verdict by dreamy Anderson Cooper, with whom I once waited on a bathroom line at the Diamond Horseshoe, staring at his massive arms. Cooper was hanging out with pals Andy Cohen and Lisa Loeb, whose song "Stay" was a big hit when I was a kid. After she happily joined all the gays on the long bathroom line, it could not have felt more odd to wash my hands in a sink right next to her.

But before all that, long before party monsters I knew party politics, participating in the kind of election day spectacle that happened in vivo in towns across the country, at least in states that still used clunky old machines where a voter pulled little levers for their candidates. When the polls closed, opposing camps gathered around electoral registrars to await the "opening of the machines." The back panels of these prehistoric, rusty old contraptions were opened up and the tallies read aloud. One side of the room loudly rejoiced, while the other suddenly soured.

Sometimes I was on the winners' team, sometimes with the mopey losers, but the path to that realm started in a shabby old building across the street from the storied Chelsea Hotel. Years later I'd go inside the iconic downtown space. But back in high school, not imagining that I would ever even set foot inside the ornate old Chelsea, I was a regular on the other side of Twenty-third Street. I had drifted leftward enough, into the ranks of the Communist Party USA.

A lot of Margaret's old friends were former party members who left when they could no longer apologize for Soviet policies. Curious about the relevance of such a radical movement to current crises, I began reading its materials and stopping by meetings. The reds on Twenty-third Street didn't advocate for the violent overthrow of the government or even apologize for failed socialist experiments around the world. The party members were plain, middle-class professional folks more interested in nudging labor unions, community organizers, and progressive Democrats further left, away from corporate interests. When they warned about authoritarian and extremist impulses stirring in the "bowels" of the Republican Party, I'd dismiss them as Chicken Littles. But whatever shade you might throw at the aging, dowdy remnants of America's socialist movement, the early days of the Trump administration made it clear that they were right all along.

My involvement with those Communists up through the first few years of college was misguided, and one that my mother abhorred, but at the time I felt inspired by the party members' talk of radical theory, mobilizing young people of color, and dissecting capitalist boom and bust cycles. It was the first place where I saw people from different races and backgrounds truly get along—not because they more or less had to, like in a school or workplace—but because of their intensely shared belief in a fairer and more just country for working people.

At Yale I became convinced that what they preached about a socialist future just wasn't in our country's political DNA, whatever the reds or grumpy, frumpy Bernie Sanders might say. So I left aside pie-in-the-sky rhetorics and moved into more pragmatic politicking within the Democratic machine that controlled New Haven. The pull here was personal, largely happening through the mentorship of a truly brilliant Yale graduate named Julio Gonzalez, then serving as Alder for the city district made up mostly of undergrads. Although critics called him Stalinist and Machiavellian, his pragmatic genius and uncanny ability to read and assess power dynamics was so impressive that much of what he taught me I still apply to my life today and certainly to my downtown forays.

Recruited through a campaign to pass an anti-child poverty referendum, I was drawn to Julio's realism, savvy, and charisma. Unlike the Margaret crew or my party comrades on Twenty-third Street, Julio actually got things done. Barely out of college, he was an elected city official and increasingly influential power broker. Julio mattered. I soon became his mentee and, according to a friend, his "enforcer." He had Jeannie's fire within him but the fact that he was Mexican meant that we related to each other in a special way. *Finally*, a role model—a brown man like me, a smart and savvy Yale graduate, respected and feared in New Haven's political hierarchies—a glimpse of a future that might be possible for me too. And he saw some value in me.

Under Julio's tutelage, I started doing voter outreach—some of the toughest work I have come across—and I wasn't very good at it. During a mayoral re-election campaign that Julio managed, we would be given lists of registered Democratic voters, a stack of campaign pamphlets, and out we went into the sticky heat of a New England summer. Interrupting people's dinners, naps, or TV-watching, we would knock on their door, flash a cheesy smile and maybe a wave, and then try to explain why our candidate deserved their vote. No hashtag solidarity or social media sanctimony transmitted from the comfort of your cozy couch. Just very long, very sweaty days that demanded a big bottle of water, good sneakers, and a passionate, articulate presence on an annoyed stranger's porch.

Maybe I'd be better at it now after years of classroom lecturing, but back then I was too shy. And campaign life yielded way too much drama. As any operative of either party will tell you, a political office quickly becomes a brewing ground for it. The stresses of pulling together rallies, fundraisers, and get-out-the-vote efforts, late paychecks, employees and volunteers having sex and then having to work together, packing on pounds with pizza and beers late at night and hoping you'll walk them off the next day. Too many things. In the course of it all, I was sent to infiltrate and spy on a potential opponent's meeting (not by Julio), escorted out of a building for passing out campaign flyers, and cursed out plenty of times by disgruntled voters and campaign leaders resentful of Yalies involved in city affairs.

I began to notice some important subtleties in the performance of power during those New Haven crusades, whether in deals brokered by Julio and his loyalists in the mayor's ruling coalition, or in helping to recruit ambitious, fresh-faced Yalies into "the Cadre," Julio's little family of political superstars. Like Starlight, Warhol, or even Michael, Julio was a social curator, a persona collector. I witnessed how Julio and his top lieutenant—a calculating Kennedy devotee affectionately called "the man behind the man behind the scenes"—would carefully try to mold and place malleable new recruits. They could see a certain spark in people and I like to think that some of that keen eye rubbed off on me.

Although totally naïve and very rough around the edges, like I had been, the Cadre newbies would be trained and inserted into whatever context Julio and his allies thought appropriate: into a sympathetic nonprofit whose support was needed for a campaign, to liaise with the Yale unions that deeply distrusted Julio, or even to run for office. Although the building of progressive coalitions was always the name of the game, the true métier of our little mafia was power.

Growing and expanding the Cadre's grasp meant placing loyalists in key municipal posts, reaching into the higher rungs of the state party, fantasizing about national influence—as O'Brien told Winston in *1984*: "an endless pressing, pressing, pressing upon the nerve of power." *House of Cards* or *Reign* intrigues and plots at the very, very local level.

As I consolidated my spot in Julio's inner circle, his lieutenant joked that I was being "seduced by the dark side," essentially tossing my lofty socialist ideals into a memory hole. I replied that I only wanted to "try on" Darth Vader's helmet, just take it for a quick spin, see what it felt like to breathe in it. Just curious. Wouldn't you be?

Wearing the helmet made some interesting things happen. I was the first person of Mexican heritage to sit on New Haven's Democratic Town Committee, part of a Cadre wave of Yalies taking city posts that undergrads didn't hold at most schools. Then I bargained my way into a wonderful two-year stint in City Hall's economic development office, doing work in land disposition usually reserved for full-time civil servants. In their office overlooking the New Haven Green, I learned about the real and practical good that municipal government could do for citizens through sensible interventions.

I remember a small, empty parcel of city-owned land in the Hill neighborhood that had become a disgusting dumping ground for garbage until the homeowner next door decided to clean it up. Even though the land didn't legally belong to her, she carefully tended to it and made sure it stayed pristine. When I joined Economic Development and the city wanted to sell off the parcel, two case workers and I went worked extra hard to clarify, ease, and expedite a process through which the homeowner could buy the parcel and add it to her property, knowing that she would enhance it even more now that she was its official owner and not just informal caretaker.

A tiny parcel, probably insignificant in the long run, but a visible improvement for a working class neighborhood. This was meaningful work that I could sink my teeth into, not the grandiose chest thumping of Margaret's crew or the old Twenty-third Street Communists. If this was the kind of end made possible by Cadre politicking, then it was all worth it. As a reminder of that time, near my bed I keep a print of my photograph of a blighted house in another New Haven neighborhood, gray and bleak yet somehow still elegant and alive.

Despite being involved in fascinating and intense work, I looked like a hot mess. Through a vegetarian diet consisting of pizza, pasta, and cheese I quickly packed on the Freshmen Twenty. My six feet of height thankfully offset the thickness, but still. My largeness, stiff demeanor, and fondness for long black coats led to a campaign pal dubbing me "the Dark Angel," a moniker that I didn't really mind. None of my work meant that I was particularly liked or popular. Instead, I was the local closet queen that refused to acknowledge his queerness and also happened to be clueless when it came to dressing. The worst example was the time that I paired a puffy dark brown jacket with loose dark brown pants, looking like some UPS delivery-man that had just joined the Village People. In my shitty all-brown outfit I met up with a friend who looked at me, bewildered, asking, "Vic, is that a uniform? Are you wearing a uniform?"

Three months after working for Julio on the mayoral campaign, an unexpected encounter triggered a determination to lose weight and thereafter fixate on my proportions. I was outside City Hall on a cigarette break (fourteen years later I quit for good) when a campaign staff member named Edna walked by and stopped dead in her tracks when she saw me, completely shocked. I had apparently gained so much weight in just a few months. SO MUCH. It was visible in my face, neck, arms, and torso, she said, then repeated it again just to make perfectly clear how plump and portly I looked.

Putting out the cigarette, I figured I'd calmly return to my office on the top floor of City Hall, shake my boss's hand, open the window, and step out. Instead, I tried to meaningfully process Edna's de-moralizing observations and plan out a healthier diet. A few months later, I started hanging out with a girl that I really liked, the one that

I'd end up dating for almost two years. Once the goal of impressing her was established in my obsessive mind, I started getting up at five in the morning, swimming for an hour, then spending another hour working out in the gym. By the time I saw Edna the following spring, I again left her too shook. She grinned and dramatically stomped away in disbelief, throwing up her hands in an excited hallelujah of approval for my newly svelte self. I yelled after her, "Oh Edna, look what you've done!"

So gradually I started to shed the anguish of my early college fumbles. In combination with my Cadre work, sociology saved me. No sexy flags, no great ideological statements, no rancorous meetings, just a way to finally make sense of the world around me. The first thing that I shoved under the social science microscope meshed both my Mexican background and my Cadre lessons. Encouraged by brilliant and supportive professors, I wrote a senior thesis about power, factionalism, and control in Mexico's ruling PRI organization, given the Orwellian label of "the perfect dictatorship" by Mario Vargas Llosa. Through my interviews in Mexico City and classes in Yale lecture halls, I learned about political hierarchies, patronage systems, and enduring despotisms, while in New Haven wards and City Hall offices, I saw raw power in action, converting my work with Julio's Cadre into a kind of applied sociology.

It was fascinating to see systems of reciprocity in Mexico that mirrored what happened in an urban Democratic town like New Haven. I saw how any class in power runs on quid pro quo tactics and a logic of *pan o palo*—"bread or stick"—either you contribute to and benefit from those in command or you are punished. This could mean exclusion from the ruling elite, at the very least. It was simple: play by the rules, be a loyal team player, produce results for the bosses. If not, *YOU CAN'T SIT WITH US!*

It was the first time that I clearly saw how similar social structures are. Politics, military, nightlife. We humans will always find a way to define, impose, and enforce hierarchy.

The most poignant collision of my past and present selves happened when Ernesto Zedillo—the former president of Mexico and great nemesis of the Chiapas rebels I supported in high school—joined the Yale faculty. He had completed his PhD in economics there, so it was a kind of homecoming for him. After one of his campus lectures, I politely introduced myself and even exchanged a few emails with him. Sitting alongside Margaret or my Twenty-third Street comrades dreaming up pointless "awareness" campaigns in support of the rebels, could I have ever fathomed such an encounter?

After finishing college I spent a year in Mexico City, continuing my political research through a fellowship at El Colegio de México. Living in a gorgeous neighborhood not far from the conjoined houses of Frida Kahlo and Diego Rivera, I wanted to integrate my Mexican identity into my adult life. But riding the Metro or hanging out with aunts and uncles during the weekend made it clear how very American I was in my attitudes and beliefs. The customs and prejudices of my birth country be damned. I did not belong there, but I did relish the research roles. And so it was in Mexico that I decided to give grad school a try. I remember so vividly sitting in my uncle's living room—having just interviewed an old guard Mexican senator in the bustling capital—and realizing how amazing it would be to do this as a career. I had to make it happen.

I knew that politics—on the street or in City Hall—wasn't for me. I wanted to study, to dissect, to understand. Julio was disappointed, I think, as were the other allies in the mayor's ruling coalition who had supported my ambitions. But still a shy, closeted wallflower, I wanted the removal and detachment that I thought the academy could provide.

My time in Julio's Cadre imprinted me in a way that I still feel today. His shrewd combination of realism and tough tactics was impressive and part of me wishes that we had both kept on fighting the good fight together. Julio had an ability to read people's needs and ambitions and align them with the fulfillment of his own ends, something that Gaga, Warhol, and Michael understood too.

But I also realized that achieving big things requires alliances cultivated with people very different from you. As smart or attractive or rich as you are, it's impossible to reach for the highest rungs without a cadre. Making it Up There requires establishing and sustaining a harmony of interests. If your crew doesn't realize that their ambitions and mobility are tied to yours, if individual excesses are not controlled, if sex, jealousy, and drugs overwhelm your cadre, the whole fame game can fall apart.

I grew up living with my brother, parents, and grandmother, a devoutly Catholic woman whom I remember being an avid watcher of afternoon talk shows. During dinner she would recount whatever wild stories had been featured by *Sally Jesse Raphael*, *Geraldo*, or *Donahue*. I sometimes did homework with these talk shows as background babble: guests would confess terrible secrets, followed by my grandmother's appalled reactions. It seems strange yet probable that a very young version of me scribbled on loose-leaf paper in my Trapper Keeper while my grandmother gaped at Michael Alig and his club kid friends prancing onto a talk show stage.

Many of those talk show appearances are now on YouTube, a de rigeur Google search for most after watching or reading *Party Monster*. They're curious visual artifacts, signaling a rare moment when an underground New York subculture popped into the American mainstream, so much so that the FCKNLZ culture troupe reperformed and reinterpreted the appearances at New York's Museum of Arts and Design in 2012. The club kid king and his minions were clearly out of their element as they faced a blinding national spotlight very different from the camera flashes of familiar downtown photographers. Dressed insanely and spewing manic defenses of their supposedly harmless hedonism, they horrified a studio audience plucked out of Middle American households yet inspired bored misfits or closeted kids all around the country.

Alongside Michael's crime, the talk show stints kept the club kid scene from tumbling down a memory hole. Looks were displayed, skills learned, connections made, and careers launched during what some consider a nightlife "Golden Age." As former Pat Field collaborator Artie Hach told me, "I met everyone through going out," gesturing at his Emmy. "That's why I question like, 'How do people meet people now?'" The club kid moment was no accident. Despite the freedom and pleasure-seeking of the scene, the participants understood hierarchy and control as they vied for the favor of their carnival's Caligula. Michael and Julio would have a lot to discuss.

Their downtown moniker originated in Amy Virshup's *New York* magazine story in 1988. Titled "Club Kids: Rocking with the New Music of the Night," she described the antics of Michael, Zaldy, James St. James, and Mykul Tronn. She wrote, "Clubs—the kind where you danced, anyway—were supposed to be dead, killed off by AIDS and the new gentility. Outrageousness—celebutante boys in chiffon dresses, girls in nothing but Saran Wrap—was out; conservative was in." This was 1988. If only her readers could have foreseen the lavish lunacy that would be soon be unleashed.

This was the age of the last celebutantes, a growing drag scene, and the ambitious upstarts who partied with Warhol and then kept downtown animated after his death. Desi Santiago, the ex–club kid turned successful art and fashion star, understood these lineages well. During a break from working in the studio he shared with Zaldy, the former Desi Monster explained, "We were looking back at Warhol and that was the trampoline, the catapult to where we were. And now that was going to be the catapult to another thing, twenty years from now." The club kid catapult would be the new role of huge nightlife venues as cultural incubators for fresh musical trends, sartorial innovations, and new aesthetics of distress and decay.

I won't ever fully understand the club kids' night carnivals at

Limelight, Tunnel, Palladium, and Club USA because I wasn't there. I was starting high school in Westchester while Michael's midnight empire rose and fell as he and his acolytes became arrogant, addicted caricatures. Before that, however, they were cobbling together a grand new clubland chimera. As Ernie Glam explained it to me, "The whole club kid movement was like an appropriationist movement where it basically just took all these other youth culture movements that preceded it, and threw it in a blender and mixed it up, and then like just vomited it all up and then here was the club kids."

Deaths bookend the club kid era: Warhol succumbing to complications from a gall bladder procedure in 1987 and Angel Melendez's murder at the hands of Michael and Freeze in 1996. Both were gay men from non–WASP families, searching for meaning and belonging. The outcomes of their tales could not be more different. Warhol's art and iconicity defined a whole moment of downtown history. Angel ended up in a cardboard box floating in the Hudson River.

Warhol had an affinity for nightlife as a stage for his pop persona, but ever the devoted voyeur, he preferred a detached, tongue-in-cheek perspective. At Area, Anthony Haden-Guest's *The Last Party* reported that, "Andy Warhol did an elegant piece, which has been inadequately documented, for understandable reasons. It was a sculpture that wasn't there. He was given an alcove and if he was in the club, he might stand in it for a bit." But as Frank Owens's *Clubland* documented, the Pop king did preside over a kind of passing of the torch: "Andy Warhol and *Interview* invite you to the grand opening of the Limelight," read the launch invitations. His *Interview* lieutenant Bob Colacello later attended an opening event with megawatt names Reinaldo and Carolina Herrera, who were scandalized by the church-cum-club. "This is desecration! We cannot stay here. I am getting ill," the designer maven told Bob. They soon left.

But one person's desecration is another's liberation. The wild Limelight scene loosened up, and sometimes tore away, social strictures on individual identity. It often devolved into mindless preening and posing for the big wigs and photographers, but not always. When we spoke, James St. James told me that he missed dressing up with friends, throwing on wacky garments and cute accessories, passing around vodka and coke lines. "For me dressing up was never about getting laid. It was never about being fabulous," he recalled. "It was about amusing myself. And if I could crack myself up while I was getting dressed, then that was a successful night."

As fun as it all sounds, it's important to remember how the power of throwing around Peter Gatien's cash animated Michael's machine. As he wrote in an April 24, 2012, letter to me, "Peter let me spend about $2,300 a night on club kids, which gave a lot of kids jobs + the freedom + ability to hone their skills + looks. It was an actual profession. Plus, we'd hire kids on Thurs, Fri, + Sat at all 4 clubs. It was an industry! But when we couldnt pay them, at the very least, they'd get drink tickets." Gatien was no Medici, but factor in a much lower cost of Gotham living and you see the power of funding manic nightlife art via the largesse of Michael's one-eyed patron.

To no one's surprise there emerged an enormous sense of entitlement, one that Michael even complained about in the *Party Monster* documentary. Christopher Comp's own disco name—bestowed by Ernie Glam—was a nod to all those cute, spoiled, *compensated* kids who were ushered into parties for free and never paid for drinks. Before coming out as gay, Christopher dated women and moved to New York with his high school girlfriend, who would become the club kid Pebbles. Having always wanted to move to the city, the club kids' *Geraldo* appearance stirred the urge further. Nightlife was enthralling for Christopher, whether attending Susanne Bartsch's "absolutely overwhelming" Copacabana party or the Outlaw party at Penn Station where he and Michael were arrested. Inspired by KISS, Kabuki theater, and horror films, Christopher gradually honed the clean, severe black and white aesthetic for which he is still known. Drug addiction followed, however, yielding a habit that he wouldn't kick until 2008.

Due to his current line of work, Christopher asked to be identified by his club kid name, as did Lollipop, who worried about her nightlife past damaging occupational relationships. Lollipop was yet another West Coast transplant who started clubbing in her teens and became enthralled by the magazine *Details*. After seeing the talk show appearances, she dreamt of maybe, somehow meeting the club kids one day in New York. After moving to the city to attend FIT, she chose a disco name that represented both the signature accessory of her look and her dance floor function. "Everybody's like out of their mind on ecstasy so they need something to stop their teeth grinding," Lollipop told me, so she filled her backpack with lollipops and started passing them out at parties.

The energy of those parties has been well documented elsewhere. The general vibe seemed to be what Kenny Kenny told Frank Owens: "You felt like you couldn't be judged by anybody for anything. It was perfectly OK to walk around naked, for instance. Basically, any kind of sexual behavior was OK; any variation on sexuality was OK. In retrospect, it was destined to become a nightmare. But at the time, at least for a while, it felt beautiful. It was kind of like the hippie thing. We were lost children who had found this surrogate family."

Not everyone thought it was beautiful. Go to any panel about downtown history and see what happens when you mention the hard-on-crime mayoral administration of former prosecutor Rudy Giuliani. As the force most often blamed for ending the Golden Age (alongside Michael), his name draws hisses and boos, even more so when "America's Mayor" lent his sneering support to Donald Trump's presidential ambitions. His mayoralty saw no value to nightlife. As Frank Owens argued, "Giuliani thought of nightclubs not as pop culture playgrounds that brought significant economic benefits to the city—not as important social safety valves where young people went to release the stress of urban living or as valuable incubators of musical movements (house, hip hop, punk) that had swept the globe—but rather as wholly sinister venues that promoted rampant antisocial behavior."

Later downtown generations sought it out and eventually tried to actively restage parts of it. When singer and Gaga friend Breedlove settled into New York years later, he and his pals sought out the scene that they had heard about for so long. "I've heard that there were club kids somewhere," he told me. "We were looking for them because we were also inspired by the idea of the late eighties, nineties New York club kid at that time and I really kind of wanted to find people that were like that and I couldn't find anybody that was getting dressed up like that at that point."

Although the club kids were a distinctly American and downtown phenomenon, thinkers and pundits trying to make sense of the club kids often point to theorist Dick Hebdige's work on subcultural style, in which he dissected a British punk "nihilist aesthetic" characterized by a "polymorphous, often willfully perverse sexuality, obsessive individualism, fragmented sense of self." In 2013, punk counter-cultural aesthetics were controversially enshrined in an exhibition at the Metropolitan Museum's Costume Institute. A movement that railed against "the system" and vibrated with aggressive, anarchistic, and angry energies was elegantly packaged and fêted at a Fifth Avenue gala for the wealthiest and most famous among us. There was Sarah Jessica Parker—Carrie Bradshaw herself!—rocking a Philip Treacy mohawk and Giles Deacon gown.

So too with the Limelight crowd. For the last few years one could find club kid costumes in Halloween stores, including a bright blue "Lil Club Kid" wig for babies priced at $12.99. Pop stars like Gaga, P!nk, Kesha, and Katy Perry carried on club kids' emancipatory rhetoric too. Even from the confines of prison, the Party Monster saw this imprint. In an April 24, 2012, letter to me, Michael wrote, "I've always felt 'We R Who We R' + 'Firework' were both very club kidish, in their message of shining + everyone being a star."

The high bourgeoisie picks from their party culture too. A friend of mine was browsing Barneys New York online when she stumbled upon Sies Marjan's "Club Kids" silk jacquard pencil skirt priced at

$1,490 and a "Club Kids" silk bomber jacket at $1,990, both emblazoned with colorful party scenes. When she sent screenshots, I was stunned by the flagrant, unvarnished nature of this direct appropriation. Like punk before it, the DIY stylings of a youthful scene had been bent and twisted to fit capitalist profit-seeking. When Barneys opened a massive downtown store in 2016, they even commissioned an ad campaign featuring Lady Gaga, Ladyfag, Muffinhead, and others. From bargain bins to Barneys, a subculture can always be mutated into a luxury brand.

It's a little strange to see nightlife faces during normal daytime hours, stripped of the false eyelashes, layers of bright make-up, teased-out wigs, and club couture. Often they're barely recognizable, if at all. At one of my favorite Thai restaurants, Room Service in Hell's Kitchen, I was looking for drag scene queen Linda Simpson and since she was out of look, I literally walked right past her. I apologized profusely and in her deep baritone, the Minnesota native forgave me.

That was strike two for me. A few months prior, Linda threw me out of her campy-kitschy bingo night at Le Poisson Rouge, where M was working as Linda's on-stage assistant and had kindly guest-listed us. BFF Talal came along and at first we behaved ourselves as we watched M do his Vanna White routine next to Linda in the basement lounge. But after way too many glasses of Prosecco, we started throwing shade at two rather rotund and frumpy contestants. Dressed in plain cardigans, the drab out-of-towners joined Linda on stage to claim their prizes: two kitschy little yellow cows. Something got into us and we started shouting, "Two cows! Two cows! Two cows!"

I know. Don't hate me. It was mean and we embarrassed Linda, M, and ourselves. We deserved to get tossed out.

So I was grateful when Linda was willing to forgive my Prosecco-fueled Mean Girl antics and still meet me for dinner. And then I almost fucked it up by walking right past her. Thankfully, the rest of our conversation was faux pas–free.

New York had always beckoned, Linda told me, especially after reading about the Warhol crowd. She's now a revered downtown godmother and when it comes to drag, she has seen it all: from the Pyramid star system of Lady Bunny, Sister Dimension, and Tabboo, to Love Machine hosted by Larry Tee, Lahoma van Zandt, and RuPaul, to the more "slick" and trans Boy Bar scene. She even launched the beloved politics-meets-pop scene magazine *My Comrade* in 1987.

With all this seen scene history, how does Linda explain the wild success of her old C.U.N.T. compatriot RuPaul? Now the world's most famous drag queen and one of the breakout stars of the club kid era, Ru can be credited with pushing drag closer to the mainstream than ever before. Glossy ads for her TV show adorn the subway walls and sides of buses during my morning commute. How does Linda make sense of it all? "Some 'right place, right time.' She's very motivated, very dedicated to her stardom," Linda said of Ru, "She's very beautiful, that has a lot to do with it. She's a really good package as far as a performer."

Linda had mixed feelings about the colorful and catty carnival of catchphrases that is *RuPaul's Drag Race*. She said, "I think it's really helped drag and kind of killed drag at the same time, you know? Because it's a certain sort of drag. It's more Midwestern, really, in many ways."

To see *Drag Race* ads dot the transit system would have been unthinkable during the club kids' heyday, as drag queens had to carry baseball bats or run through dangerous ungentrified neighborhoods just to avoid an awful bashing. Sadly, these attacks still happen, but places like Lips and Lucky Cheng's monetized drag into a commercialized shtick palatable to suburban tastes. What could previously have been considered a part of the underground avant-garde is now a gimmicky platform for shrieking bridal parties and the endless selfies of sweet-sixteens.

The TV show itself had a hard time getting off the ground. As *Drag Race* and *Party Monster* producer Fenton Bailey told me, "From when we did 'Supermodel' with Ru at the very beginning of the nineties, we were almost since then trying to sell *Drag Race*, so it took ten years basically and frankly, we'd given up. We'd been to Logo three times and they said, 'No, it's too gay, it's too this, it's too that.'" A development director at Fenton's company encouraged another try and the hit series was launched, later moving over to VH1 for its ninth season.

"If you can't love yourself, how in the hell you gonna love somebody else?" "Everybody say LOVE!" So go some of RuPaul's tired mantras, but on his show everybody throws SHADE. It's even a competition. There's a whole segment in season two where Ru asked them to insult each other. The queen who would go on to win the show, Tyra Sanchez, said that she doesn't read people, to which RuPaul mockingly retorted, "Of course you don't, Tyra, 'cause you're Christian."

What followed were cruel remarks exchanged about the queens' teeth, legs, feet, face, body hair, skin color, and age. Some reads: "Darling, how old *are* you?" "You are a *gringa puerca*." To a Laotian contestant, "What are you doing here, mama? Go back to Chinatown, girl!" Ru cackled throughout.

I get it. It's playful. It's just a show. But Linda kicked me out of her bingo night for throwing similar shade. The world rightfully decries President Trump for his insults. Say those things on Twitter and it's cyberbullying. Say them in the workplace and you might get fired. But shove it all under RuPaul's "Everybody say LOVE!" reality TV brand and, hey, hand the man an Emmy. As disgruntled *Drag Race* contestant Phi Phi O'Hara told *Vulture*, "I felt like we're not people to her. We're just game pieces for her show and she didn't care enough to know who we were."

A queen more senior to Phi Phi agreed. As Linda said, "You don't get that far in show biz by being just all about love, you know what

I mean?" Still, she admitted, there must be an authentic element in there, somewhere. "But some of that shit that she says I think she kind of believes," Linda added. A veteran of the Boy Bar drag scene, DJ and rock performer Miss Guy remembered a different RuPaul mantra from yesteryear: "In those days before she was famous, it was, 'Everybody say ALCOHOL!'"

RuPaul's current relationship with her club kid past is distant. Her shows feature Lady Bunny and maybe Susanne Bartsch's name will come up, but certainly not Linda Simpson, Michael Alig, or her onetime sidekick Flloyd.

To me it's extremely ironic that while prepping for the 2009 VMAs, Flloyd spent so much time with Gaga but never mentioned any of his history with people like RuPaul, Michael Alig, Deee-lite, and others. His relationship with Ru could have been an important conversation piece for at least two reasons. First, at that point Gaga desperately wanted the blessing of the established drag community, particularly nightlife veterans in downtown New York or the LA club circuit. The formal blessing wouldn't fully come until years later when RuPaul and Gaga performed for a poorly rated 2013 Thanksgiving TV special. And second, according to Flloyd, Ru understood the price of fame all too well, especially the tossing of friends down the memory hole.

I asked Flloyd about all this in his East Village apartment. He once worked for Kickstarter in what he said was an amazing job cleaning their offices and in the course of the work learned how to make his own cleaning products, oils, and soaps. At one point during our chat, he took various bottles of mint water and lavender water and started spraying them everywhere, quickly coating my face in wonderfully aromatic scents. Today, so far from cleaning stage blood off pop stars, Flloyd cleans people's houses so he can pay his rent, though his long-term goal is to be a comedy writer.

Flloyd is one of the most gracious hosts that I have come across, offering me an abundance of tasty snacks throughout our chat. Let's attribute it to his background, his kind southern hospitality. But if I mention Atlanta, what comes to mind? For me, it's *Designing Women*, a show that I absolutely adored, but not quite drag queens. And so you might be surprised that a key sliver of the club kid scene came from the Big Peach: Larry Tee, Lahoma Van Zandt, Lady Bunny, Flloyd, and RuPaul, who back in the day was in love with Flloyd's best friend.

Their tight but drama-filled friendship was typical of artsy queer youth, triggering a massive falling out at one point. Like the always hardworking Gaga, Ru's fame is not surprising to his peers, given his nonstop hustle back in the day. Flloyd remembered, "Ru was the consummate salesman. He always knew that you couldn't make money unless you had a product and he always wanted to be a singer, always wanted to get that contract." At the time Flloyd was dating Lady Bunny, who really wanted to meet Ru, a rising scene persona, and therefore pushed Flloyd to make peace with him. Bunny's suggested drag detente worked and the three soon became "inseparable," a gender-bending Atlanta troika emulating the Supremes, Flloyd recalled.

Despite their intense early bond, Flloyd spoke snidely of Ru as a wannabe "gay Barbie," "queen of the control freaks," and "childish and petty." Although leveling strong barbs at his old Hotlanta pal, there were hints of reverence for what Flloyd acknowledged is an extremely savvy mind, adept at remembering faces and knowing who in a room is valuable: "He's good at the business. He's good at schmoozing."

Flloyd also felt extremely wounded at having been displaced as Ru's sidekick when he first landed a talk show. They were all fans of Johnny Carson, he remembered, as they sat around dreaming of their glory days to come. "I was Ru's Ed McMahon," Flloyd said. "We talked about it forever. That's like a promise that he made me, was that I was his sidekick." When Ru finally landed a talk show with VH1 in 1996, Flloyd expected their dreams to finally come true. Instead, when he asked his friend about at last co-hosting the talk show, RuPaul replied, "What planet are you living on?" Flloyd recalled. "He was super rude."

Friends told Flloyd to sue Ru but he declined. The wound is still sore twenty years later, now that he occasionally sees footage of *RuPaul's Drag Race* on Logo and spots Michelle Visage next to Ru, loudly laughing as the judging panel spills tea. Imagine how this must sting a person. "That's where I'm supposed to be. Michelle Visage took my place," Flloyd said, munching on crackers in his small kitchen. "I see her and I'm like, 'Who the fuck is she?' What is that? Where did that come from? How did that *thing* step in front of me?'"

As Flloyd and I talked about promises made down south and broken up north, his boyfriend sat quietly in the living room looking through his phone, while their cat crept quietly around the apartment. Like others who flirted with fame before it capriciously eluded them, Flloyd's tone turned rather somber, although also slightly defiant. His gushing flows of gabbing gave way to quiet pauses when I could hear the cat scratching something in the corner. He said to me, "I think about what could have been. You know what I mean? Kind of have to think about that, right?" No, I tell him, that's a dangerous game. Can I get an amen up in here?

I turned on my tape recorder while M finished packing up his camera equipment in Amanda Lepore's tiny Hotel 17 bedroom, adorned with red curtains, a shopping bag overflowing with receipts, and, naturally, copious amounts of make-up. M had finished photographing Amanda for a magazine project that I was working on with F and she seemed really pleased with M's idea of aiming several big spotlights at her. "It's really cool," she told M, who savored the praise from downtown's glamour goddess.

While M hauled out his gear, I asked Amanda about the allure of the sexy and glamorous blond bombshell, especially the only celebrity that I think truly deserves the "icon" honor, Marilyn Monroe.

"Blondes have the most light," she said. "The most extreme girldom." Amanda so empathized with Monroe's tightly controlled place in the Hollywood studio system that she now saw herself as "Marilyn's revenge," a trans woman who can enjoy and love everything that Monroe could not. But while Amanda relished the benefits and openness of a new moment in trans visibility, she was also intensely nostalgic for an era in which she would most likely *not* have had her celebrity, or perhaps not even been able to transition. So why pine for yesteryear's Tinseltown? "It just looks better to me," she explained. *"And more tasteful and expensive."*

When friends took Amanda to the club kids' Disco 2000 party for her birthday, she fell in love with what she remembered as its countercultural, genderfuck vibe. "I had that sort of like punk rock 'n' roll kind of in me because I had to fight to be who I was also," Amanda told me. "It was a fight all the way as a child. I related to these kids." As Amanda fell into nightlife's embrace, she was promoted from go-go dancer to host, a job she still does all over the world.

Today, rare is the host that will go beyond sitting, gossiping, and drinking to actually greet new guests, dance, and mingle like Amanda does. So what made her such a welcoming host? "I think it's because I enjoy being there," she replied, citing her friendless childhood, endless scorn, and a marriage to an extremely possessive spouse. So nightlife gave Amanda a family context. She said, "I just don't get sick of it because I guess I lacked—*wanted that* when I was a kid." It holds true today. Known throughout clubland for always being gracious and kind, during our chat Amanda punctuated even the most serious statements with a giggle, or her sometimes honking laugh. And when I first dyed my hair blond about two years into my post-Gandhi makeover, Amanda blessed my bleached enterprise, kindly telling me that I looked good as a blond.

A sister in Amanda's clubland family was another future transsexual icon and nightlife host: Sophia Lamar. Go to YouTube and watch her *Donahue* appearance from back in 1993, alongside Michael

Alig, Richie Rich, Jennytalia, and others reveling in confrontational banter with Phil Donahue, who labeled their scene "a new kind of entertainment." Sophia was subdued, notwithstanding her massive coiffure, compared to bold declarations by Michael and Richie, who incessantly gestured at the audience with his hand mirror.

Sophia told Donahue that she was actually a "club personality," paid to be a "decoration" for the night, even back in the day unwilling to fully align herself with Michael's crew. No one today is surprised by this early defiance. Read her tweets and you'll find no cheerful updates about her day or meals. Or Amanda's playful comments and lipstick or kiss emojis. In April 2017, Sophia wrote, "I'm not here to fight you, I just want to tell you @ how shitty you and your aesthetic are. But I know mediocrity rules." Go follow Sophia's account and be prepared for her hilariously scathing takedowns of people that she encounters at her parties, rough readings that she's more than ready to do in person too.

Neither her supporters nor her haters would be surprised to hear that her West Village apartment, at the time of my chat with her, was a dimly lit, thoroughly black and gray affair, complete with a black cat that crept around the apartment. At one point the very cute feline maneuvered behind my head, nuzzling my ear to Sophia's shock: "She's being so friendly to you! I'm so surprised! She's so not social at all."

At Christian Siriano's 2013 Fashion Week show, Ashlee Simpson asked Sophia for a photo. She turned to a friend, *"Who is this white trashy girl?"* But she appreciated Simpson's warm demeanor and told me, "I really like her." Her set of likes also included Banksy, Kanye West, and fashion designers who were "chic, modern, rock 'n' roll," although these likes were smaller in number than the people who have attracted her wrath, like nightlife's ever-present scribe. "I never read Michael Musto," Sophia said. "I think Michael Musto smells *musty*. He's too old, too out of touch."

The Cuban exile instead looked to the Brooklyn warehouse scene as an innovative space incubating a mixed crowd, less shiny and posh perhaps, but more gritty and underground, more DIY than Pat Field readymade. But Sophia is not hopping on any bandwagon. She began throwing parties in Brooklyn before it became a gentrified and pretentious hipster haven. "People thought that I was crazy because I was one of the pioneers to go there," she remembered, having built the Electroclash scene alongside fellow club kid Larry Tee, Spencer Product, and Tee's then boyfriend Conrad Ventur.

Sophia spat out the word *gay* like it was a slur, despite having a wide fanbase in the community, reserving special venom for the basic, clueless, fame-hungry gay sheep that flocked to her parties. Her critique touched on a debate that I often discuss in my gender and sexuality courses and that pops up each June around Pride. To what extent should a "gay identity" even exist? Why posit an entire culture on what happens in the privacy of one's bedroom? Sophia, at least, had taken a stand: "Anything you do based on your sexuality is awful. *It's horrendous.*"

Beyond the self-limiting and contrived nature of the gay identity, Sophia criticized the sense of entitlement that accompanied young gay men in a time of greater expressiveness and visibility, before the Trump presidency sparked hints of a more militant moment. She saw this at her parties, where young muscle queens would arrive eager to disrobe: "They go there and they take their shirt off. And I was like, 'Sir, this is not a beach, and I don't have a lifeguard on duty.'" Her aim was to elevate the party dynamic, to expose this basic boy to a corpus of music outside the Top 40, and to educate him about the depth of culture that exists outside of Logo, Grindr, and whatever happens to be circulating on Facebook.

But Sophia admitted to a frustration at her inability to halt the tide of immature sheep and their desperate bids to take Instagrams with her as some trophy won during their night out. "Nothing frustrates me more than preconceived ideas and this entitlement," Sophia claimed, beginning to imitate her peon guests. "'Because [party promoter] Erich Conrad is there and Sophia Lamar is there, I'm going to take my shirt off and this is going to be gay, gay, gay. Whoa, wait a minute, what is that music? I want Rihanna! I want my Gaga!' You know? *'Fuck you, faggot!'* " She pulled back a little, sniffling, realizing how angry she became at the mere thought of these boys.

One accounting for Sophia's attitude emerged via fellow clubland veteran Astro Erle. "Now her nickname out is *'So-bitter Lamar,'* " he claimed. "New York City will make you bitter." He linked this to an ordeal at a club, which he said fired both Sophia and Amanda for being trans women. After a kerfuffle, Amanda got a larger settlement, initiating a divergent path between the two friends. Amanda went on to become David LaChapelle's muse and work on other major projects, while Sophia, according to Astro, had to settle for small nightlife gigs in which she was paid one hundred dollars here and there. For Astro, this unfair quality didn't justify her aggression. "It's not cool to be bitter [. . .] There's only so many freaks, so we have to stick together."

Sophia's loyal devotees celebrate her as a rare, authentic downtown icon, while her detractors claim that her brutal character is, well, a decoration, one meant to distract from the middling career of an aging Cuban transsexual.

How did Amanda make sense of her old friend's vitriolic voice? "She likes to speak her mind. I like to keep myself happy," Amanda said. "I couldn't think that way because I think, like, I would just get depressed. If I thought that way then I would have to jump off a bridge or something because, you know, I wouldn't be well."

The "club personality" that in 1993 coyly smiled at Phil Donahue as she described her modeling ambitions is still a nightlife decoration decades later. I went to her party at Leftfield on the Lower East Side and saw her energetically dancing, drink in hand as she twirled around a gorgeous young boy. Sophia compared party hosting to casting a film. "To me, a party is like a movie," she observed. "I'm doing casting. And some people are very unnecessary for the scene. *'You*

are unnecessary for the scene, sir. Miss, we don't need you here.'" Would
she actually say that to someone and politely expel them? Or would
the person who rants so viciously on Twitter ultimately acquiesce
to the demands of her profession? Sophia admitted, "People are very
gregarious. They want to be around people, even if they hate them."

Although many won't recognize Lila Wolfe's name as a mainstay of
the club kid coterie, most interested in their scene would recognize
her figure in some of the famous photos from that period, wearing a
tight leather bustier next to Michael Alig or sporting white men's
briefs or tape on her breasts alongside her friend Walt Paper. That
young, native New Yorker, at one point called "Tapedtitty Tantrum"
on a party flyer, is now Dr. Wolfe, "the number one chiropractor in
New York," according to her. It occurred to me that this was quite
possibly true as her receptionist directed me toward Lila's spacious
corner office in a Wall Street high-rise. Walking past a large aquar-
ium of colorful fish, a broadly grinning Lila munched on tiny chocolates, offering me several while I gawked at the gorgeous view that
she enjoyed daily.

She grew up in an artistic household, one that quickly threw her
into a world of museum visits and gallery shows. "My first toy was
a magic marker," she said. Her mother freelanced at an ad agency,
where she was directed to go after school so that, ironically enough,
she would stay away from drugs and trouble. Fatefully, it was her
mother's twenty-one-year-old gay secretary who began taking Lila
out to clubs at the terribly young age of thirteen. Her wide smile
grew larger as she recalled the two stops made on her very first night
out in New York: an Outlaw party underneath the Fifty-ninth Street
Bridge and then Red Zone, where her escort quickly breezed past the
velvet rope, teen Wolfe in tow.

Her garb on that first night was "really wack," Lila remembered,
sporting wedge sandals, palazzo pants, and a political T-shirt com-

menting on the Israeli-Palestinian conflict, which prompted curious questions from none other than club heavyweight Rudolf Piper. Lila pursued the task of becoming a door person with enough tenacity and charm that she would eventually become the gatekeeper of the VIP room at Disco 2000. She met Michael Alig right at the beginning of what she called "a fantasyland of fun." Despite being close to the outrageously clad Walt Paper and Desi Monster, Lila never drifted toward some of the more alien or devilish looks of other club kids. Contrasting her aesthetic with the provocative and ghoulish ensembles of Karlin Supersonic and Jennytalia, Lila sought to conserve a "curvy" femininity consistent with her figure and akin to that of Diane Brill.

Amanda Lepore became a kind of disco sister, giving Lila advice when she worked at the Belle de Jour dungeon. Still a virgin, Lila was tasked with duties that included spanking and laughing at men in diapers, feeding them dog food, and getting her boots licked by submissives. She stayed for only six months, feeling totally ill at ease: "I didn't know what to do, torturing a guy. It really put me off men for a while." Still, she made good money and developed an awareness of others' sexual needs. Amanda herself disliked being a dominatrix. "I wasn't really happy," she explained to me. "I was, like, depressed most of the time."

But how was a young teen able to wriggle free of parental control and plunge into nightlife madness? "I would dope my parents' salsa with sleeping pills," Lila casually explained to me while her sore-necked patients waited outside her office. After her parents consumed their spiked snack and passed out—a shot of NyQuil added in to their daughter's ministrations—Lila would sneak out, rage all night, and creep back home before they awoke. Soon hooked on coke, she nervously watched others disintegrate from their drug abuse. The influence of her family prevented her from totally derailing at this moment and she gradually sought an escape from the tragic fates that awaited many of her friends.

Lila's post-clubland life now revolved around chiropractic work with a client list that included everyone from janitors and construction workers to hedge fund managers and A-list celebrities. After weaning herself off the club life, she hopped on a flight to Georgia to begin chiropractic training at Life University. When she talked about this work, her body language and tone changed. It was a distinct "Dr. Wolfe" identity popping up, one slightly at odds with her old "Tapedtitty" self. Talk of the magical abandon of hedonistic revelry was displaced by phrases about "energy" and "healing." And yet she saw this labor as an extension of her nightlife work, her contribution to an environment that relieved people of the pangs of modern life. Gone were clipboards and guest lists, only able hands and a welcoming smile were needed for this healthy haven.

Although Lila still attends her friends' concerts and gallery openings, along with "a Ladyfag party here and there," she was considerably sour on how culture changed since her days as a door person for storied soirées. Running her fingers through her platinum blond bob, Wolfe shook her head, gazing out toward the East River that her office overlooked. "Now you can just buy fucking platforms," she said. "You know, it's so tired. Unless you're a midget you don't need them." I laughed, then asked about that fabulous young secretary at her mom's office, the one who ushered her through the shiny gates of clubland. "I think he's dead. Crack, or something."

The next time you're at a Manhattan restaurant, activate your Terminator vision. Look around. Scan and zoom. See the couple on vacation? They're intensely instagramming grinning selfies but don't have a single meaningful thing to say to each other. Watch the elderly widow sitting by the window. She's a regular and all the waiters know her story, although they don't necessarily care.

Note the youngish professor also looking around, looking right back at you. I have a small audio recorder, iPhone, and sunglasses in front of me. I'm waiting for a man who has painted the faces of the most famous people on the planet. But the man who will eventually walk into the Midtown East diner has rather disheveled hair, wears no make-up at all, and is wearing a faded black hoodie and a rumpled white T-shirt with more than one stain on it.

The make-up artist known as Kabuki Starshine is also often hunched over, maybe the product of years of stooping over people while he precisely applied their make-up. Or it's just the natural posture of a soft-spoken, almost fragile demeanor. But let this be clear: the fingers of this man have worked on the cheeks of Michael Jackson, the brow of Madonna, and the eyes of Lady Gaga. And still he admitted to feeling so awkward when meeting random nobodies.

I first asked Kabuki for a chat when we worked together on the Jane Forth photo shoot with Darian Darling and Veronica Ibarra. Zooming ahead to 2016, Kabuki, Veronica, and I would reunite in the same space when M•A•C launched his very own make-up line called "Kabuki Magic." The gorgeous Lendita Berisha accompanied me to the unveiling party, filled with industry professionals who had their own make-up exquisitely done. Kabuki, even as the fêted star of the evening, was humble and gracious as always.

Back at the diner, we ordered food and Kabuki jumped right in, stating, "I was a club kid when I was fourteen." Even as a boy in Florida, he went to school wearing make-up, becoming known as "that Boy George kid," and "famous but [having] no friends." Gym class was tough since he was uncomfortable taking his clothes off in the locker room. How could he, being "a tranny" with "subtle make-up on and everybody thinks you're a freak?" And yet the fact that he was labeled the local Boy George gave him a certain appeal as a micro-celebrity to others at the margins. "The four-hundred-pound girl that had the gay uncle that lived in New York would call me up," Kabuki remembered, his plate now yellowed by exploded egg yolks.

Boy George and David Bowie showed him an exciting new range

of possible identities to perform. But should he play it safe, or follow their lead and really experiment with his identity? "That's going to be so boring if I play it safe," he remembered thinking. Early on he considered the possibility of being transsexual until deciding that he didn't need a sex change in order to be a gender-bending "androgynous but not being in drag" persona. But ultimately Kabuki wasn't lured to the city by any romantic vision of downtown tribes. Since he was unwilling to cut his long hair just to find a job in Florida, he needed to move to New York: "I didn't want to lose my personal freedom of identity."

Being so femme, Kabuki's arrival did not imply a warm embrace by downtown gay hubs, but through a friend who knew Michael Alig and Flloyd, he discovered a sliver of wild clubland that to him resembled a living, breathing John Waters movie. At his first Limelight night, Kabuki was pulled to the front of the line. Finally, a place where he belonged. He was introduced to Michael and told that he could be paid, in essence, to go out and party. But he needed a disco sobriquet, to be supplied by his friend Jodee Jingles. Michael greeted the freshly baptized Kabuki Starshine with a recognition of the new addition to the night, saying, "*Oh fabulous.* Out with the old, in with the new."

To Kabuki, clubland was "punk, Dadaesque, there are no rules," albeit a world that was carefully curated. He became fast friends with Kenny Kenny, Olympia, Keda, and Zaldy but still couldn't shed the shriveling shyness of his character, recalling, "I was even more socially awkward then than I am now." This should not be confused with shame, since Kabuki was proud of his exquisitely crafted make-up being impeccable at four in the morning. But how was Kabuki trying to position himself in this Dadaesque demimonde? He sought to be "a drag queen with no tits. I was a femme Aladdin Sane, that was my ideal. Bowie at his most glamorous, most feminine."

The next big break in Kabuki's career as a make-up legend was getting a job at Pat Field's famous boutique, the longtime haven for nightlife personas in need of a daytime living. When it came time to style the women of HBO hit *Sex and the City*, Pat called on Kabuki to be the number two make-up assistant on set. Kabuki asked me to keep his comments about work on the show off the record (as well as comments about his direct work with Gaga and Rihanna), although he did speak fondly of later working with Macaulay Culkin, Seth Green, Chloë Sevigny, and Marilyn Manson on the 2003 *Party Monster* feature film.

But perhaps the apogee of his career involved working with the King of Pop himself for his last two photo shoots, for *L'Uomo Vogue* and *Ebony*. Kabuki beamed while reliving the experiences in his mind, using the word *"sympatico"* to describe gigs with Michael Jackson, someone also known for a bashful quality despite enormous talent and wild looks. Kabuki flashed his own childlike smile as he declared, "I really liked him. He was super great to work with."

Kabuki recalled sitting down to do Jackson's make-up, intent on building up a good rapport. Suddenly Jackson murmured, "Do you have any candy?" Four suitcases of make-up and tools were on hand but this was the last thing that Kabuki was prepared to offer his client. "Well, let me see what I can do," he told Jackson, scurrying to procure a few Twizzlers and Halls from his advance team. For the second shoot, Kabuki came prepared. Knowing of Jackson's penchant for the 1970s, Kabuki's friend Flloyd bought him a bag of candies from the decade, which left Jackson reeling with glee. "Michael Jackson was like over the moon with this twenty-five-dollar bag of candy from the '70s," Kabuki remembered, relishing the delight that they brought to the childlike King of Pop.

Eventually Kabuki decided to mention his work on a film with their mutual friend Macaulay Culkin. When Jackson asked which movie it was, Kabuki immediately feared a gaffe. "I was kind of like, 'Oh now I put myself in it,'" he remembered, "'cause I knew [Jackson] didn't want [Culkin] to do the movie." When Kabuki told him that the film was *Party Monster*, the King of Pop laughed nervously.

"And then he said, 'That was about a couple of gay guys, right?' So that's Michael Jackson's review of *Party Monster*." Not wild nightlife, not drugs, not murder. A couple of gay guys. Although the interaction said much about Jackson's complex relationship with queerness, it didn't diminish Kabuki's enjoyment of the photo shoot. "It was exciting to watch him dance to his own music in an improvisational way," he told me as we finished breakfast. "I was just thinking the whole time, like, 'How many people get to see this?'"

Although never a club kid or theatrical dresser himself, Steve Lewis was the savvy director of beloved nightlife haunts like Limelight, Tunnel, Club USA, Palladium, The World, Red Zone, and Life. Alongside Peter Gatien and Michael Alig, Steve was responsible for the now legendary Disco 2000 as the smooth Svengali who kept the machinery of the night humming. He remains involved in nightlife but mostly from the design and consultancy angles and as writer of the "Good Night Mr. Lewis" column in *BlackBook*.

While nightlife mavens like Susanne Bartsch and Ladyfag may show up at their parties with flashy fineries and an entourage of hangers-on, Steve saunters into a joint in a rather staid suit, hands in his pocket, jaw muscles bulging like he's chewing on something. A true OG, he casually checks in with the notables in the room and tosses suave compliments and up-and-down looks at any beautiful women around. Steve squints at you when he talks, taking measure of how much he can trust and/or throw you. He is one of maybe three people I know who is truly comfortable speaking with almost anyone, be it Klaus Nomi and Joey Arias on the old St. Mark's Place, a rock drummer getting wasted with two blondes on his lap, a nosey writer like me, or an A-list celebrity. During a visit to my NYU class, he wowed students with Up There tales of hanging out with Beyoncé and Leonardo DiCaprio or throwing together last-minute gigs with Prince.

During a steamy summer evening on the terrace of the Lower East Side club DL, my bestie Talal and I once came upon Steve absolutely salivating over a gorgeous young brunette with a massive tattoo across her ample chest. Steve repeatedly brought up the subject of tattoos, mainly hers and his, giving him an excuse to tear off his shirt and reveal all the quotations and colorful things inscribed on his body. This was Steve truly enjoying a summer night out, slightly disheveled, relishing the moment and the sight of this woman's flesh.

Right across the street from the DL is Hotel Chantelle, which Steve helped to design and where I first met him. F and I were going to the popular Pogo party hosted by Darian Darling, Miss Guy, and others. Steve was slouching by the door, arms folded, chatting with the clipboard-toting doorwoman. Recognizing him right away, I introduced myself. Though polite, he and his gatekeeping colleague quickly chastised F for foolishly wearing flip-flops to a club. (Glasses can fall, shatter, and cut up your feet.) Thankfully he looked past F's gaffe and handed me his *BlackBook* business card.

A few months went by and Steve and I met up at Chantelle before his DJ set. We walked to a nearby bodega where he fueled up for a long night, purchasing a Yoo-hoo and two bananas, then continued our chat on Chantelle's smoking terrace.

Steve is a master of the science of the velvet rope, a true professor of the night in his own way. NASA creator Scotto lauded Steve, telling me, "There's very few people that have such a distinct vision about exactly what to do and got it right so many times. He revolutionized New York nightlife until [Mayor] Giuliani ruined it." Steve could be a scholar-in-residence at a university's department of sociology. If only he shelved some of his more salacious (but hilarious) stories. If only academia didn't primarily uphold the impenetrable and obscure as worthy of teaching.

Visiting Michael in upstate prisons with Steve was always a true adventure, one that started around six in the morning and ended around ten at night. During the course of the day trip he might curse me out, but usually my face would end up aching from laughing at Steve's sharp, nutty, and totally unfiltered humor.

During one prison visit, something in his high-end designer slacks—probably the zipper—kept setting off the prison's understandably sensitive metal detectors. In the public screening room, Steve even dropped trou to show the appalled guards that he wasn't hiding some slender shank anywhere. After they yelled at him to please pull up his pants, we had no choice but to leave and drive to a nearby dollar store where he bought purple XXL bargain bin sweatpants for him to wear to see Michael.

During another drive back to the city, an unexpected dinner detour led us to a wonderfully cozy old school diner tucked into a bend of the Susquehanna River and what felt like a total time warp. While Steve would inevitably flirt with the waitress, I swallowed a feast of turkey, mashed potatoes, greens, biscuits, and pie, mulling over our prison chats with Michael. If you're ever in the area, try Dobb's Country Kitchen and please bring me back some pie.

Years later, after Michael was released, I'd be back at Chantelle with Steve and my urban studies class in tow (all of age). Since he had designed the space through his nightlife consultancy, he gave us an amazing behind-the-scenes tour of the club, showing us the brightly lit back offices and kitchens. The students took to him right away and I wasn't surprised. Sometimes called "Uncle Steve," he has also been a guiding light to young party throwers like Emily Bachman from Bang On! and Lisa Brubaker, a nightlife operator now based in Los Angeles, where she produced the *Glory Daze* Alig documentary for which Steve consulted.

A native of Chicago, Lisa's accent reminded me of Hillary Clinton's: *boxes*, for example, rendered as *bAHxes*. Armed with finance expertise and a love of dance music, she quickly mastered both the aesthetic and managerial aspects of clubland via marketing and publicity work with nightlife and style brands. For her, the science of nightlife boiled down to the three B's of why people go out: "beats, booze, and bitches."

While we spoke Lisa rattled off names of parties, DJs, and club directors who helped to shape her experience. What explained her ability to become a nighttime curator and door person? "You generally have to kind of be an extrovert," she said, alongside knowing what kind of crowd the club wants, having a good woman-to-man ratio, maybe being more lax at the beginning of the night, but as traffic increases becoming more discerning about who gets in.

It's this curatorial bent to nightlife that Steve has mastered. There's a temporal aspect to his industry too. For most people, clubland is a life course phase, something done to have fun or procure sex in your twenties and thirties. Eventually, patrons start a family and only return to a club for a birthday or bachelor(ette) party. So the industry always needs to attract a fresh clientele that is young, hot, horny, and loaded with disposable income.

Some of them require their own night lessons, Steve said. Women get into a club, see how fellow females are dressed, and then simply start mimicking, as if having flipped through a fashion magazine. For men, it's tougher. A promoter may need to pull a dude aside and tell him where to get a haircut, or where to buy the right pants and shoes to help him get laid. "A lot of these people are very good looking people," Steve told me, "but they have no style. But they can *learn* style."

Although Steve aspired to the badassery of an old-school rock 'n' roll dude, fondly remembering Max's Kansas City and CBGB, he didn't ramble about them incessantly like a nostalgic old bitty. For him, the business is a lifestyle, a vibrant faith whose sexy ministrations occur in the small hours of the night. Rather than lament what's long gone, to me he dished out the names of top hotspots where you should go, places like Le Bain, Home Sweet Home, and The Box. What did seem to anger him were the drugs that killed off the nightlife era over which he presided. If borders, schools, or prisons can't effectively control trafficking, how does law enforcement expect clubs to do it?

At the time of our chat, Steve was happy to finally be building up his DJing chops, proudly telling me how he opened for Mark Ronson at Life. So what's the rhythm of the night, I ask him? How does a legendary clubland curator like Steve help mold the experience for his guests? "I'm not sure," Steve said. "As a DJ I try to fucking create that energy and DJs are supposed to. A lot of the DJs today are just staring at their computer screens and not at the floor." Plenty of other factors can affect the room's mood, including weather, big news headlines, or, if it's the end of the month, bills that need paying. A promoter or manager can mold the mood by sending out go-go dancers at a certain time, telling the DJ to start amping up the tempo, or manipulating the lighting systems. "But in the end the crowd has its own feeling of the night," he said. What song marks the apogee of his set? Nirvana. "Smells Like Teen Spirit."

Only a few minutes after sitting down with Astro Erle on a sunny café patio, a phone call from his boyfriend interrupted. Astro told him that his glass of wine with me would only take about forty-five minutes. Somehow that time mutated into an all-night, booze-soaked ordeal with Astro. Richie Rich and his two dogs were soon added to the mix, followed by more white wine, a very wobbly stroll down Avenue A to Eastern Bloc for vodka sodas, and even more drinks at the old Lucky Cheng's, during which Richie painted my nails blue—using his saliva to correct mistakes—and Astro became embroiled in loud verbal spats with a lover and one of his "daughters," who ran away crying.

But it was all very classy at first, I promise, daintily sipping wine outdoors at the now gone Yaffa on St. Mark's Place.

Originally from Los Angeles, Astro reached for the stars but never quite escaped the struggle of his early years as a punk and a hustler prostituting on Santa Monica Boulevard. Astro was later a go-go dancer and party promoter in San Francisco when visiting East Coast club kids told him, "You need to move to New York. Michael Alig would love you."

His sobriquet would pair his given name with his fondness for all things spacey, stellar, and silver. Moving to New York with thirty piercings on his body, Astro was initially shaded by the voguing queens of the pier scene. His response? *"Fuck you, honey, I'm a fucking alien."* Eventually a coworker at Liquid Sky told him, "You're so astro," to which the newly christened Astro Erle reacted with his trademark expression, *"GOOORGEOUS!* That's my name."

As I slightly baked in the hot afternoon sun while chatting with Astro, Richie Rich soon swished by, having just walked his dogs in Tompkins Square Park. Astro called out and he joined us, relishing the opportunity to jump into an interview.

Known primarily for the Heatherette fashion label he co-launched, Richie credited David LaChapelle and Patricia Field with nurturing his fashion career. Alongside RuPaul and Kabuki, he's perhaps the club kid alum most connected to pop celebrities. Wielding a gilded mirror and sporting a bright red pout and barrettes, Richie told Donahue, "We're all future superstars, if not now." During our chat, he casually mentioned a plane kiki with Pam Anderson, a dinner with Vivienne Westwood, palling around with Fergie and Kelly Osbourne, or appearing on *America's Next Top Model* and *Project Runway*. Although he told me this in his notoriously nasal whine of a voice, it indeed sounded casual, no anxious desire to impress.

During our prison kikis, Michael would obsess about a select few friends and what they thought about him. Richie was one of those people, the individual who most incarnated club kid ambition. Whenever Richie's name would pop up, the snide resentment seemed to ooze out of Michael. In a March 31, 2012, letter to me, Michael wrote, "All the attention + fame he craved + felt would satisfy him, did not. He still feels empty inside. And not only that, he's afraid, because his shtick is so youth-dependent: he can not afford to grow old. And yet, it's inevitable. He's losing (or lost) his hair. He has a missing tooth in front. His face is sagging. And all the filler + plastic surgery in the world wont restore his youth."

When I finally met Richie on that Yaffa patio, he seemed to have all his teeth. He wore one of his signature caps so I couldn't really assess his hair situation. He was also dating Ross "Saucy Rossy" Higgins, a much younger model with whom he would soon split. Richie told me that the parties that he and Ross attended were extremely boring, since they just shoved him into a corner to host. He became a colorful creature for the club's filler crowd to stare at. "Animal Crackers Glitter Zoo," he called it. I asked about the unique allure of the original, livelier scene that launched his fame. "We ran around without fear," Richie said. "We weren't scared of shit. I just cared that my lipstick didn't smear." Staying away from addictions helped him to survive too.

Although Richie named Pat Field as an original supporter, her former creative director Sushi cited business grievances for a rupture with his old compatriot. "I don't talk to him either," he said as we looked through Sushi's club kid trading cards. Sushi claimed that he gave Richie "two thousand or three thousand or something" when Richie started Heatherette, and "he never paid me back." "Oh, he's terrible," said Sushi.

Back at Yaffa, Richie was now tipsy and I was close to straight up drunk. But Astro must not have eaten a damn thing that day because he was beyond wasted. He loudly announced to Richie, me, and St. Mark's passersby that he had nine boyfriends and loved to eat ass. Richie joined in, asking if Astro and I had ever eaten pussy? (No and yes.) Astro was so gone at this point, yelling, "Where the FFFFFUCK are we? Are we in the city?" Like Michael, Richie enjoyed a delicious torment moment, so he told Astro that we were in Williamsburg, Brooklyn. He then commanded, "Show him your dick!" Richie's nasal tones vanished in favor of a surprisingly hearty evil laugh, revealing his absolute relish at Astro slipping into complete stupor. Soon, I started cackling too. We were a mess.

Earlier, the boyfriend called because Astro, a sometimes barber, promised to cut his hair that day. To my knowledge, Astro never made it to the appointment. I really hope he didn't.

"Victor, did you see my herbs?"

I looked down into a corner of Ernie Glam's terrace to see a few potted plants and nodded approvingly. I had stepped onto the terrace for a cigarette while Michael Alig, Ernie's husband David, and two guests remained inside. Ernie had somewhat awkwardly used his herbs to pull us away from a tense conversation about some of Michael's new and unsavory business partners.

Ernie and I first chatted about his clubland past a year earlier, sitting at his dinner table, not imagining for one second the many evenings that I'd spend at that same table working as Michael's assistant. And Ernie had no clue that Michael would eventually move in with him after his prison release, although he did float the possibility over dinner.

Like Amanda Lepore, Ernie is known for always being polite and courteous. He'll calmly and articulately relay the most outrageous club stories as casually as if he was reading a menu. None of Michael's manic hand gestures or obnoxious giggles. After graduating from the University of Pennsylvania in 1984, Sacramento native Ernest Garcia moved to New York, inspired by a childhood love of the X-Men and the Avengers, defenders of the city, and became the club kid Ernie Glam. Then, as now, he harbored dreams of a fashion career and started taking courses at FIT, piecing together his own nightlife looks.

He's responsible for some truly outrageous outfits, including the assless unitards that Michael made infamous. It was a release, he said, a way to let off some erotic energy during the sexphobic AIDS crisis of the 1980s. The crotchless gear he designed was too much for Ernie but Michael, always the exhibitionist, wanted it badly, turning it into his feathered penis look, complete with sequins and feathers loosely affixed to his private parts. And so Michael became a kind of benefactor for Ernie's outré fashion creations. "He has like this electric charge to his personality," Ernie explained. "I guess he's like one of those crazy catalysts, where you might not do something if you're on your own, but if you're with him then you'll do it."

His night moniker came from a love of glam rock stars like David Bowie and Alice Cooper and the flamboyance of disco divas like Donna Summer. The reborn Glam gradually moved into downtown circles, ending up at the Pyramid with RuPaul and Lady Bunny or Boy Bar with The Connie Girl and Perfidia, and fawning over icons beloved to him like John Sex and Grace Jones.

After classes at FIT he would change into his club looks and head over to Tunnel, where he would partake of Michael's seemingly endless supply of drink tickets. With friend Cynthia Social Lies, he threw a party that failed but signaled to Michael that Ernie was worth absorbing into his nighttime mix. It's a classic move for anyone interested in building an empire: buy off the upstarts, thereby squashing the competition. Julio would have approved.

Working together cemented their friendship, largely because good ol' reliable, Ivy-educated Ernie could help with daytime projects like decorating a club. They'd go on to vacation together in Berlin, collaborate at Red Zone, and even move in together. As part of the living arrangement, Michael offered Ernie $250 to be Clara the Carefree Chicken, named after Aunt Clara on a favorite show of theirs, *Bewitched*. Inspired by magazines *The Face* and *i-D*, Ernie also signed on to work for the Dadaist club kid magazine *Project X* and soon quit his day job at a shipping company to become a full-time club kid.

Now a journalist in Westchester, Ernie still regretted that the fashion career never happened, a long held dream that evaporated through too much time partying and not enough grunt work. Today Ernie is back out and partying, wearing wigs, make-up, and accessories of all kinds, in addition to self-publishing both a novel and a book of nightlife photography, starring in two YouTube series (one with Michael), and working on exhibitions of nightlife ephemera.

Ernie fell back into the scene once Michael left prison and moved in with him, injecting a bit of the frenzied *Project X* and club kid heyday into Ernie and David's quiet Bronx household. But when we first met, Ernie swore off the likelihood of going Glam again. Other club veterans could pull it off, but he insisted that he couldn't. Still, the urge was brewing inside him. "I would feel like it wouldn't look good on me," he said. "Why? Do you think it would look good on me if I did it?" All Ernie needed, even in his fifties, was a crazy catalyst.

After I screen *Party Monster: The Shockumentary* in my classes, I start my lecture with a brief "Where Are They Now?" segment. Dropped jaws and gasps always follow when I show a photo of Robert "Freeze" Riggs as a doctoral student at NYU. No bright red dye in his hair, no leather choker or fetish gear, just glasses and a white collared shirt.

The second biggest gasp goes to Walt Paper (Walt Cassidy). By the time of the film he had already toned down his look, foregoing abundant facial piercings and hair braids sticking out from a bald cranium like antennae, making Walt resemble a genderless insectoid alien. Today, he is a bearded, hypermasculine hunk of chiseled muscle, as any peek at his Instagram or Facebook will quickly reveal. The students are shook, and some blush, at the sight of the very handsome, tattooed man who shed his extraterrestrial drag punk self. It's a perfect sociological demonstration of how malleable identity really is.

During a nearly three-hour chat over lunch, Walt explained his move from a SoCal beach disco scene to a Missouri farm, spending a good deal of time discussing his father, an industrial psychologist and Navy spy plane veteran plagued by Cold War nuclear anxieties. More thoughtful and philosophical than most interviewees, Walt peppered the whole conversation with talk of *space*, reflecting his interest in the flows of energy, whether in clubland or now the gym, where he used his flesh to make a statement about masculinity.

Walt was raised to live his truths, unencumbered by constraints on sexuality or appearance, and drifted toward the aesthetics of Agnes Martin, Kenneth Anger, Anita Pallenberg, Robert Mapplethorpe, and Rudolf Nureyev, among others. After a year studying tribalism at Kent State, he came to New York in 1991 to pursue painting at the School of Visual Arts. Walt quickly fell in love with downtown's outré characters, whom he lovingly called "street witches."

His journey to the very center of club kid lore started primarily via Linda Simpson, who asked him to contribute material to her magazine, and soon earned his disco name from the illustrations he produced as decor for the space. His whole downtown identity stemmed from the production of an ornamented nightlife context, a realization that helped me to understand his preoccupation with space. The fit was perfect. Walt remembered thinking, "This is it! This is all I ever want to do: is just work in a nightclub and then make my art during the day."

Walt soon started go-go dancing and promoting at Limelight and Palladium, educating himself about his downtown forebears and their pathos, like Brigid Berlin's manic obsessions or Edie Sedgwick's profoundly beautiful fragility. In his mind, he fell into the second generation of club kids, alongside Desi Monster, Christopher Comp, Sushi, Sacred Boy, Pebbles, and others. They were the so-called "products" of the original pioneers attached to Michael and James.

As we munched on crab sandwiches, Walt totally soured when I asked about contemporary culture, calling Lady Gaga a "regurgitation" and dismissing downtown Manhattan in favor of grittier outer borough spaces like Brooklyn's The Spectrum and Jacob Riis Beach. He also fondly remembered an abandoned building near Tunnel inhabited by crack addicts, whom Michael would pay to set up the structure as an after-party space. He practically beamed at the thought of crack house homeless hospitality: "You're on the river. It's almost like crude. It's raw and elemental [. . .] It's not a hotel with a jacuzzi on the top of The Standard."

Walt's club kid friend Desi Monster also morphed from nightlife freak to bulky hunky artist and, like Walt, also talked a lot about space. Desi walked the walk: for a big Lords South Beach commission, he once dressed up the entire Miami hotel like a black dog, his muse.

Growing up not far from the city, in Newark, New Jersey, Desi had more exposure to clubland but like so many others, read *Details*, acquainting himself with tales of James St. James, John Sex, and Diane Brill. The lore of it all pulled him in. As he told me, "What always really interested me was the mythology, I think: how you create your own myth, really."

With his older brother serving as a point of entry to downtown culture, Desi began writing his own myth by wearing industrial goth looks to high school. He would help his young female classmates with their make-up or design prom looks for them, leading to livid accusations that his following was actually a Satanic cult. The ghoulish guises protected him. "I always had this armor of fear around," Desi remembered, "that *'People, just keep the fuck away from me.'*"

Finally jumping down the clubland rabbit hole felt like home, he told me. Part of the second wave of the movement alongside Walt, "We were sort of Michael's children," he explained. Desi moved into an apartment shared with other club kids, an experience that many remembered fondly. Astro also loved living in a clubland commune. As he recalled, "You can just like borrow eyelash glue, or a lipstick, or a shoulder pad, or an ass pad, or a panty, whatever." He searched for a point of comparison. "It was like a—what are those called?" he asked me. "What do those college people do?" A dorm, I said.

One of Desi's roommates, Christopher Comp, gave him the Monster moniker, a nod to his affection for being a frightening "shape shifter" wearing prosthetics and masks. "I was a new creature every night," he remembered. He took the transformative ethos to a higher level, throwing himself into corseting and piercing, even taking hormones to distort his gender, and later learning metalsmithing through a sculpture MFA. Throughout it all, the core of his aesthetic has always been "Latino freestyle goth," he explained. "I'm goth till I die, till I'm undead."

Desi praised the club kid moment for its originality. "It wasn't mimicking what was out already in the zeitgeist," he said. "It was its own thing." And that thing served as a glorious point of departure for a life as a successful artist, a career that included working with Guido Palau on mannequin masks for the Metropolitan Museum's blockbuster *Alexander McQueen: Savage Beauty* exhibition. Or collaborating with Michael Jackson on his never-to-be-staged tour. What did it mean to work with MJ? "He hugged us all. He really was like a child," an already pensive Desi told me, becoming even more wistful. "This non-gender, non-race being, who had seen so much and experienced so much. It was like meeting The Man Who Fell to Earth, really."

From being a "child" of the club kid king to a collaborator of the King of Pop, Desi easily looked past the dark end of the club kid moment and instead celebrated its emancipatory power. As Desi framed it, "The ability to create your own identity, and to shift yourself, to shift your gender, to shift your body. *And you have this power.* How can it not become a thing? How can it not grow? How can it not be wanted by people? People are going to be tired of being beige all the time."

•

It's fascinating to see how the veterans of the club kid scene grew up. Armen Ra cited Amanda Lepore as his best friend and argued that they both demonstrated a pristine longevity. "Her and I were more concerned about keeping our composure and getting our beauty sleep," he said. "And it shows because we're both stunning and it's twenty years later and most of our colleagues didn't fare too well." Sophia Lamar stood as a downtown guardian against nostalgia for her past: "To me the idea of being a club kid right now, at this time— 2013—is like saying, 'Oh I want to be a hippie.' It's like, 'What's the point?' That was something that happened a long time ago and it's over. Try to make your own movement and be creative." She easily dismissed the dismissers of today's scene: "You got old. You got tired. You got jaded."

But before that happened, her misfit crew defined a valuable downtown moment. Far more fabulous than Julio's Cadre ever was, far prettier than I'll ever be, the club kids inspired people all over the world—the outcasts, the queers, the hunchbacks that James St. James summoned—to abandon the beige. It also imprinted culture long after it was over. Several kids moved on to pursue marvelous careers unstained by Michael's crime, now prominent within their respective industries. And plenty of people—like Lindsey from Indiana, today's nightlife newbies, the Haus of Gaga, or me—were intensely attracted to the club kids' artistic assaults on the beige.

I connected with some better than others. As Latin gay men with Ivy degrees, Ernie and I have some things in common, although our nightlife tastes really differ. Kenny and I also clicked in a certain way, both knowing what it is to become embroiled in grand falling-outs with past collaborators. One of the coolest things to come out of my visits to see Michael in prison was my friendship with club godfather Steve Lewis, developed during all those long drives up to see the apostate to their shared nighttime faith.

I suppose the reds back on Twenty-third Street might also call me an apostate, that idealistic high school acolyte who abandoned

Marx for Julio's mafia. And eventually I did cross that street. As a polar vortex descended on the city in late 2016, I tried to do a slightly Christmasy red eye shadow and gold eyeliner for a party at the Chelsea Hotel. The beautiful DeeDee Luxe, a performance artist at The Box and *Sleep No More*, had invited me to be her guest at a fête thrown by Tony Notarberardino and *Vogue* honoring an artist's exhibition opening. Before that, we met for a drink at El Quijote downstairs. I marveled at DeeDee's perfect skin and curves, thin hands, and her fingernails' shiny black lacquer accented with tiny gold embellishments. They seemed to majestically handle the monkfish, cheese, and olives that we munched on.

DeeDee's good-girl-next-door looks meant that her wild performance acts could snowball into visual assaults. The clash of sensibilities made her such a compelling stage presence. DeeDee coyly giggled as she described props like a squirting black dildo or a curious encounter while performing in the immersive spectacle *Queen of the Night*. "One time Barbara Walters gave me a milk bath and she goosed me—she like went up my butt," she said, again chuckling as she recited her tale of an unexpected sponge.

Loving her stories, we kikied longer than expected and later learned that, alas, we missed the crescendo of the party upstairs. But when we did arrive, it was still quite the turn up. Extremely pretty kids, exquisitely dressed and decidedly not beige, jigging and twirling around Tony's amazingly furnished home, just below Susanne Bartsch's apartment. Here was a marvelously styled and sparkly place, lavishly ornamented yet not kitschy, objects old, foreign, and ironic alongside the mandatory black-and-white photos—all quintessential downtown décor.

Tony greeted us warmly and we chatted about his forthcoming book of portraits taken at the Chelsea, whose subjects include Susanne, Steven Baldwin, Debbie Harry, Sam Shepard, and Dee Dee Ramone. He suggested that we retire to his equally fabulous bedroom for a quieter moment to speak. Tony turned the artificial fog on before jumping onto his bed. Smoky nightclub effects in the boudoir, I kid you not.

DeeDee's boyfriend Eric showed up and we fell into nightlife shoptalk right away, dishing about bottle service prices, sky-high rents, and his role in making the Gramercy Park Hotel's Rose Bar a huge hit. His mannerisms, tones, and talk of being an Ian Schrager disciple immediately reminded me of Steve Lewis. He admitted it himself, before I got the liquid courage to point out the resemblance. While all four of us kikied on the bed, a staffer joined us and asked to take my photo. Really? *My* photo? (Edna, once again, thank you!) We refilled our drinks in the kitchen—white wine for DeeDee, Eric and I went for the tequila. I asked about Rose Bar and he mentioned a friendly, down-to-earth Heath Ledger playing pool and the *Gossip Girl* crew stopping by.

A music icon's daughter, sporting a chic pillbox hat, lounged around with the cool boys and girls getting drunk around her. There was endless movement from one end of Tony's apartment to another. Group selfies were taken. Joints were lit. Then chatter about another little party in Janis Joplin's old apartment downstairs, so we all scurried down for a peek. The apartment was charmingly appointed and better music was playing, but we beelined to Janis's balcony. We were silent, feeling the exhilaration of standing next to the famous L-shaped HOTEL CHELSEA sign. It was frigid outside but we really didn't care.

We dashed back upstairs for drink refills. Tony had a velvety screen propped up to serve as a backdrop for a burlesque show earlier in the evening. I wanted to see the view from his sixth floor window so while the others talked I had a peek behind the screen. There it was: my old comrades' drab party headquarters, dark and empty, right there opposite Tony's window. What I was and what I became, staring at each other across Twenty-third Street and two decades.

Somehow I traded in the unhappy days of pushy politicking for nights with a fresh-faced crop of ambitious young upstarts eager to take their place in the hierarchy of New York cool. As I rejoined the party, a couple was making out while a nearby hipster dude puffed on a joint. Tony gossiped with a conspiratorial air, Eric gave DeeDee a loving squeeze, and most of the young crowd swayed happily to French jazz music. The kids would be all right.

5

MIDNIGHT
MATRIARCHIES

Five years of grad school felt like being lost in a thick fog. Unsure and unsteady, again trying to figure out the rules of the damn game. Grasping for a way through the haze of classes, papers, data sets, and CVs. Trying to discern the parameters of a habitus. Several professors and students at Columbia were themselves beige children of faculty at elite schools. For them, it was all a simple rite of passage, the realization of a pathway that had more or less been open to them all along. They enrobed themselves in the habitus as easily as the gray wool sweaters from Banana Republic that they always wore.

Intimidated by the academy's tweedy world of receptions, symposia, and lectures, I focused my energies in a way that I didn't in college, doing well in each course and trying to go above and beyond in every paper I wrote. At the start I struggled in my statistics classes. The part of my brain that processed mathematics felt like it had dried up, but I tried my absolute best and learned the basics of stats programming that I would later develop for my dissertation. It wasn't easy, but I met every deadline and did well, earning distinction in my qualifying exams, winning graduate awards, and being among the first in my student cohort to publish research.

Despite the showy pretense of an open community of intellectual exchange, academic departments could be pretty siloed. Professors and their acolytes formed competitive tribes. Scholars who visited from other universities to present their work were made to run intellectual gauntlets. Their research presentations became opportunities for faculty to one up each other, cap and gown gladiators showing off how expertly they could shank someone's findings. The grad students were in on it too, trying to show everyone in their department who was really top dog.

A senior math professor once gave me the following description of the vicious egos swirling around quiet university hallways. Within an old building named after some wealthy benefactor, you're at a department reception in a lovely wood-paneled hall. Hors d'oeuvres and Pellegrino neatly arranged on white linens. Around you, very potent brainpower wrapped in brown blazers, clunky shoes, and disheveled hair, fumbling through awkward chitchat. You endure your colleagues' awful wine and cheese breath as they make corny jokes or tell you about the totally obscure topic that has become their new obsession. Walking across the room you suddenly feel a wet spot on your side. Did some goofy nebbish spill wine on you? Nope. You look down and realize: at some point, you were stabbed.

Propriety, publications, and prestige are the name of the academic game. But uptown or downtown, ivory tower or skid row, the people are just as shady.

My first-year cohort was small, and I quickly befriended N, a young Slavic woman who grew up in France. Her family was also from a working class background, and although we quickly bonded via our perceived Otherness, she was a pretty blond woman always being hit on by the straight, bespectacled men in the doctoral programs. They would tediously bumble their way toward her with overtures to "meet up for coffee." After our early morning stats class, N and I would have a bagel in one of Columbia's many overpriced cafeterias. Our petty, unseen middle finger to their ridiculous prices and rude staff was a stubborn refusal to pay extra money for butter or cream cheese, instead relying on the free salt, mayonnaise, or mustard as condiments.

Undergrads don't always realize that like any human organization, gossip swirls endlessly around Ivy departments. Over our bagels à la Dijon, N and I traded the choicest bits: which professor had slept with which student or which one cheated on his wife with another professor at which conference, which grad students were dating each other, or which ones had slept with undergrads, and so on. It added a splash of color to our dull days on campus, mostly spent running regression models in the clinically illuminated stats lab, reading, writing, and napping in the library, or trying to digest Lefebvre, Merton, Simmel, Marx, and other big theorists.

Some of the other grad students were way too uppity, as if petty departmental politics actually mattered beyond our nerdy wannabe community. To be a department chair is a spot that might seem somewhat prominent but in fact is rarely coveted. It means dealing with budget-obsessed administrators, managing numerous committees, and kicking very senior professors out of their offices when they're close to retirement. I fell into the uppity mind-set for a while, but thankfully snapped out of it once I realized the pointless cesspool that departmental politicking can be. The academy is a world of great prestige and learning but little power and even less fabulousness. I arrived with Julio's tactics in mind but they needed real adapting to work there.

Other students fetishized the scholastic lifestyle, wrapping themselves in the identity of the intellectual: the pretty boys loved to strut around with brick-like theory books and worn leather satchels, hanging out in the cafés and pretending to read, but actually hitting on senior undergrad women or the few non-mousey grad students.

They sometimes slept their way through a Master's program cohort, pretending that they intended to stay on for the solitary, unglamorous life of a PhD student. Eventually, though, they dropped out to find a magazine job or make some tedious documentary film about whatever backwater town they're from.

While at Columbia I thanked the stars that I came across the extraordinary genius that is Harrison C. White, an academic godfather whose students went on to dominate parts of American sociology, pushing the entire field in a more quantitative direction. His first name reflected his storied lineage to two US presidents, William Henry Harrison and Benjamin Harrison, although he would dismiss his genetic ties to two American heads of state by saying that they were only minor figures in our history. A prodigy, Harrison entered MIT as a teenager and stayed on to do a PhD in theoretical physics there before doing another PhD—this one in sociology—at Princeton, launching his career with a fascinating study of the sociology of sleep.

Because he was so close to retirement, Harrison didn't take on students as advisees, although he did recruit his own little cadre to work on the rewrite of his book *Identity and Control*, the grand statement of his theory of identity. Working with a genius like Harrison on heavy theory-building was an amazing collaborative process for his acolytes. We exhausted ourselves with thinking through his frameworks via case studies ranging from the chaos and argot of a children's playground, to a view of our personhood as an "uneasy balancing of disjunct identities," to the similarity of Catholicism and Communism in the "underlying architecture of control" implicit in their sprawling organizations.

Alongside Harrison, my faculty advisor David Stark was an encouraging and thoughtful mentor, recognizing that I was willing to work hard at my projects. But he couldn't see how ill at ease I was in many of these settings. To his credit, he was not a gossip, but that also meant that a catty old queen like me couldn't really connect with him. After taking Stark's graduate seminars, I also became his teaching assistant, watching and learning his marvelous lecture style up close. Eye contact with everyone in the room. Cold-calling students to keep them on their toes. Slides heavy on blown-out images filling up the PowerPoint screen. Limited lines of text. And no lecture notes to read. You need to have it in your head. You have to feel it raw right there as you deliver the lecture. As I tell my students, if I'm a good professor at all it's because of David Stark. *I learned it from watching him.*

So much depends on your mentors: getting office space, outside funding, publishing co-authored articles, recommendation letters, introductions to bigwigs at other schools. Finding your way out of the heavy fog depends on *them* lending you a guiding hand. I was more confident and focused than when I started college but it was still damn tough. Classes were small and intimate and everyone was extremely competitive, ready to piss all over each other's work in order to impress the faculty. So much of what I learned from Stark, Harrison, and others I carry with me to this day. But the career that we all envisioned for me—the 'spiritual hologram' of my self as a successful, tenured professor at some big school—has long since evaporated.

After I finished up the required years of coursework, I decided to write my doctoral dissertation about the US Army officer corps. I was curious about studying the defenders of a far-flung American empire, carrying out an in-depth study of the raw stuff of military hierarchy. The salutes, the ranks, the uniforms with the colorful emblems, they're all meant to make perfectly clear who's in charge, who reports to whom. The whole slew of symbols and systems fills the underlings with a new sense of personhood tied directly to their mission and organization.

My dissertation examined why a few Army officers became the superstars of their organization: the generals wearing those shiny stars on their shoulders. The project grew from my obsession with the puzzle of the High, Middle, and Low in Orwell's *1984*. Why are social orders always structured as pyramids? Why and how do some people end up at the top, others stuck in the middle, and the lowest languishing at the bottom? Why do some ambitious politicians achieve high office and others fade away after a few jingoistic campaigns? And why do some artists and performers become global icons seared into public memory and others end up bitter nobodies agonizing about *almost* making it?

During my year of fieldwork in Washington, DC, I built an original data set extracted from government records at the Library of Congress and Army archives at Fort McNair. I also worked at the Army Research Institute for the Behavioral and Social Sciences (ARI), carrying out a study using their own personnel databases. A six-day workweek at the three different sites was grueling, but I couldn't say I minded Metro commutes alongside unbearably handsome and brawny service members in their digi-camo uniforms.

ARI was based just south of the Pentagon in Crystal City, Virginia. Despite its cool sci-fi fantasy name, the place was just a drab collection of plain office buildings filled with military contractors, service members, and federal civil servants. Around my neck I wore a little Steve Urkel–esque pouch to carry my Metro card, a pink photo ID needed to access the ARI building or ride the defense bus shuttles, a plain white access card to open the door to my particular floor, and a snazzy ID with the Department of the Army seal that doubled as a visual identifier and a tech access card. You could only use the computer assigned to you by inserting that Army ID into a little slot on the keyboard.

Visiting the truly magnificent Library of Congress on Capitol Hill was also a chance to stop being the jaded, know-it-all New Yorker for a bit. Getting off the Metro alongside the women- and men-in-black who traffic in our nation's secrets, I was now the tourist gawker, staring at their bureaucratic uniforms: the men's crisp suits and colorful ties, the women's sensible flats or painful heels, white blouses capped with dangling pearls. When I later became a fan of the *House of Cards* book and series, I'd think back to riding the Red or Blue lines with the governing class, wondering about all the juicy political gossip they must be carrying around.

At all of these sites I worried about being read and dismissed as the bald brown spic faggot from New York. So I tried to butch it up by lowering the register of my voice, standing straight as an arrow, and even requesting heavy starch when I took my dress shirts to the dry cleaners. It really made them as stiff as paper, so putting on a shirt in the morning felt more like folding myself into an envelope.

My favorite person at ARI was a retired lieutenant colonel named Pam. Pleasant and more relaxed than the others, she was also a devoted worker. At first I got the impression that Pam was brushing me off as a weird, swish interloper, but I was politely persistent. I'd ask if she had a space of time to talk so I could pick her brain about her experiences as an officer: her deployments to European bases, training alongside men, all the manuals and regulations that codify Army careers, and being an African American mother in the course of her rise through the ranks. Aside from these chats with Pam, the rest of my ARI time was spent huddled over in my gray cubicle, writing programming code, crunching numbers, and writing up analyses.

With my crisp envelope shirts and little ID pouch, I looked so so nerdy. Gandhi-in-khakis carrying around binders of Army regulations and personnel policy. My wire-frame glasses, baggy pants, and a shiny bald head gleaming brightly in the white office lighting made for a big, hot mess of a look and I knew it. All of this piled on top of a lingering confusion about my sexuality. To punish me, the universe even placed a very cute frat-type boy in the neighboring cubicle, his hotness diminishing me even more. Naturally I did my best to ignore him.

Only six years after 9/11, the whole defense establishment was still on edge, certain that all its facilities were comprised and vulnerable to attack. After I missed a mandatory evacuation training session with a very minor clearance level of FOUO (For Official Use Only), I learned that the only place to make it up was the Pentagon.

Picture me during my first visit to the headquarters of history's most powerful defense forces, really uncomfortable in my envelope shirt but totally awestruck at the grandeur of the place. I walked in, swiped my ID, and was handed a map to navigate one of the world's largest office buildings. Butching it up as much as I could, I moved around stiffly, though agape at the throngs of square-jawed, high-ranking officers and the monumentality of the whole place. I had to ask for directions, but finally made it to the wing of the building where my security training was held. I'm probably not allowed to talk about the meeting's content, but I can say that the sensation of that first day was unlike anything else.

Thanks to the ARI gig I was able to pay off my college loans fairly quickly. I even started a little investing. Although it could be a really solitary job, I was given an enormous amount of freedom to play with their datasets. My work was overseen by two bright and pleasant supervisors who were extremely open to my ideas, but it was hard to picture myself there as a permanent researcher. Cluster after cluster of cold cubicles, beige people milling around the gray maze, carrying papers, files, binders. Always an ID to show or tap. Security officers at every corner. Me trying to not be so damn swish. The work could be fascinating, sure, but a lifetime in all that grayness?

I did not belong there.

Still, I was making good money and absorbing as much as I could about our imperial capital and its people. I was involved in interesting research with smart colleagues who had a ton of great stories (some just as salacious as those of Steve Lewis or Ernie Glam, although the contexts could not be more different). And yet some nights, on the Metro ride home, I would feel so deflated, gloomily listening to Tara King th.'s "The District Sleeps Alone Tonight." I was lonely, anxious to finish my data collection on time so I could leave the fog of grad school, and feeling totally unsure about how to explore my feelings toward men.

But damn it, I finished. Data in hand, I moved back to Columbia in 2008 and wrote a dissertation that offered original and solid findings about why certain officers made it way Up There as medaled Army generals. But the study was bone dry, as many statistical studies tend to be. It put my poor brother to sleep. And rather than study immigrants, sex workers, or differently abled children, the groups that so many sociologists loved to analyze, I chose to study a tribe that most of my colleagues hated: the disciplined, uniformed group of people who maintain our national apparatus for organized violence. In a tight job market already shrunken by a recession, this didn't help my job prospects.

Washington taught me about the ideal of service, something that in his own way Julio exemplified for me but that isn't expressed as intensely in snarky, jaded New York. I saw the sacrifice and proud commitment of Pam and others who offered so much to a country that, at its best, gives us the freedom to make real our spiritual holograms. They defended a society that lets us try to be what we truly want to be, fail at it, and try again.

What does exist in New York as much as it did in those well-guarded Washington buildings is hierarchy. But back there, the contours of the pyramid are clear. The shiny silver eagle on your shoulder will tell everyone that you are a colonel and that a subordinate must salute. Here in New York, figuring out who matters, who leads, who's going to last and for how long is a much tougher affair. Sure, for some like Warhol, Gaga, or RuPaul, their rank is clear. But what does it really take to make it Up There and stay there?

Hot summer night, mid-July 2012, Walt Cassidy and I exchanged double air kisses with the door person before entering Frankie Sharp's popular Westgay party at the now gone Westway club. I had invited Walt along to gage his reactions to new nightscapes that had emerged since his days as a club kid. Walt is as contemplative as his physique is chiseled, armed with a fondness for introspection not limited to our interview context. As a vigorous Facebook poster, the former Walt Paper is no wallflower, instead endlessly musing about his moods. His intense scrutiny of his own lived experience, coupled with his storied past as the androgynously alien Walt Paper, made him an ideal candidate for making the rounds of downtown's Tuesday night parties.

As I often tell my students, being a good interviewer means becoming a mirror for people, giving them a chance to gaze intensely at their selves as they try to articulate what they see. I mention Dorian Corey in *Paris Is Burning*, who offered insights as she applied her make-up. But as Walt and I walked through deserted SoHo streets en route to Westgay, he became one of the rare people to try to flip that interview mirror, asking *me* if I had ever been in love. After saying yes, I tried to change the subject but he persisted, asking me where I had met the boy. I laughed and again ducked the question.

Once inside the steamy club, Westgay's rooms smelled like beer, sweaty men, and the chemical used for the fog machines that pumped in the required ambiance. Dressed in a tight white shirt, Walt was thrilled when he bumped into a former bandmate and other clubland pals. While go-go boys in mesh jock straps bounced around on the catwalk behind us, Walt noticed the buff dudes in distressed tank tops and snapbacks, many of them intensely ogling him. To an attractive white hunk like him it seemed to mean little, being accustomed to lustful gazes while he inhabited the upper rungs of the downtown hierarchy. But as we had planned to do, after a few BudLights and some swaying to house music, Walt and I ducked out.

We caught a cab over to Susanne Bartsch's On Top party at The Standard, then in its second year and considered a hit summer party. Now successfully situated in LA, Justin Tranter remembered On Top as "a little bitchy," since in New York, "being mean is cute," he said. It is, but it's also the party where I met my best friend Talal, pulled together a birthday party for a singer-songwriter friend, and hosted the launch for the magazine I co-guest-edited with Michael Alig. And it's where, on a windy fall night in 2011, F made it clear that he didn't love me the way that I loved him. So for all these reasons and more, On Top is still a very special downtown spot for me.

Thanks to Walt's clubland standing, we bypassed the long line of people waiting in the hot night at The Standard's entrance to Le Bain and were quickly let in by Susanne's doorman, an old friend of Walt's. We walked through a dark corridor painted with neon body parts illuminated by black light. After an elevator ride up filled with the *ntz ntz ntz* of dance beats booming louder and louder, the doors at last opened to a dimly lit space with sweeping views of Lower Manhattan, bodies writhing in the shadows and faux-fog, the air tinged with a faint smell of chlorine from a jacuzzi. An exhilarating antithesis to Crystal City and Pentagon corridors in every way.

During our lunch several weeks before, Walt had exuded a been-there-done-that attitude about the state of nightlife. For him, Susanne's parties were "generally structured around posing." They were always that way, he remembered: "People would come together, and they would stand around and they would drink and they would look at each other and they would pose."

Walt and I excused our way through clusters of those posing people, stumbling upon a tipsy Richie Rich, an ever-drunk Astro Erle, and an ever-sober Amanda Lepore. Like other revelers Amanda glistened. But unlike the others she shimmered not from sweat but from the various sequins, studs, and glitter covering her tiny body.

Darian Darling, another On Top host that summer, avoided the chlorine-tinged air in favor of her own space on the breezy roof, where each week she could be found surrounded by doting hangers-on. The de rigueur double air kiss greeting was often followed by her signature and slightly nasal, "*Oh hiiiii.* What's going on?" After introducing her to Walt, whom she seemed to find enticing, we circulated around the crowded rooftop, flashes from phones dotting the midnight space. Walt started to enjoy himself as he bumped into more friends, made out with a few men, and inspected the mash of personas pulled together by Susanne.

Walt's claims about the decline of nightlife into a manufactured haven of "regurgitation" were belied by Susanne's success. In her mid-sixties, she was still comfortably situated as New York's nightlife queen. A woman half her age could envy her physique, yet Susanne shows no sign of bequeathing her throne to any of the young upstarts on her payroll. Like any seasoned student of power intent on defending an empire, Susanne coopted and purchased worthy competitors rather than waste time and energy trying to eliminate them. The weaker, inept wannabes who resist being absorbed into her midnight kingdom soon realize the pointlessness of their efforts. Julio would love her.

That night at The Standard I said goodbye to Walt as he stood in the embrace of a young man wearing a massive headdress that to me looked like a $14.99 Party City ware. It was obvious that Walt's interest in the job of investigating contemporary nightlife had waned. He was perhaps now focused on completing a job of a different kind.

Anyone who truly knows and goes downtown can do a Susanne Bartsch impression. Consider it a litmus test. Her pronounced Swiss German accent is a flourish that only adds dramatic bite to her already expressive character, one that incarnates fabulousness. For someone playing the fame game, it fulfills the need for a signature flare.

The state of the downtown elder's reign is healthy. One can trace a glittery arc from the success of her hit 1980s Copacabana parties to recent seasons in which she held court at venues like Greenhouse, Marquee, Gilded Lily, the SoHo Grand, Verboten, and, of course, The Standard. Employing beloved nightlife artists like Joey Arias, Amanda Lepore, and Muffinhead, in a Bartsch crowd you might find Alexander Wang rubbing elbows with young art students, or spot Lance Bass and Perez Hilton milling around, or turn around to see the absolutely tiny Hayden Panettiere sipping her drink next to you.

From the very beginning of my night lessons, I have been fascinated by Susanne. I love watching her at work on the dance floor: manically texting, air kissing, dancing, waving, handing drinks to people. *The Advocate* proclaimed her "The Mother of All Club Kids," while *Vogue* described her as "a pioneer on the New York club, art, and fashion scenes since the '80s," albeit one, *WWD* stated, who is "of-the-people, for-the-people." Chic, fabulous, pretty people, that is.

Her shadow extends beyond New York. Ex–club kid turned fashion star Zaldy remembered working on Gaga's Monster Ball and being struck by the resonances with downtown royalty: "There were some things where I'd be like, 'Wow, that's so Susanne Bartsch.'" Sushi, ex–club kid and former creative director for Pat Field, mentioned something similar, "I was watching [Gaga on] the Grammys show, [and thought,] 'Oh my god, that's like a Susanne Bartsch outfit!'"

And don't forget Susanne's major Museum at FIT retrospective, a documentary film, a M•A•C eyelash line, and photo shoots for *Vogue Italia* and plenty of other fashion magazines that have cemented her status as the "queen of New York nightlife." It's the title with which she's most associated but one that she avoids. "I think it's stupid," Susanne told me when we spoke in her gorgeous Chelsea Hotel apartment, "I don't really care what they call me, just come to my events. That's all."

But what about another title, maybe the one most cherished by all downtown people: ICON. "That I find flattering," she remarked. In the truest sense of a word so overused today, to be an icon is to be an object of veneration, if not worship, to approach divinity. To this she aspired, "You can't be more than that, really. Right? What else is there? *Immortal.*"

Susanne is separated from gym impresario David Barton—although they remain close—and their son attends Brown University. She has worked hard to maintain the demimonde diadem on her head. Wait outside On Top and see a lavishly made-up Susanne sweep into the venue with her young assistants in tow, whispering orders or maybe throwing a little shade in that well-known accent of hers. Once inside, watch her oversee the scene that she assembled. When the dance floor is full and arms and heads are flailing and bouncing underneath the throbbing lights, when she isn't assailed by a dozen people asking for a photo or a drink or a job or some other thing, Susanne relaxes and flashes her very warm smile, as proud as any mother.

During its debut talk-of-the-town season, On Top became a new target for one of my frumpy Ladyland friends and me. We were so anxious about getting in that we would show up ridiculously early, a little after ten, usually wearing cheap necklaces and ill-fitting blazers. The doorman look unenthused as we meekly approached him, but when it was that early in the night he could afford to be less discriminating. Once in, we nursed beers for two hours until the truly It people trickled in between midnight and one o'clock. When I finally mustered the nerve to introduce myself to Susanne back in 2011—just beginning to budge out of my high Gandhi phase—she basically grimaced and walked away from me. I was humiliated and offended, but years later, after leaving Gandhi Vic far behind, Susanne and I now kiki a little.

I have hosted at a nightlife party only three times in my life and all three were thanks to Susanne. Hosting meant that I was given either a bottle of vodka or drink tickets to dispense and made responsible for bringing in people. It's a tougher gig than it sounds. The attracting of people requires a certain flare and grace, whether the pulling of voters to the polls that Julio demanded of me, or pulling people out to a party, precisely what Susanne's midnight alchemy thrives on.

The first time I hosted for Susanne was after my "Wearable Art from Warhol to Westwood" panel at the Gershwin Hotel, which I organized as a response to the Metropolitan Museum's blockbuster *PUNK: Chaos to Couture* exhibition. I asked Susanne if we could do the after-event at her Catwalk party at Marquee. She agreed and then themed the whole night around Warholian wearable art. It was a lavish treat, but hosting a table with bottle service also meant two things. First, I couldn't leave the table unattended in order to dance or stroll around and see everyone's eleganza. Second, a steady stream of people who wouldn't normally give a flying fuck about me were suddenly so nice and affectionate just so I'd pour them a free vodka Red Bull. Ugh.

The other two times were at On Top. The first time was for the 2014 launch of the magazine I edited with Michael, a few months after he was released from prison. Because of his mandated curfew he couldn't attend, but there was a big kerfuffle about whether or not he was technically "hosting" in nightlife again. This was during the time that I was bickering with Joe and Michael so I arrived to the party already frustrated and exhausted. But one highlight was getting to skip around all night handing out drink tickets to my friends. Doing that night after night? I saw how it could really go to someone's head.

The second night of On Top hosting was for a friend's birthday in 2015, when he and his music troupe performed. A ton of my past students from FIT, Columbia, and Hofstra came, as did F, who acted pouty and claimed that I was ignoring him. Each time that I hosted, Susanne was amazingly generous and professional. Hosting really means running around double air kissing people all night, making sure they feel welcome, introducing your friend groups to each other, saving your booze or tickets to reward the people who really matter, trying to score more, enjoying yourself but not getting *too* drunk. It's no simple thing. Susanne does it like no one else can, and always dressed to the nines.

In addition to how she speaks, another signature might be what Susanne *says*. When acting as MC at her parties, she's known for some hilariously raunchy and explicit sex talk. When my best pal

Talal and I went to her SoHo Grand birthday fête for longtime collaborator Brandon Olson, Susanne declared to the packed salon that he was the one who taught her how to suck and fuck. From then on, that's how we affectionately thought of our dear Brandon: Good Ol' Suck and Fuck.

Susanne's career draws attention to the whole point of nightlife, which at its best is a kind of graduate school. A would-be performer, artist, or fashion designer becomes a party regular and maybe starts hosting. Just like Harrison would mentor students, someone like Susanne takes the young wannabe under her wing, giving them a stage on which to strut and display their creations, week after week. The music, drugs, booze, and sex make it all a fabulous networking space, no? Better than some stuffy job fair in a hotel conference room. But it's also a proving ground. Can you be the popular social butterfly at the best parties in town and still be productive during the day, churning out an actual product to sell?

For Susanne's ability to find and develop talent, to be a kind of nightlife university dean, eyewear designer Kerin Rose Gold called her a "clubland A&R." Astro Erle told me, "She will fucking bring in the new kids. She will fucking discover the new talent." James St. James also applauded, "I know Susanne and I know that she *loves* throwing parties and *loves* being with the kids and *loves* feeding off of that creative energy, and it just makes her more and more creative."

Susanne's close friend, the great chanteuse Joey Arias, remains a fellow downtown nexus, after having first moved to New York from Los Angeles with *PAPER Magazine* co-founder Kim Hastreiter and then collaborating with Klaus Nomi. His long friendship with Susanne started when Joey felt inclined to start his version of drag at her legendary Copacabana parties. Doing a spot-on impression of Susanne, Joey remembered her immediate response, "Put the tits and the heels on, bitch, and come dance!"

This doesn't mean that her realm is one big utopia. Steve Lewis commented, "She works hard." But there is a price to be paid, he added: "In order to do what she does she has to be a bitch." Others see her just sticking to regurgitation. When I visited Sophia Lamar's home, I mentioned going to On Top. She quickly interjected, "Susanne Bartsch is not the current scene. That is a repetition . . . a way for her to make a living and stay relevant. But that's not the club scene." Ferocity plus success will yield enemies. Off the record, an old collaborator called her "*Sleazanne*."

When I arrived at her Chelsea Hotel home for a chat, Susanne wore a fuzzy blue bathrobe and mom jeans while getting extravagantly done up for her now defunct Sunday party Vandam at the now vanished Greenhouse. Her hair stylist, make-up artist, and personal assistant / companion, all attended to the assembly of her fineries while she texted her party doorman, making sure that key notables were properly placed on the guest list.

Meandering around the apartment, we were just chitchatting as she turned a corner and I followed along. I assumed that it was her kitchen but she actually entered her bathroom and removed her robe. "OH my god. I'm SO sorry," I said, covering my eyes and stepping back. She and her assistants all laughed at me. Really? A professor of the night accustomed to seeing Susanne in sheer garments was shocked to see her in a bra and jeans at her home? Blushing, I sat down and settled in for our interview. She returned, robed, and submitted to her make-up guru's ministrations. "*Ahhh-sk me whatevah.*"

Despite the chaos of pulling the right look together, Susanne and her aides clearly loved it all. Her devoted hair stylist Raquel told me, "It really is like a photo shoot every Sunday." Is it all planned out though? "It's like painting, creating a piece of art. I love it," Susanne said. "I think it's my art form. I don't really paint, sing, or act, so it's kind of my form of expressing myself."

To build rapport a little, I told the Bern-born Swiss miss that I had family in Winterthur. But she instead talked about needing to leave Switzerland because it was all "too predictable." She moved to London, before coming to New York for a love affair with a painter who initially held the lease to the Chelsea apartment. But she missed London's New Romantics scene, so she began importing English wares after talking to her favorite London designers. "Why not import what I miss?" Susanne concluded, setting up a downtown boutique that quickly garnered glowing press.

The next move was a fashion show. I started to ask if anyone showed her the ropes, but she cut me off. "No." Learning by doing, she pulled together her first runway showcasing eighteen fashion designers at the Roxy. "I was like on the floor the night before, exhausted," she remembered.

The next logical step was to get into nightlife so that her clients would have a place to wear their fineries. It's good business, no? Sell them both the looks and the stage on which to wear them.

Here a nightlife trajectory began, reaching an apogee with Susanne's legendary monthly party at the Copacabana, brimming with muscle boys, vogue stars, drag queens, and Brazilian samba dancers. "Incredibly glamorous and decadent," she called it, comparing it to Studio 54. She spoke about it like any proud mom might talk about a child. As she remembered: "People calling to see if they could land with a helicopter on the roof to come to the party. And it was really the true mixing of downtown and uptown and the gays and the straights. Everybody went, from Reinaldo Herrera to Carolina Herrera to Bette Midler, Faye Dunaway and Michael Musto and a little queen from Brooklyn or from the Bronx. It was less Brooklyn at that time."

Drag veteran Linda Simpson fondly recalled the Copa parties. She said, "I think Susanne's good at mixing different sorts of people." According to Richie Rich, who worked as Susanne's assistant for years, a proximity to megawatt stardom at her parties didn't faze her. "She's around the elite," he explained to me, "but she doesn't care. She'd rather have the tranny that spent five hours doing her make-up showing up with glitter on." When I asked Susanne to explain the Copa's success, Susanne invoked that elusive nightlife goal: the truly mixed party. "I love when people mix, when you can achieve that mix of people, when they come and they feel comfortable with each other."

Today she preserves a dance floor democracy threatened by the bottle-model system. But does Susanne's success emerge from the mad love of it all or a keen business sense that ropes in the elites? "The money does not motivate me. It never has. *It should*," she insisted, suggesting that she would have plunged into the bottle service world if business truly were her motivation and not the circus-like revelry of On Top. It's the joy of the night, people dancing, flirting, laughing. It even makes her forget her own problems, she said. "If it's a successful thing, a good night, I feel high the next day from it."

Michael Alig and Susanne have a few things in common, although the king of the club kids and the queen of nightlife could not be more different as people. Susanne is tempered by maturity, motherhood, and a sense of responsibility that simply doesn't exist in Michael.

But like him, she loathed limits, especially those born of a sanitized and gentrified New York. Her assistants and I all laughed when she declared, "You can all take your clothes off right now and nobody's going to like get upset. You feel like doing that—I don't mean we're having an orgy but—it's just like, '*Do what you want.*'" Today's social media technologies added to strictures meant to be shirked: "You can't even put your own nipple on Facebook," she said unhappily, adding that dating apps simply mean that people don't need to go out like they did before.

Susanne possesses a sense of what makes parties fun while still being willing to try new things. She excitedly showed me a flyer for her "living art" Catwalk party, headlined by Gage of the Boone, Brandon Olson, and Muffinhead, who's a "major genius," she said. Downtown mainstay Paul Alexander, who briefly hosted for Susanne, noticed her ability to spot and adopt young people's trends, telling me, "'Cause this art thing [of hers], it was happening in the

Brooklyn parties. The kids were doing that and she was smart enough to notice and be like, 'I'm gonna do some art parties.' "

Her past nightlife collaborator Kenny Kenny also compared downtown royalty like her to Michael, but felt a greater proximity to him because as a gay man, he experienced bashing, fear, and abuse. If one was to lump them together as sadistic overseers, Michael was more of a juvenile jester, rolling around in his slop of cruel silliness like a pig. His revelry could be contrasted with Susanne's ruthless efficiency. It's darker, Kenny said, she had to derive some real, tangible benefit from the puppeteering, not just shits and giggles.

On Top's original success was tied to Susanne's alliance with Kayvon Zand and his nightlife troupe, the Zand Collective. Their arrival at Le Bain was an event in itself. While Talal, M, F, and I drank and smoked on the roof during the first bit of the party, the big lingering question was always when the Zands would arrive. You would hover by the bar, and suddenly, out of the elevator: a burst of dark plumage, leather, straps, masks, and vinyl wrapped around thin, pale bodies, snaking its way through the crowd, eventually immersing itself in the steamy jacuzzi. Meanwhile Susanne joyfully oversaw the black baptism in the bubbling waters.

Kayvon's noir star shone brightly at that time, picking up write-ups for his infusion of goth club kid realness back into nightlife. He was accompanied by the blond bombshell burlesque performer Anna Evans, now his wife and mother of his daughter Zara. Back then, Kayvon's lavish looks won people over, but they didn't quite grasp that he intended it to be a package deal: what he was really peddling at his parties was his music.

Growing up in a Persian household, Kayvon escaped North Carolina through modeling gigs in London, Milan, and Madrid, and eventually found his point of entry into New York nightlife via Kenny Kenny's Happy Valley party, just like Ladyfag. At that point, Kayvon endured a difficult time while dating a man. He told me, "I was in a relationship with a guy. I never speak about him because it was such a bad experience." Why? An absence of support for his musical ambitions. The boyfriend told him, "You could never be a singer. You could only be a model."

Something similar happened in his break with his old nightlife queen. Kayvon told me that Susanne had originally promised to act as his manager and help with his music. "Her intentions were really initially to help me. I do think we had a friendship," he explained. "I do think that she liked me as a friend but I think the moment I became someone who could potentially [be a] competitor I wasn't seen as a friend anymore." He also cited a growing sense of independence, even as his ideas helped to make On Top a hit. "Susanne wanted to continue maybe things the way that they were with me and I feel like I was growing and I didn't really want to be a hired gun anymore," Kayvon said, his demeanor growing as dark as his long black robes.

There are parallels to other stories. While Susanne imported fineries from the London scene, her longtime nightlife partner Kenny Kenny imported its cattiness when he became her doorman. It became a mark of his nightlife persona, one that I experienced twice. When I first introduced myself, he wagged his finger in my face, told me that he was working and not giving interviews, then turned away. The second time he gave me a glaring once-over, eyes bulging, to indicate that my look was totally unimpressive. Kenny was right. It wasn't. So I upped my outfit game.

He brushed me off the same way that Kayvon, Susanne, and others originally did. But persistence was the price of admission for my night lessons. By late 2016, Kenny and I kikied over mango slices, hummus, and berry confections at Muffinhead's apartment, or at the Waverly diner, where the minute I sat down across from him, The Great Kenny Kenny told me that I looked *fabulous*.

As noisy NYU kids filed into the Waverly, Kenny made his signature glare-and-pout combo before telling me about collaborating with Susanne. Back in the day a mutual friend told her to hire Kenny, so she sought him out at the Pyramid and a new downtown alliance was born. "It was good with her for maybe two years," he said, relishing the memory of becoming known in a vibrant pre-Giuliani scene. They cut a look as a dazzling downtown duo, he said, "I became kind of an Edie to her Andy."

But working so closely with Susanne was both a blessing and a curse. "She's a very manipulative, tough person, opportunistic," Kenny told me as he buttered an English muffin. He identified a matrix of insecurity, competitiveness, and a need for control in Susanne as she built the foundations of her nightlife empire. "I started work for Larry Tee too at Love Machine," Kenny recalled, "and she asked me not to work for him and she would pay me *just* not to work for him." While I devoured fries and coleslaw, Kenny complained about the "hos and bros" behind him as they got louder and louder. When I tried to pull him back to our chat, Kenny worried that he was getting too bitchy and blamed me, insisting that I brought it out of him.

But he kept right on spilling Susanne tea, explaining, "She has a relish or a need to cut you out of things." So why keep working with her for all that time? Money. Although they're still in contact, their close bond is most likely forever destroyed. "I've never met anyone quite as competitive and manipulative," Kenny calmly explained. "Because she can make you feel like you're her best friend and at the same time, turn around and stab you in the back."

Whatever detractors might say, the proof is in Susanne's pudding. Her reach only appears to grow. Approaching the 2016 holiday season, the city, and the whole world maybe, was still trying to make sense of Donald Trump's electoral victory. Amidst the fear and uncertainty, one of the first really frigid days of winter coincided with what my former Barnard student Alexandra Warrick called a "crocus moment." When commissioned to design a Christmas window for the iconic Bloomingdale's store, Susanne decided to assemble a Leigh Bowery universe with sparkling planets designed by nightlife stars, all orbiting their neon nightlife god. Downtown had gone uptown in the most extravagant way.

Alexandra came along to the unveiling as my plus-one, wearing a plush yellow faux fur coat that attracted comments and petting from strangers all night long. After dancers did a light-up hula-hoop routine on the red carpet in front of the windows, the curtains went up and there was Susanne's glittery gaga galaxy with Bowery in his famous light-bulb look. After her assistants fussed to make sure her look was impeccable, Susanne beamed while standing in front of the window honoring her forebear and tribal leader. At the party upstairs, light-up champagne flutes and candies revved us up. Susanne's invitees naturally stood out as the more curiously dressed so we all easily found each other and kikied. While arranging ourselves for a photo, the General Manager of the whole store—of Bloomingdale's itself!—asked to squeeze into our mix.

Susanne held court in a corner, clearly feeling the fullness of her victory, but always ready to do business and invite people to her upcoming Boom! party at The Standard. One glass of champagne, more photos, and then off to Miami for a sold-out party with Amanda Lepore, Joey Arias, and Muffinhead. But before she jetsetted off with her chic assistants, a Bartsch blessing was bestowed. Susanne complimented *me* on my gold make-up that night AND the glistening green-and-gold look I wore during my most recent On Top outing. I mean, it's like Alexander McQueen telling you he likes your outfit, or David Bowie saying that he enjoys your music. Call it a night, I told myself, you're not going to top this.

At the end of Christopher Nolan's Batman trilogy, the hero tries to convince a nemesis not to detonate a nuclear device that will wipe out his city's innocent residents. The villain slightly deflates him, retorting, "'Innocent' is a strong word to throw around Gotham, Bruce." She might be right. It's very easy to romanticize and overstate the goodness of an iconic space, which happens downtown all the time. I hear a lot of talk about "family," as people are eager to mark themselves with a group affiliation and thereby have an identity. There's nothing wrong with that. We all do it. But *family* is a strong word to throw around downtown.

World of Wonder co-founder Fenton Bailey found a community at the Pyramid and a grand inspiration in downtown chronicler Nelson Sullivan. But as he explained to me, "I wouldn't say it was like a family. I mean, it was just a group of similarly creative, eccentric people, who were all inspiring in different ways." But all the family talk can efficiently bind people together. The Lady calls her Haus of Gaga a "pop-cultural family and living Warholian factory," thereby interweaving the familial with the commercial in service of *her* iconicity. Even in Orwell's *1984*, the all-powerful Party "calls its leader by a name which is a direct appeal to the sentiment of family loyalty," Big Brother.

Family is also a word often used to describe the House of Field, named for Patricia Field, the semi-retired but still legendary Father of the House and the Emmy-winning, Oscar-nominated fashion impresario best known for her work as *Sex and the City* costume designer. Her styling for *The Devil Wears Prada*, *Confessions of a Shopaholic*, and *Ugly Betty* are also among her biggest credits. At its peak, the House was many things beyond just a company selling wares online and at now shuttered boutique spaces. It became a vibrant nightlife micro-mecca, an informal talent agency, a vogue ballroom troupe, and a hip one-stop pop shop for It kids, stylists, and celebrities needing rare and extremely cool clothing, accessories, jewelry, hair styling, and make-up.

Pat's eponymous boutique closed in 2016, triggering frenzied laments about the end of an era. Before that, she straddled the downtown and uptown worlds like a couture colossus. As costume designer for *Sex and the City* she helped to configure a new vision of glamorous urban femininity—picking up an Emmy in the process—while as a nightlife tastemaker she launched the careers of multiple downtown superstars. House of Field veteran and The Ones bandmate Paul Alexander said, "She was always a trendsetter," attracting stylists from around the world. "There were things that you would see we had in the store and the next season you would find it in *Vogue* by some European designer," he explained.

Her profile is maybe a little more mass than Susanne's, a natural outgrowth of her work on an iconic TV show and big movies. In my fave photo of her, Pat is consulting with Meryl Streep done up in her imposing Miranda Priestly garb. Pat is a curator of both clothes and creatures. Although a *New York Times* article called her a "punk den mother," she was also, said *Observer*, "an expert when it comes to fashion finds" for the more mainstream, or "wardrobe mistress" to elite visitors like Caitlyn Jenner, according to *The Independent*.

A former employee's fawning documentary film about the House of Field featured other past staff mostly upholding Pat's downtown crown. Titled *The Little House That Could*, the film wound its way through the festival circuit, winning several awards. Directed by Mars Roberge, now a Los Angeles DJ and video editor, the film included interviews with Field children profusely recounting the ways in which Pat inspired, sired, or hired them, alongside Susanne, Chi Chi Valenti, Kenny Scharf, Muffinhead, and Martine (although the film missed the last great star of the store, Leo Gugu).

As I wrote in my *Pop Mythology* review of the film, many documentaries are ultimately paeans to their subjects and Mars's saccharine homage is no different, even comparing the House of Field to the Warhol Factory. Pat's longtime wig stylist Perfidia recalled styling a wig for Superstar Holly Woodlawn, who told him, "Wow, this really feels like the Factory. There's transvestites working here and no one's judging them." And Pat, in her often imitated, gravelly voice, joyfully recounted Warhol walking into her store and exclaiming, "Pleasure to meet you. You're famous!"

Sadly, former visual director Artie Hach reported that the ostensible star of the film thought little of the whole documentary project. The Father of the House gave Mars essentially no time, which is why the tiny interview segments in the film about Pat's own company were done while she was getting her bright red hair styled. "She couldn't be bothered," Artie said. "She didn't respect his artistic integrity I don't think."

I don't blame Mars for creating a wistful remembrance of his old downtown refuge. On the phone from LA, Mars told me that he couldn't relate to his straight colleagues and their endless talk of sports. It was all a very, very far cry from working alongside proud downtown freaks and styling a star like Britney Spears. So surreal that moment was, Mars remembered, that when she purchased a cheeky Page Six Six Six shirt and some pants, he inadvertently suggested, "You should get those, 'Those look like something Britney Spears would wear.'"

The House of Field also modeled a new version of family, with Pat, a lesbian cis gender woman as the Father, and the late Codie Ravioli, a trans woman who fathered three sons before transitioning, as one of the individuals who served as the Mother. The family business encompassed nightlife stars gainfully employed during the day, becoming a haven for multiple generations of drag queens, transsexuals, club kids, queer artists, and others. Citing his own very femme presence, Armen Ra told me during a phone chat, "Pat's just kind of the savior of everybody downtown. It's the only place we could really work." He gushed over her role, "She's the glue for New York's downtown."

Another prominent House of Field member, Jojo Americo, is from Westchester, like me. He hung out in the same White Plains mall that I frequented as a grade school kid. In addition to being a jewelry designer, he was responsible for the stylishly wacky window décor at Pat's boutique. It was love at first sight for Jojo and the store, remembering how the staff "looked like they just landed from Mars!" He felt similarly about Pat. "I just remember being like, 'Wow, she's the fucking coolest lady I've ever seen!'" A friend hooked him up with a job and he stayed there for sixteen years.

During a kiki before her death, Codie Ravioli chain-smoked and gabbed away in a deep, raspy voice, just like Pat. It was January 2013, on a day so unbearably cold that she canceled our lunch and instead invited me over to her cozy home, where she sat cross-legged on her bed as her two dogs jumped all over us, often kicking my audio recorder across the room. Only nine months later, the Mother of Pat's House would be dead from a heart attack, shocking downtown, which gathered at a packed memorial at XL featuring appearances by The Connie Girl, Brie, and Laverne Cox.

Codie had started her downtown explorations as a teenager, quickly falling into an underground community of mohawks, platinum blondes, and shaved heads and picking up a disco name after she showed up to a rehearsal eating raviolis out of a can. During our chat, the Queens native furiously pointed and gestured—in between fidgeting with her long blond hair—while spilling high-quality tea about everyone from Cher to JFK Jr. to Madonna. But Codie was especially proud of her work for Pat's store, managing the wig department and working in the salon as a stylist. She proudly upheld the staff's reputation of being catty to people whom they didn't believe were worthy of shopping in the hip boutique. "*Oh, we were bitches!*" Codie said. "If you weren't dressed right, we didn't talk to you."

She remembered defiantly kicking out people who were explicitly rude, even if they happened to be a Camelot scion like John F. Kennedy, Jr. While dating Darryl Hannah, he accompanied her to the store but wouldn't stop muttering that the employees were "fucking freaks." Codie flipped out at the son of the assassinated thirty-fifth President of the United States, yelling, "You know what? Enough! You can wait for Darryl outside. 'Cause that's really fucking disgusting." Darryl looked on, supportive of Codie, who kept right on going, "You know, ya mother might have had class but you had none of it! *None of it.* Get the fuck out!"

Like other store employees, Codie also performed at Boy Bar. Grinning, she proudly crowed about having Michael Kors thrown out of the hip locale for getting "nasty" during a discussion of men's fashion. She yelled at him, "*Eww*, who are you? Fuck you!" She also gushed when recalling a night out drinking with Cher, but then soured on Danceteria-era Madonna, whom she casually dismissed as "just an annoying fag hag."

In addition to her beauty, Codie was a trans pioneer and advocate, proudly showing off her three handsome sons like all moms do, but also mentioned being HIV-positive, something that she intended to reveal on a reality show then in the works about her family. Codie excitedly told me about managers, sizzle reels, network conventions, and pitches. "But World of Wonder did turn us down," she threw in. "Well, they're assholes, so it's OK." Both in her home and in the House of Field, she inhabited new models of belonging and living, so it's a real loss that the country missed the chance to watch Codie live her unique and powerful truths on their screens.

I first introduced myself to Patricia Field at Leo Gugu's party at Eastern Bloc, where she was polite and more or less friendly. I was with F, who was always a huge fan and showed her the clutch purse he bought from her store. But despite my attempts, she wouldn't speak with me on the record. I first emailed her in January 2013 and her reply indicated that she wanted to schedule our chat for March. Curiously, she asked for more information about the other people I might have interviewed about her. Despite several follow-up emails from me, her assistant told me that she wouldn't be available for a chat after all. She did accept an invitation to speak to one of my NYU sociology classes in 2014, alongside Warhol star Bibbe Hansen. With her signature red hair and chic reptilian skin loafers, she spoke vividly to my enthralled students about the intersection of style, sexuality, creativity, and personal expression.

I had always been really curious about what Pat was like in person, someone who really made it Up There, surely earning a tidy sum while configuring a new urban glamour by dressing Carrie, Samantha, Miranda, and Charlotte. On his blog, Paul Alexander wrote, "When I first met [Pat Field] in the 80's and all through the 90's she would pull the looks. She still does but now she puts it on Carrie Bradshaw and Samantha on *Sex and the City*. Carrie dresses like how she dresses and Samantha is like how she would want to look. That's the main reason those two characters look the best, they both are the type of woman Pat Field really is."

But while downtown folks angrily gripe about the lost rawness of a gritty city now dominated by uppity Carrie wannabes anguishing over does-Big-love-me dilemmas, Pat's legacy remains largely immune from the taint of the stiletto-latte legion.

Sushi, Pat's former creative director and an ex–club kid, claimed responsibility for introducing Carrie Bradshaw's iconic nameplate necklace into the show. After he and Richie Rich had them custom made, Pat spotted Sushi wearing his. "I made it in Chinatown and I was wearing it and she asked me to make one for Carrie," he remembered, still resentful that Pat never publicly credited him for this idea. His mood growing darker, Sushi told me, "She should be giving me a credit, so that would help *me*."

Sushi started working for Pat after Limelight closed and he visited the store with Amanda Lepore looking for jobs. He quickly rose from a floor salesperson to creative director, soon bringing in boyfriend Artie Hach to do the windows as visual director, work that morphed into becoming Pat's personal decorator plus a styling gig for *Sex and the City* that would earn Artie an Emmy. Not bad, right? Artie explained her enormous success and their aesthetic compatibility by pointing to a disregard for limits, similar to Susanne and Michael. "She breaks all the rules," Artie said. "There are no rules in fashion, to Pat, at all."

With his gleaming Emmy watching over us, Artie told me about the impossible time crunches and endless set drama that his styling work entailed. "Sarah Jessica [Parker] was amazing. She was a lot of fun to work with," Artie said. "I remember one time she ate some-thing before a fitting and then she looked at me and she goes, '*That never happened.*'" Thus, in the HBO show's simulacrum of postmod-ern New York, morsels belong in memory holes, not mouths. SJP's character, styled by Pat, Artie, and others, left an imprint on Man-hattan women. Jojo Americo remembered thinking, "'Holy shit! Ev-ery fucking girl is strutting down the street in a real dress by a real designer with Manolo Blahniks.' I was like, 'This is nuts!' [. . .] 'Look at what Pat did!'"

Most other Pat Field employees loathed Carrie's fans, however, finding themselves in similar Codie vs. JFK Jr. store battles. After being deposited by tour buses, the disruptive out-of-towners would point at trans women and call them men, make a mess of the fab merchandise without buying anything, or put on wigs and snap pho-tos. Mars Roberge understood the antipathy but pointed out a de-cline in sales once the show ended and the trickle of tourist turds dried up: "The fans of that show is really what made that store survive from 2000 to 2010 and the staff hated them, but I was the one that would deal with them."

But past the cute anecdotes about SJP and downtown women's chic attire, as I spoke with Pat's old employees, I became tangled up in a knotty spaghetti of naughty she-said-he-said. I noticed huge contrasts between her massive success and the dead end destinies of some of the House family members left behind. Like Susanne, Pat was accused of initiating purges, so I was interested in the people cleaved out of her fashion empire and cast into the memory hole like some tired last season garment.

When I met Sushi at his large Brooklyn loft, he greeted me in his pajama shorts. I could see that he was a little hung over as he chain-smoked like his old boss Pat—puff, puff, puffing away throughout our chat. Sushi told me that while growing up in Japan he became completely obsessed with New York culture, eagerly applying for ex-change programs. Eventually transferring to school in the city, he soon started clubbing with close friends who were also excited to dress up outrageously for their night outings.

At the Roxy, Sushi soon met Michael Alig, who rewarded him for his fabulousness with drink tickets. The problem was that Sushi had no clue what a damn drink ticket was and kept right on paying for drinks. When Sushi introduced himself to Michael with his full name, Atsushi Sakai, it was quickly re-rendered à la Alig as just *Sushi*, who remembered thinking, "He's making fun of me!" Falling into Michael's clubland family, Sushi grew close to Desi Monster, moved into a club kid apartment that included Desi, Aphrodita, and Christopher Comp, and started an eight-year relationship with Artie.

At the House of Field, the new power couple displaced a previous wave of elders that included Jojo Americo and Perfidia, who sensed resentment from the new kids. "They were mean to us old school people 'cause they were so insecure," Perfidia recalled. "They were really, really intimidated by us and what we had done before." Sitting in a restaurant off Houston Street, it didn't take much for both of them to fall into rehashing the internal House intrigues and squabbles that followed, which Jojo described as "clawing, backstabbing, and killing."

I visited Artie after he returned from a traditional Incan cleansing ritual in Peru and he was ready to address his own tortured egress from the downtown legend's orbit. "Patricia Field is being extremely negative in the way she's behaving at the age of seventy-two and I pray that she finds integrity in her life." Artie claimed that owed monies, abusive treatment, and broken promises were to blame, including verbal commitments to a 25 percent ownership of the real estate of the final store locale. Whenever actual paperwork for Pat's promises was demanded, according to him, she became "belligerent."

At the height of his time as company head, Sushi was essentially in control, "She used to call me, 'Sushi is the boss.'" He told me that he quit. Others claimed that he was fired. "But I still love it because

I'm good at it," Sushi said, lighting yet another cigarette. "You know, I could do it with my eye[s] closed." Perfidia disagreed, telling me, "How does a dumb Japanese guy buy dresses for some girl, and you know like he's just copying what he thinks Pat likes? I don't know, I thought his merchandise was probably the saddest era of Pat Field ever." There's no love lost between the Field family generations. Perfidia said, "I'm sorry for [Sushi] but I think his karma was really rotten."

"I needed to be treated with a little more fairness, especially if I'm the one who was running the company for so long," Sushi explained. "She's difficult to work with," he added. Even her defenders mentioned her proclivity for verbal confrontations. "She was so tough and could wreck you but then it would make you want to do better, of course, like a parent," Perfidia told me. "She unfortunately has that verbal abuse thing."

For Artie, Pat's Greek-Armenian-American heritage created within her a natural inclination to structure her business as a family. But could it have also been a calculated commercial strategy? "She wanted me to be family so she could take advantage of me," he said. Artie seemed to be missing the peace of mind that the Incan cleansing ritual should have bestowed. Instead, he had serious beef to hash out. "I hope people see this," he said to me. "Like, you give your life to Patricia Field and then she throws you in the garbage."

Others felt tossed into the memory hole while Pat's profile and pocketbook expanded via more Up There gigs. "I kind of was angry at Pat because she didn't take me," Perfidia said. "Here [I'm] the beauty expert of the store, she gets *Sex and the City* and she goes to some other beauty salon and hires somebody? That totally floored me and that was the beginning of the end." Why the tossing aside? He believed that Pat just wanted to keep him at the store doing what he did. It pushed him to seek work on other projects. Lesson learned. Paul Alexander compared Pat to downtown contemporaries like Madonna and Marc Jacobs. "I don't think that you get to be successful by being terribly fair," he said. "You need to be fair to yourself but not to others if you really want to succeed, unfortunately."

So much for family. It was unfortunate that Pat backed away from a chat with me despite initially seeming interested. She has so much to say. But while turning me down, Pat did something that no one had done before: she told me whom to interview *instead*. Although unexpected and a little odd, I jumped at the chance to talk to Derrick Xtravaganza, a Brooklyn native and member of the legendary House of Xtravaganza. You perhaps saw him in the music video for "All Night," Icona Pop's homage to *Paris Is Burning* featuring the latest generation of the Xtravaganza family. It signaled Derrick's return to the scene after a long hiatus. As he told me, he pulled away from the vogue scene when the AIDS epidemic ravaged his community, triggering a deep depression. "I cut ties with the ballroom scene and I moved to New Jersey, got my life together, got a job, and didn't look back until 2007," he said. "But I never stopped practicing."

Curiously, when he first saw a vogue show, the femininity of the moves discouraged him. But the "butch queen" competition category was different, he said, becoming enthralled by its "masculine, hard moves" and the playful making of shapes with dancers' hands and body movements. Ronald LeMay and Jerome Pend'avis Magnifique were the key influences in his training, but Pat Field and her house loomed large on his early horizon. "Every now and then I would go to her store, like I wanted her to know who I was," he said of Pat, who finally presented him with a trophy when he walked for the House of Pend'avis at Red Zone.

When we spoke at a Flatiron District café, he still felt the burden of his dead friends but told me that he tried to find meaning in his own survival of the AIDS epidemic's darkest days. Imagine, he said, finally finding a family, a place where he belonged, and then to watch so many of them die. Still, Derrick clung to what he achieved. From

1988 to 1992, "I changed the vogue game." As we spoke, it seemed like Derrick was slowly coming back in vogue, having just returned from judging a St. Petersburg dance competition of young women in Russian vogue houses.

New York's ballroom scene could yield a whole other account of downtown families. But even though she wouldn't speak with me on the record, I'm grateful to Pat for linking me to Derrick. He's another example of what Dorian Corey called "a small fame" in *Paris Is Burning*. The tricky part is whether or not any of that will satisfy a person once they set their sights on impossibly high targets. Whether you're Warhol or Gaga, Susanne or Pat, a club kid or an Xtravaganza, or anyone discarded by a fame monster, what will ultimately give you a sense of satisfaction and contentment? Is there a way to survive a memory hole with a little peace of mind?

And what happens when you come close but the prize you seek remains painfully out of reach?

Like Amanda Lepore, Paul Alexander is one of those nightlife folks who will always offer a pleasant smile and greeting. Once you become a downtown habitué and you see people out and about regularly, you can tell when people aren't having a good night. But Paul will still be courteous and offer you his bright warm smile even if that happens to be the case.

Anxious to speak with him about his time as a House of Field star and performer with The Ones, we met up near the Chelsea Piers and walked into the breeze blowing in off the Hudson. In a soft, very deep voice (which I envy given my nasal tones), Paul talked about migrating from Jamaica and growing up in the Bronx, where he liked to play dress up with his mother's clothes. She let him explore freely and unencumbered as he became curious about fashion very early on.

Paul enrolled in art and design courses in high school with the goal of becoming a fashion designer. "In my class that first day in tenth grade was this boy, Marc Jacobs, and we became friends right away," he told me, as pier joggers passed us by and we found a bench.

The tenth-graders became best friends by graduation, with Jacobs quickly becoming the favorite darling of their teachers. Why? "He has this golden aura about him," Paul explained.

As fame became the name of their game early on, the inevitable competitiveness spilled over into their college years at Parsons, given Jacobs's early recognition from major industry figures. Jacobs quickly earned financial backing and accolades right out of college, while Paul fell behind. Discouraged, he decided to drop his futile rivalry with Jacobs and turn to another love—music—encouraged by Madonna's burgeoning stardom, which Paul began to obsessively chase.

I mentioned to Paul a January 15, 2010, blog post of his titled "clouds," where he wrote, "Doesn't help that my best friend from high school is one of the most successful fashion designers in the world and I am still working on my Madonna moment." Years later, had he been able to reckon with the actual outcomes of his aspirations? "No, it haunts me to death," he said, without any hesitation. Approaching fifty, Paul wondered if maybe he had done this or that, things might have turned out differently, undertaking a Flloyd-like excavation of his past. Did he really believe that his old friend Jacobs was happy? "I don't think he is at all, but he's loaded."

In the relentless pursuit of his "Madonna moment," Paul's own career apogee came in the form of the hit single "Flawless" by his band, The Ones. The only problem was that he didn't realize that *this* was his big break, finding himself unready for the major career opening that could have altered his life. *"You had your time,"* he remembered a close friend boldly informing him. "And I was like devastated with that news so it crushed my spirit for the longest time."

Paul and Jacobs don't talk anymore. The last time Paul saw him was at a Susanne Bartsch charity toy drive when Jacobs was still dating Lorenzo Martone. Previously, Paul had a standing invitation to the Jacobs fashion shows and would kiki with him for a bit after. One year Paul committed the apparent faux pas of bringing along The Ones and that was it. "He's very particular about things," Paul said about his breach of protocol, not knowing what else could have possibly offended him to the extent that he would be banished from the Marc Jacobs standing guest list. Paul sounded rueful now, "The one year that I took advantage of like the invitation by bringing my group to be seen there, it all changed."

He repeatedly talked about Jacobs as an old friend and competitor who seemed to casually achieve what Paul never could. And yet I didn't hear the resentment and anger that I heard from Pat Field's old inner circle. So question marks started flashing in my mind. Paul talked about Marc Jacobs in intimate, sensitive ways, so I asked if they had a romantic relationship. A long pause while Paul stared at me. An off-the-record topic, so off my recorder went.

Back on, we were far down Reminiscence Road when he mentioned being attracted to the House of Field after seeing its fabulous members collect the wages of their "small fame," like being guest-listed basically everywhere. He coveted this luxury, so he sold a capsule collection to Pat Field and later became a buyer. Although he doesn't necessarily host the biggest downtown parties around, to this day Paul doesn't wait in line and usually drinks for free.

He was at least candid about his deep preoccupation with a lifelong chase of an elusive Madonna moment. But why? He gave the example of styling Mariah Carey for her "Make It Happen" music video and seeing crazed fans gasping and grasping, beaming and screaming for photos. "That's what I want: *to make somebody so happy to see you*." He became reflexive but not emotional. No big tears on the Chelsea piers. Paul wrapped up his musings by telling me, "Had I been ruthless like Madonna, and didn't care about who I was hurting, I might have gotten further."

DJ Johnny Dynell, an honorary Field, turned to the subject of fame easily, having known the Scissor Sisters, Madonna, and other downtown ascenders early on. His verdict was cautionary. "To be famous is very unnatural," he told me, using the example of a wedding. To be a bride is to be the center of attention, wrapped in a resplendent gown of lace and silk, a flawless princess made up and photographed and pleased and toasted. But at the end of the day, the bride is exhausted and most likely does not want to do it again. Fame is like *Groundhog Day* in this way. "When you're famous on that level you're the bride every single day of your life," Johnny said. "You gotta be a little bit mentally ill to want that and crave that."

We can tie it back to the human need to have and exhibit an identity, whether you're a frumpy grad student, an Army officer, an ambitious stylist, or a nightlife impresario. But fame entails a hunger for the maximal identity, the super self that everyone recognizes as living Up There, a crazed craving for the sensation of strangers moving aside for you like they did for Billy Name and his Superstar friends. Fame is a status that's intensely wanted but something for which no one can really prepare, something so desperately coveted but at times regretted, even contributing to loneliness, destitution, depression, addiction, and suicide.

And what about that moment, when the Rubicon has irrevocably been crossed, when you're in a social situation that brims with status ambiguity or conflict and first feel the impulse to react by saying *those words*? They represent the highest that a human's nose can go. The pinnacle of entitlement. The supreme snobbery. *"Do you know who I am?"*

Oh no you didn't, miss honey. But the punch line, of course, is that if you really need to say these words you're not as famous as you think you are. It's the classic arriviste mentality, but be careful in wishing for the Madonna moment like Paul did, you just might get it: the endless attention, the evaporation of privacy, friends always wanting something, the stalkarazzi, and the cloying fans like Starlight's Yotel meatball. And the fear of it all fading away someday.

Fame is so very fleeting. We see it in the tragedy of the withered has-been accompanied by whispers of irrelevance instead of the frenzy that Paul watched Mariah Carey revel in. Although much derided for its inaccuracies, Kenneth Anger's *Hollywood Babylon* captured the special anxiety that our uniquely American obsession contains: "The fans worshipped, but the fans also could be fickle, and if their deities proved to have feet of clay, they could be cut down without compassion. Off screen a *new* Star was always waiting to make an entrance." The superstar syndrome that Anger identified reproduces itself far away from Los Angeles, on Lower East Side corners or cobblestone SoHo streets. And the hunger is as powerful as ever.

Maybe surviving fame requires compartmentalizing your show and your self. Fenton Bailey, one of the World of Wonder "assholes" that Codie mentioned, has produced documentaries about Chaz Bono, Tammy Faye Baker, and Britney Spears, and of course launched Michael Alig's own fame via grisly films about Angel's killing. Fenton compared Spears's own shyness to Michael Musto's awkwardness. It was the absolute last comparison that I expected: a curvy blond pop princess dancing in tiny sequined outfits next to the sleepy-eyed, "musty" peddler of snark oddly shuffling around downtown. Fenton explained the mismatch between the Spears *person* and *persona*: "You would think that someone who would sing these very sexually balls-out songs, would be that kind of a person but actually the truth of who she is, is she's a very shy, Southern, polite, ordinary person [. . .] She sings the songs, she embodies the songs, she looks the part, but it's not who she is and she is a really shy person."

Spears is doing what behavioral scientists sometimes call "character-splitting." Gaga, for example, has been asked about the distance between Stefani and The Lady. To make sense of the experience of being famous, a *Journal of Phenomenological Psychology* article by Donna Rockwell and David C. Giles interviewed fifteen adults with celebrity status. Like cellular mitosis, the identity splits into a private self and a public figure. But it's an isolating process. As Rockwell and Giles concluded, "Fame chases old friends away at the same time that strangers are flocking toward [one of their celebrity interviewees]."

So what does it really take to build a little empire way Up There? Do you need the ruthless hunger that Paul saw in Madonna, Marc Jacobs, and others? A constant discarding of people into a memory hole? A few predictors of surviving fame are key.

First, you need a stable family life or inner circle of pre-fame friends to provide some grounding and clear reminders of where you started. Gaga and Susanne had this, for example. Michael Alig really didn't. Warhol had his mom and close besties like Brigid Berlin, a sassy heiress who didn't want or need his money.

Second, a real and consuming commitment to your craft and art, an obsessive devotion that's more important to you than the bling, camera flashes, red carpets, and fair-weather friends. True for Warhol and Gaga. Less so for Michael and others. Although they possessed wild creative talent, the hunt for the Madonna moment was the underlying obsession.

Third, avoiding drug and alcohol abuse. On so many registers, it should be abundantly clear that addiction can lay waste to a fame seeker, his or her ambition, happiness, and even life.

To this list, Susanne and Pat might add: a powerful eye for social curation, an ability to sniff out trends, a flair for grouping together people or garments. History writers will rightfully salute the Manhattan mavens as pioneers who made the city less beige and created magical moments where so many people, including me, felt like they fit in a little. It's also important to remember that the fame game can still be unfair toward women players, although extremely savvy and creative women dominate entire industries, including Shonda Rimes, Sheryl Sandberg, Oprah Winfrey, and Anna Wintour. Michelle Obama, Elizabeth Warren, Nancy Pelosi, Janet Yellen, and others stand out in the public sector, even as the shadow of Hillary Clinton's near-win of the White House (and total win of the popular vote) lingers over the Trump administration.

Glimpsing the innards of two midnight matriarchies—and seeing the human detritus left in their wake—revealed much about the price of admission to downtown's volatile fame games. The key lesson may be the importance of a steely inner strength, a stable inner core that only comes from steady, intense, and disciplined devotion to whatever it is that you do or make. As I tell my students, put luck, looks, labels, and Instagram likes aside. The proof is in your pudding.

6

BOXED IN

I absolutely live for dinner kikis with Bibbe Hansen and her husband Sean. They're all too rare occasions to catch up about whatever's keeping us busy, but also a chance to dish out the latest bits of gossip swirling around town. Every now and then a yesteryear morsel about Warhol, Edie, or some other Factory star will spin through our Spill the Tea session, or maybe a mention about her star son Beck, word of any big upcoming gallery openings, and updates on the downtown dramas of the day.

About six months after my post-Summer of Alig convalescence with them upstate, we met up near my NYU classroom after I finished class. It was one of those insanely frigid New York nights when it's so cold that it actually hurts to be outside, when you walk two blocks to the subway muttering curses and spitting out promises to move to LA.

Though tired I was eager to see them and exchange news. I dashed over to meet them only to find that Bibbe and Sean had brought along some little mid-twenties interloper I'll call T. He was very cute, yes. Short and thin. Wavy brown hair and wonderful lips. But also a total newbie, freshly plopped into the city from somewhere out west. And big surprise! Yet another aspiring singer-songwriter. Some friend of his recommended that he look up the great Bibbe Hansen and so there he was on the corner of Waverly and Greene. *Ugh*. We grown-ups had stories to tell, situations to dissect, and I knew that T would have nothing to add to our conversation.

After a day of teaching I was hungry and cranky. Throughout our dinner at Dojo, my go-to for soy burgers and beers, I ribbed and tested T nonstop, asking for his thoughts on obscure downtown figures and trying to overwhelm him with sordid nightlife soap opera stories. Callously, I refused to admit that I was once essentially in his newbie shoes. But to my surprise he held his own pretty well. Oh, and that goofy, clueless smile of his. I spent the dinner hiding my eye-rolls but also picturing what his stomach looked like.

When we said goodbye I flung my business card at him, poked his chest, and said, "This is my number. If you're smart, you'll text me. *If not, you don't belong in New York.*"

Can you believe I'm single?

But he did actually text me! So we made plans to get together. By this time I had become very close to my dear Rose Wood and she invited me, plus one, to Snoop Dogg's private Fashion Week concert at The Box. I decided to invite T and briefed him on the night's protocols. After a quick pregame at a nearby bar, we walked down to The Box, where Rose greeted us at the door. Fashion Week at The Box with a cute boy! But despite having T as my date, I was in total business mode. Since it was a very Up There fête for Fashion Week, my Terminator mode was on HI, trying to spot who was there and with whom. At certain points I practically became liquid metal, oozing in between all the cocktail dresses and chic blazers packed tightly together. While I scanned the Box booths I also kept an eye on T, who happily danced with a few pretty girls eager to ditch their stiff rich dates and bump and grind with a hot gay boy.

I got caught up in a conversation about performance bookings and the lighting system. After a bit I turned around and there was T up in the very center of the stage, turning up hard, hands pummeling the air. That's my date up there, people! He's with me! I grinned. Like a fish to water.

But then he started unbuttoning his dress shirt. He kept going, pulled it off, and with a dramatic flourish flung it across the stage. I was mortified. Never mind his muscles and chest! I ran up to the stage, picked up the shirt he flamboyantly tossed into a corner, and yelled, "OH my god, put this on right now! *This is NOT that kind of club!*" He shrugged, complied, and kept on dancing.

We hung out and drank until the acts started. In one number a group of brawny dancers flipped around, finishing up as a torrent of bubbles cascaded onto the audience. The club was suddenly black lit, creating a curtain of neon turquoise orbs falling on us, a thrilling effect. And because of that black light, as the orbs burst, bright white splatters appeared all over our faces and clothes. Surrounded by the glowing little explosions, T turned around, screamed, "I love this place!" And kissed me. Shocked and swooning, I thanked the heavens for The Box and Bibbe Hansen.

Snoop Dogg came out to perform, surrounded by the gorgeous Hammerstein Beauties twirling around him. The crowd lunged forward to take photos and Snoop made jokes about passing a joint around the club. T and I held each other. Box co-owner Richard Kimmel would later tell me that Snoop was booked often because of their close friendship. The odd couple bond shared by the frizzy-haired theater impresario and the blunt-toting lanky rapper emerged because they "really hit it off," Richard said, calling him "super bright" and a "real gentleman."

T spent the night with me. We hung out a few times after. He even came along on Steve Lewis's behind-closed-doors tour of Hotel Chantelle. Unfortunately T and I spent too much time talking show biz and ultimately intentions were misunderstood. One sunny Saturday he invited me over. I got a bottle of gin and his favorite amaretto liqueur and showed up at his place in Flushing, Queens. But after a nasty tiff at three in the morning, he flushed me out the door. I left behind the amaretto and took the leftover gin with me. Fair, no? When I summoned an Uber, the driver couldn't find me, so I scurried around a desolate Queens street, shoes untied, buckling my belt, a half empty gin bottle tucked under my arm.

In a hammed up, C-list cable TV movie's melodramatization of the night, I would have fled his apartment wearing a flimsy negligee, barefoot in pounding rain. Mascara running down my face, one hand clutching my wig, the other desperately hailing a cab that pitied my humiliating outer borough expulsion. In reality, I went home quietly, though regretful that I wasted that Box night on T.

So you won't be surprised to hear that when a Shanghai luxury magazine asked me to write about my top New York hotspots I had to give the number one slot to The Box. Plenty of other venues popped into mind, like The Standard, Flash Factory, Marquee, or Cafeteria, but six years after I started my night lessons the small theater-cum-club on the Lower East Side is still my favorite place. And it has beaten the odds of the downtown fame game to become one of the city's premiere nightlife spots for a whole decade as of 2017. At their Valentine's Night ten-year anniversary gala—bald Vic in khakis long since left behind—I stood in the jam-packed venue as the curtains peeled back to reveal Pussy Riot as their special guest performers.

As Richard Kimmel explained, his club took up the Moulin Rouge mantra of providing "low life for millionaires." In doing so, it stepped into city lore, being filmed as Chuck Bass's "Victrola" club in *Gossip Girl* and becoming the model for the mafia's club in Fox's Batman saga *Gotham*. Gaga and Tony Bennett used The Box for their jazz album's photo shoots. Debra Messing filmed some of her police drama there, while Baz Luhrmann shot it for his Netflix series *The Get Down*.

Back during my high Gandhi phase, I had zero hope of getting in on my own but over the course of my downtown nights I became a bit of a regular and ended up taking along colleagues, friends, and former students. But I also had to reckon with the results of my social standing in places like this. I had access, yes, but I'm not a performer, a promoter, or a club kid, so where did the professor of the night go from here? I couldn't let myself get boxed in.

I ended up at 189 Chrystie Street for the very first time in 2011 because of my friend M. One of the hosts had a certain soft spot for him, so tagging along with M made getting in easier. The first few times, I arrived after first hopping around gallery openings, bars, and parties and I really had to struggle to sober up in order to not be a hot mess inside. I was overwhelmed by the outrageous acts but much of it was a blur of bodies and lights after way too many vodka crans. Knowing no one there and still looking pretty busted, had it not been for the host's affections for M I might not have ever experienced the magical nights that the little theater offered.

Like their Halloween ball in 2016, for which Rose Wood told me that she would debut a brand new act that she very much wanted me to see. I wore my usual all black ensemble and donned a shimmery iridescent mask. Some friends tagged along, including Alexandra Warrick in an elegant cocktail number, Lendita Berisha in a fetishy feline look, and Ava Glasscott dressed to the absolute tee as Harley Quinn, right down to the faux tattoos on her thighs.

The spectacle started once we were led inside, where I have *never* seen so many statuesque, nude women in one space before. They twirled around wearing only capes and masks as we all settled into Kayvon Zand's table. The Box had invited their best (and richest) clientele for an all-out visual bonanza of a masquerade. We sat through fire acts where we could feel the heat of the flames on our faces, saw women bathing in pools of faux-blood, and muscular male tumblers tossing each other all over the stage.

But then Rose took it to a whole other level. In a regal black gown accented with silver ruffles, head covered in a long black veil, she became a vampiric Victorian lady of the realm passing around to the audience chocolate-covered strawberries on silver platters. A bald, insane-looking fellow was her creepy Igor-like companion. After ascending the stage, the strawberries did not satisfy her haughty highness, so she lifted up her dress and defecated onto a platter. The lunatic lover then placed the shit in a serving bowl, setting it on fire. The simmering shit was then presented to Rose, who dipped a spoon into the shit dish and ate it. Satisfied at last.

The crowd was left appalled. When the silvery Salò number had its first full run several weeks later, it really pushed buttons: someone attacked Rose and the police were called. So the creative minds behind the venue are also boxed in by the rules of the downtown fame game. Their lavishly louche brand of entertainment had to be provocative and wild enough to capture an audience of super wealthy globetrotting clientele who have seen and done it all. But it also had to refrain from crossing a certain line whereby that same clientele is totally offended and grossed out. It's another spin on the conundrum that ensnared Warhol, Alig, Gaga, and others. In any kind of art, how far is too far?

As former Box director Craig Klein saw it, nightlife is the business of "re-gimmicking liquid distribution." How can you get people to come to a place and buy alcohol that they could consume more cheaply on their own? It all comes down to the *sale of the social*. Music, ambiance, lighting, performers, go-go dancers, fancy booths, attractive hostesses, and even the embossed cocktail napkins are all ways of pulling people in.

To sell the social, each of your senses has to be activated, the olfactory included. My colleague Gayil Nalls studied the unique role of our sense of smell in social settings. In nightlife, pheromones released by sweating bodies very close to each other, intermingling with perfumes and colognes, have an effect on a space's collective vitality. At The Box, whiffs of marijuana mixed with the scents of the artificial fog, the sparklers' smoke, or even the smell of teen spirit. A totally underage boy once ran up to me and happily declared that his boyfriend had just fucked him in the bathroom downstairs, leaving our older host rather jealous and pouty.

Like its sister locations in London and Dubai, the venue with the toughest door in town was crafted by what history will call an avant-garde of theatrical sensation: Simon Hammerstein, Richard Kimmel, and Randy Weiner. Richard told me that the torture of uncertainty outside at the velvet rope is quite intentional: "Anyone would have to admit that you feel very satisfied when you get through that experience and it only heightens your enjoyment and your relish." When the door person lifts the velvet rope, your pulse quickens as you enter a gorgeously illuminated space filled with beautiful people. Stunning hostesses explode sparklers, signaling that someone purchased a magnum of champagne or some high-end liquor, a parade of sparks now winding its way through the crowd.

Aside from the right look, the appropriate attitude at the door is also necessary. One night in 2017 my friends and I bumped into Lindsay Lohan in front of the venue. I suppressed an excited shriek of "LOVE YOU, LINDSAY!" and instead tried to play it cool for the imposing bouncers at the door. My pals and I ended up dancing on stage (and after one too many vodkas, I tumbled off, right in front of Richard). From the stage we could see Lindsay in her booth, vigorously tapping away on her phone. Wouldn't she have had more fun dancing up there with us? Next time, Lindsay!

Around 1:30, staff members will tell everyone to find a seat, while others hand out small containers of popcorn. Soon a beautiful, impeccably made-up Mistress of Ceremonies bursts out from behind the red curtains to sing opening numbers and wind up the crowd. "*What's up, motherfuckeeeeers!*" Then coy jokes about blowjobs and cocaine: both are encouraged.

The rest of the night is broken up into a first act, second act, and late show. The acts range from violent and grotesque displays to beautifully performed works of illusion, contortion, and acrobatics. A fire breather might follow the infamous squirter, who fingers her vagina until shot glasses are filled with her emissions and handed out to the crowd. The acts would be gross yet engrossing, encouraging even the most jaded New Yorker to put down her phone and absorb the scenes.

A crowd favorite is Narcissister, a thin African American woman who always wears a mannequin-like mask over her face. In one number, she appears nude and dresses herself with clothing pulled from her orifices. I have also seen her extract a ringing cell phone from her vagina. Later, a waifish Pee-wee Herman character might snort cocaine and end up break-dancing and twirling around the stage, stepping toward the front row to shake our hands. A young aerialist named Desire might end up naked, twirling on a hoop from the back of her neck, or DeeDee Luxe, wearing a nun's habit, would wield a burning bible and a glow-in-the-dark crucifix dildo.

On any night at The Box, I would be most eager to see Rose Wood. In her homage to Anna Wintour, Rose wears a wig modeled on the infamous brown bob of the *Vogue* editrix. Like other performers, she enters from among the audience, a spotlight from above following Rose as she shoves her way through the crowd. She struts up onto the stage, approximating the same imperious look of the woman that the fashion industry fears so intensely. Here was a stage version of a figure that has become so mythical that Meryl Streep, America's greatest actress, was needed to approximate her frigid persona in *The Devil Wears Prada*.

On stage there is a toilet, which our Anna needs to use, all while Nelly Furtado's "Man Eater" beats through the house. Naturally, she defecates not into the toilet but into the panty hose that she holds open around her thighs. After emptying her rectum Anna pulls her hosiery up, smearing the faux feces all over her ass. But toilet paper won't suffice for the clean up job, so instead she rips a few pages out of *Vogue* and rams them up her anus with a plunger.

The first time I saw the act, two people walked out. Two others vomited. My friends and I cheered wildly.

I'm reluctant to say more, knowing that at some level it's pointless. You need to be there all dolled up, sipping some vodka. You need to breathe in the perfume off a beautiful brunette's neck, as you try to have a semblance of a conversation while music pounds all around you. You have to make it to the second floor. Glimpse inside the lounge with the stripper pole. Pull back the curtain of a booth and accidentally spot a dude getting blown in the dark. You need to look through the pulsating lights at the person across the room that you think is just the hottest human being ever. You may do a double-take as you spot a topless woman smeared in white paint dancing with a shirt-and-tie venture capitalist who has definitely had one too many. Later she'll have a long subway ride home to Queens on the N train. He'll stumble outside totally wasted, hop into his idling SUV, and pour himself into his TriBeCa bed.

These moments all point to the potent formula that The Box managers found for pulling in a star clientele and achieving a mixed party, the holy grail of nightlife today as much as it was in the heyday of Limelight, Palladium, Area, and Studio 54. Acknowledging his own status as "a corny white guy," for co-founder Simon Hammerstein, the recipe for a truly mixed party was the shared and common human impulse to tell stories. To do this, a venue needed "every color under the sun," he told me. "You need all different persuasions and backgrounds. And then you have a show that makes everyone scream in shock and yell in unison. All of a sudden you're like, '*Shit, we're all the fucking same*. We all feel.'"

Not everyone enjoyed the mix, though. Craig derived no enjoyment from typical nights at the place he helped lead for two years: "Who am I gonna meet there? Who am I gonna be inspired by? The fucking owner of Spotify? I don't give two shits what he has to say." Most club operatives understood the importance of what Craig called "the douchebaggery." Steve Lewis thought they could be improved, but for Craig the social divide simply could not be overcome. "Have you ever tried to have fun in a room full of guys that wear a backwards hat? You can't," he said.

Long before the pop fame of Caitlyn Jenner, Rose Wood's own journey to becoming The Box's Mother and most notorious performer started as a gradual reckoning with her gender identity. Born Jon Cory, she initially toyed with the idea of being a rabbi. Although deep-seated questions churned within her for years, it was only until about the age of forty that Rose decided to fully live as a woman and initiate a transition. A breast augmentation procedure would follow years later, along with feminization surgeries on her face. Her new name was chosen as a reference to her daytime career as a top artisan and antique furniture restorer to the stars, now counting A-list household names as her clients. "In the world of woods," she explained, "Ebony is the king of woods and rose wood is the queen of woods."

Now friendly with everyone from Jude Law and Rita Ora to her Chelsea Hotel neighbor Susanne Bartsch and India Rose James, London's Princess of Soho, she can also tell wonderfully juicy stories peppered with references to the Cockettes, Willy Ninja, or Balthus. You will feel the need to take notes when chatting with her. But she has been called The Box's "Queen of Filth" for setting her penis on fire, inserting a Jameson bottle into her anus, and urinating on audience members, among other things. Several of her performances incorporated faux feces that she manufactured herself: a number in which Rose portrayed a homeless person featured eight different kinds of self-synthesized shit. On separate occasions Rose emptied condoms of simulated semen on Ridley Scott, Leonardo DiCaprio, and a prince of Saudi Arabia, a kingdom where queens like Rose could be beheaded solely for existing.

The overwhelming terror of her stage self could be contrasted with her maternal gentleness, extremely incisive thinking, and a background as a New York University math major, one who came from a Jewish family of ophthalmologists in New Jersey. Helping the childhood turbulence over her gender identity was a family that upheld "charity and culture," letting her meld a love of performing with charity work in a children's correctional school. This kind of service continued while she ran an AIDS organization for eighteen years.

I first met Rose back in 2012 at the Alcone make-up store in Hell's Kitchen, while F and I were visiting Veronica Ibarra. I could only imagine the comments that she heard while walking to the store: the front half of her head was shaved, the dark hair on the back half grown out long, and she wore a white tank top—muscles bulging, large breasts prominent. I had already seen her perform and wanted to interview her, so I introduced myself. She looked over her shoulder, eyeing me suspiciously. Once I explained who I was, Rose was extremely pleasant and almost immediately agreed to an interview. Her packed performance schedule meant that about two years flew by, and I regret now that so much time elapsed.

In December 2014, Rose penciled me in for about an hour after her show, around four in the morning. Our chat at the now closed diner Sugar turned into five hours, triggering a very close mentorship that became one of the best friendships to emerge from my downtown outings. In addition to more of those sunrise kikis at Sugar or Veselka in the years to come, Rose was also a guest speaker at my sexuality class at Columbia, kindly dedicated an immersive Box act to my mom, and passed on countless articles and essays to read. To celebrate her sixtieth birthday in 2017, Rose debuted a new act and afterward had a stagehand bring my friends and me backstage. Giving her a tight happy birthday squeeze quickly covered my face in streaks of her fake blood, the bright red mixing with my glittery green eye make-up. You can imagine the baffled looks I later got while walking into Veselka for Rose's birthday breakfast.

It was bound to happen. When we spoke at Sugar for the very first time, Rose's arms and hands were also covered in red streaks, following a wild show in which she masturbated until she bled. I told her about Kabuki Starshine's use of shaving cream to remove fake blood from the body. Rose explained that straight bleach was the way to go. Apparently a quarter of her performances involved fake blood so she was accustomed to these brutal self-treatments.

Despite her gentle demeanor, Rose told me, "I'm 100 percent a monster," one who believed in the educational and stabilizing power of fear. "That's the purpose of horror: send you back to some sense of what's normal for you," she said. But I was amazed at how she stayed so calm in the face of so many hateful comments and bashings over the years. How had she not become a raging misanthrope? While performing at The Act in Las Vegas she couldn't even walk the street during the day, instead buying groceries at five in the morning. Someone else, like me, might have become totally embittered, or dependent on any substance that would alleviate the pain of living, or maybe just ended my existence flat out. But not Rose. Worried about so many threats, friends convinced her to at least wear a wig in public.

There was also plenty of abuse from supposed downtown allies, including one burlesque veteran who told her over lunch, "We don't respect you." Drag legends were originally cruel to her and even trans organizations protested, claiming that she portrayed trans women as crazy and dangerous. She reminded them that her daily existence on the streets was a struggle and that she maintained deep mentoring ties with trans women in the midst of their journeys. "I'm still a soldier," Rose reminded them.

As if frightening stage acts were not enough, during our chat Rose confessed to having been celibate for *thirty-five years*, by choice, and having masturbated only five times in the course of those decades. Why? For her, sexuality had no primacy within her identity. Via meditative practices she gained a certain mastery of her body

and mind. With the whole premise of her art being that she is neither a man nor a woman, "I don't have a real body identity," Rose
insisted. "I see part of my role as to break up a lot of these identities
for people."

The mutability of her sexuality was curious, given that she talked
about "turning on" someone, not in the sexual sense but in terms
of *activating* a person's mind, pushing them to feel something that
they hadn't before. The site for this activation was the stage. It was
Rose's home terrain, although the spotlight didn't enthrall her. Like
Gaga, she studied the nature of fame. But unlike Mother Monster, the Mother of The Box didn't quite live for the applause. As
Rose explained, "If you look at the musicians—the Lady Gagas and
things—they're doing it for people they don't know. There's no direct
relationship with them. It's for the world: 'I want to be a household
word.'" She understood the abstract and unusual nature of fame—
the desire to be known and loved by those who are unknown to
you—and found no value in it.

Although seemingly winning at the downtown fame game, she
eschewed any public persona. Zero social media presence. She explained, "It's better if just people talk about an experience they had
and somebody else wants to come and have that experience, rather
than people reading about it." Rose even took down a website that
was up a few years ago. So none of Penny Arcade's Facebook rants,
Walt Paper's self-worshipping Instagram photos, or Michael Alig's
Periscoping of his domestic routines. She professed no desire to be
known or to be Up There, instead trying to give the people in the
room a sensation that was impossible to feel unless you were actually
there, staring up at her on stage, worrying that some of that shit or
Jameson spew was going to fly your way.

Rose's audience—her victims—rule Manhattan. Their Prada
loafers and Manolo stilettos touch pavement only in the short strut
from their huge SUVs to whatever door is being held open for them.
And so Rose's smile grew even wider in describing her "court jester"

function, enjoying the immense contrast between her show and the guests' elite status. The wealthy elites can drop around $60,000 on a single night, showing up in designer regalia also worth thousands. "And what are they spending their money for? What do they get for all their fabulousness?" Rose asked. "A homeless person throwing poop at them." She laughed her classic Rose laugh, mixing total bemusement with a light sigh of satisfaction.

Waiters refilled our coffee mugs as Rose recalled a particular Box patron. Tattooed and potbellied, this regular was a billionaire who could easily buy the whole venue itself. He enjoyed running around wasted, at one point even trying to join Rose on stage until the bouncers stopped him. One night she joined the audience to watch a fellow performer. The drunken captain of industry jumped on Rose from behind and whispered in her ear, "You're a king. No one knows. But you're a king. I know." Able to buy any and every thrill he could imagine, he was still quite poor, Rose realized. Since his identity was tied to his pockets, he found himself surrounded by groupies picking at that infinite wealth. "He's lonelier than you," she told me.

After this kind of encounter with billionaire brutes who buy their way around Manhattan, where did Rose go? Although she's Susanne Bartsch's neighbor at the Chelsea Hotel, she spent most of her time at her workshop a few blocks north, where the smell of varnish stung your nostrils as you walked in. The other thing that greeted you was a wall of boxes containing costumes and props. Rose, also a talented calligrapher, beautifully labeled each one, creating a cardboard wall elegantly emblazoned with words like *Faggot*, *Serial Killer*, and *Throwing Poop*.

The main room was like any workshop, brightly lit, shelves with glue and chemicals, wires, a loud factory fan blowing. But a small room off to the side was its own realm. The whole place felt nonsensical, like in a dream where one minute you were in a bedroom, then open a closet door and were somehow standing by a lake. Rose's studio felt like this. A door to the side opened to a tiny, dark room that she used to meditate, nap, and prepare her wigs and make-up. Incense and photographs of yogi mentors hung not far from the wig that she used to impersonate Anna Wintour. A blue wig sat on the shelf, waiting to be coiffed. The tiny, dimly lit room felt peaceful, totally unlike the harsh lights and sharp cutting machines of the workshop room.

This space was a far cry from the stage that she dominated while most of New York slept. "Everybody loves a spectacle," she noted, and for sure she created displays that amazed stars and sultans alike. When Gaga took her friend's bachelorette party to The Box in early 2015, she invited Rose over to her table after watching her perform. To have been a fly on the wall for the meeting of those ladies! She who mastered the science of fame and she who couldn't be bothered with it. To be obsessed with remembrance and to welcome the oblivion of a memory hole. Before I left our first Sugar kiki, I asked Rose what epitaph she might want. Not flinching or hesitating, she replied, "I would rather that they misplace my body and don't find a place for it."

Getting out of a cab near the South Street Seaport, I looked around at a neighborhood that I hadn't visited in a long while. The silvery sinews of Frank Gehry's One New York tower glimmered nearby, now the shorter neighbor of a grandly looming One World Trade Center. A narrow cobblestone street led to the coffee shop where Simon Hammerstein asked me to meet him. After buying an obscenely expensive juice made out of exotic fruits that I probably couldn't identify if you placed them in front of me, I sat and looked around at the cutely dressed patrons sipping their lattes, discussing last night's drama.

I was very unsure about what to expect from The Box's notorious bad boy co-founder and the grandson of the man who wrote musicals like *The Sound of Music*, *Oklahoma!*, and *The King and I*, works from which my mom could easily sing a number of songs. Like the names of past presidents, mayors, or Donald Trump, Simon's surname is sprinkled across Manhattan, as in the Hammerstein Ballroom in Midtown, huge advertisements for musicals in revival like *Cinderella*, or the Rodgers and Hammerstein Archives at Lincoln Center.

After a few moments in the café, Simon barged in, talking excitedly into his phone. The scion of the legendary Hammerstein clan wore baggy cargo shorts, a black T-shirt, and sneakers, his hair wet. I stood up to shake Simon's hand but he only mumbled my name and walked past me, saying something about needing to blow his nose. He grabbed a napkin and went back outside, still chatting on the phone.

A few minutes later he returned, bought two coffees, and asked about gluten-free cookies. After Simon sat down and asked about our mutual acquaintances, the first thing that struck me was his curious accent, the product of being raised in both New York and London. He spoke of *puhfohmunces* at The Box, for example. He carefully scanned and studied me, smiling broadly through his beard. After this initial vetting, Simon invited me to his apartment only a few blocks away and on the way over described the previous night's romp in bed with a woman, using the same casual tenor that he might use if describing the day's weather. Michael Alig immediately came to my mind, since he has the exact same readiness for confessing sex secrets within moments of meeting a stranger.

The rustic bachelor pad of the heir to a mantle of American theatrical royalty was modern yet manly, bohemian yet bro. Surrounded by colorful old posters of his family's productions, Simon curled up on his huge couch and started rolling cigarettes. He slipped off his sneakers and plopped his bare feet up on a table adorned with bright orange tulips. While gulping down his two coffees, we discussed his trans-Atlantic lineage, one that began with a teenager's obsessive love for raves and led to an entertainment empire that spanned New York, London, and Dubai, and now had its sights on continental Europe and East Asia.

Unfettered by parental control but burdened by his family identity, fourteen-year-old Simon fell in love with nightlife. "There's this other universe of creatures, of cartoon characters," he remembered, realizing: "Not everything is as button-down and combed and pressed as watching New York during the day." He showed up to his first rave in bland clothing and encountered partygoers dressed as Muppets, but eventually left with a pacifier in his mouth following some experimentation with party favors.

Simon became hungry for the transcendent experience that he discovered, searching for a new one to be consumed each night: "I would roam the streets listening for bass speakers in the basement, literally." He soon came across a young RuPaul dressed as Wonder Woman holding court with other queens. "We were in the bathroom and watching them talk to themselves in the mirror, talk shit to each other. They were doing their whole dance, their act, their living theater."

Starting around 1993 he began throwing his own raves in Brooklyn and Queens and befriended techno DJs. With his budget-starved friends Simon had significant clout to wield: his family fortune. He was open about this symbiotic relationship and laughed as he recalled, "I knew they were kind of trying to exploit me but I knew that I could get on top." So with his babysitter's husband as his bodyguard, he carefully watched the door money coming in to make sure he wasn't cheated. With his own money he covered the warehouse rent, flyers, DJ equipment, lights, and projections, charging twenty or thirty dollars at the door and spending thirteen cents on water bottles that he would then sell for three dollars.

As he plunged into the rave scene, he fondly remembered the club kid world, saying that he "lived at the Limelight," rubbing

elbows with Michael Alig, Peter Gatien, and Larry Tee back in
the heady days of Disco 2000, before the killing of Angel Melendez bled through. Did they know who he was? Simon confessed,
with some embarrassment, to his disco name being *Super Simon*.
Although unbearably hokey by the standards of both then and now,
he just chuckled, saying to me, "I was living it, baby." Simon also
frequented places like the Palladium and the Roxy but was not
known as the Hammerstein heir. "No one gave a shit about me,"
he recalled.

He partied hard until he was eighteen years old, at which point
he had a nervous breakdown from too much drug use and "too much
beef" with others, leading to a ten-year hiatus. When he eventually returned, his tastes shifted toward the model-bottle crowd. Two
factors aided in The Box's birth. First, Simon had no interest in
working for someone else. Laughing merrily, he explained, "I always liked being the boss, even as a teenage rave producer. 'You're at
my motherfucking party.' I had a Napoleonic complex from a very
young age."

Second, and this was vital for understanding his venue, the establishment was founded not as a club, but as a theater: having no
experience in variety or vaudeville, Simon simply wanted a venue in
which to pursue his vision of "edgy realism." He now insisted on the
futility of plans, claiming that his pre-opening schemes for The Box
were the opposite of what he does now.

The ultimate push for a shift toward non-traditional theater was
a pre-opening birthday party for André Balazs, owner of The Standard hotels and the Chateau Marmont in Los Angeles. The hotelier
requested Joey Arias as MC for the evening but the downtown diva
wasn't available. So in stepped Raven O, who resembled a tan, buff
elf. Simon's meeting with the thoroughly tattooed Hawaiian singer
was electric, thinking, Raven was "fucking nuts and scary and got
tattoos and he's being all cunty with me and I kind of love it." Together, Simon said, they developed "a shared deep understanding of

each other and what made rich tension on stage. And a *'Fuck you. And you think you're going to judge us? Well, fuck you.* Come on, motherfuckers.'"

Thinking about their team, Raven called Simon his "other half" with whom he was "joined at the hip." And so their partnership began, later pulling in others like Rose Wood and long-running show producer Andrew Katz. As a theater they intended to stage a play. But while they mulled over which one to run, variety shows were staged late at night. They put a velvet rope outside and expensive bottle service inside, and voilà, the crazy chemistry of the Chrystie Street club started to bubble. The original game plan of a single show on the marquee never materialized.

Slowly Simon's "purely instinctual" directorial vision began seeking a way to build "a whole journey in two minutes," one that could channel his "psychosexual" dreams and yield "a dreamscape of romance and love and horror and drama and weirdness." He preferred arriving at rehearsals "exhausted or angry," even hung over from the previous night's revelry, just to provoke more visceral reactions from his team.

At several points during our interview it seemed like Simon was reciting a well-rehearsed narrative, an account of his identity that could satisfy both him and the nosey like me. Although I tried to puncture that blasé veneer, at no point was he as engaged as when we discussed Michael Alig. There were definitely similarities in their aesthetic sensibilities and private personas, their wars against conventions and limits. They were both eager to disturb and provoke via their work, alongside complicated struggles with expressing emotion and processing pleasure.

Like Michael, Simon talked freely of love and his fight to make sense of it. Fully relaxed on his couch, he spoke of his "uncontrollable love for so many people from so many walks of life" and how this love was channeled into his work. He recalled, "I also had an older gay man in my life who I loved with all my heart. And I was reconciling, 'How can I just want to marry this man so bad and be straight?' So there's so much to the limitlessness of our heart and our love for the world and everybody in it." I was totally surprised to hear that the man called the "impresario of smut" by the magazine *New York* had been trying so hard to make sense of a diverse set of desires within his identity. And like me, he had loved both men and women.

There seemed to be a sadness that flickered in Simon. His collaborator Randy Weiner said flatly, "He's a really dark dude," citing multiple sources, among them the burden of being constantly compared to his legendary forebears. If a Weiner production failed, the collapse stained only him. But if Simon failed, his entire lineage was somehow tarnished. It was a burden of being born Up There that most downtown upstarts don't face. And yet the lineage and the accompanying trust fund meant that he could start organizing his own events and parties at a very young age. Randy also pointed to other factors. "He's got a complicated relationship with women, you know," pausing for a moment, "*That's an understatement.*" Box star DeeDee Luxe expressed a desire for more involvement in the venue by Simon, saying, "He's a genius in his madness."

Can we draw a link between The Box's decade of success and Simon's emotional sensitivities, that flickering spot of melancholy inside him? At least by his own account, the intent of The Box, behind all the beautiful hostesses and expensive bottles, was an ambitious attempt to reconfigure how and why people see their place in the world. "I always like people to really look at their own opinions of other people, and really confront that, confront their own bias," he told me.

Simon's former director Craig Klein had a different impression of his vision and was ultimately fired from his job in 2015, despite sharing much of Simon's interest in the transcendence that nightlife offered. But as we ate a lunch of fried tofu together, I noticed that Craig, a straight married man from Kansas City, was so very chic, even by downtown standards. His curly hair was mussed to perfection, dangling over his left eye. He wore thin black suspenders over a white shirt with a print emulating paint splatter. Not quite the baggy cargo shorts and cruddy sneakers of his old Box boss.

For Craig, Simon was "an inspiring character." But did he enjoy working with him? "Not particularly," Craig admitted. "I think that he is motivated by something that I will never understand. I really tried to go there personally. I will never go there." What was Simon's driver, according to Craig? "Money and power." And so these two lovers of magical moments who obsessed over the visceral sensations that nightlife could deliver simply *did not* understand each other. Craig claimed to have a "more intellectual and thoughtful process," to be contrasted with Simon's brazen and callous "shoot from the hip" attitude.

Craig also offered a narrative of difference, a downtown fable that I have now heard many times: the dramatic saga of an attractive white man from a decent family background that just felt *so* alienated and *so* alone, but found his way in nightlife. Imagine Holden Caulfield at Tunnel, or Travis Bickle in skinny jeans waiting in line outside Marquee. In this sense, Craig had an unrecognized but common cause with men like Simon, Michael Alig, M, maybe F to an extent, and other young privileged men with looks, talent, and their peculiar alienation. Craig had explored the punk rock and goth scenes, not feeling accepted in either. He explained, "In a weird way I'm very, very social but I'm also very reclusive, and also very introverted." To me, men like Simon and Craig casually dominated downtown. But scorn seemed threaded through their narrative, a way for them to own and process their internal pain.

So if Simon could not succeed in overcoming social gaps with his own staff, how could a very door-conscious place like The Box achieve a truly mixed party? Let's call a spade a spade: in no way is a fully representative cross section of New York what the venue wants. The exclusivity of the door is meant to enforce the fact that the experience is something that must be earned. Is the place interested in difference? Yes. But also in the elite: in the prettiest, richest, and most successful people that the city has to offer.

The next time you're out, think about this puzzle of how people mix within a space. Maybe Simon hasn't fully realized his halcyon vision—and dissenters like Craig have been tossed into a memory hole in the meantime—but what he and Richard Kimmel oversee is not like every other club. Their joint has that peculiar frisson, generated by a convergence of the weird and the wealthy, the strange and the sexy, prostitutes and professors, royalty and Rose Wood.

"Um, hi Victor. It's Michael. We're outside The Box and they're not letting us in. Um."

The rest of the whiny voicemail from Michael Alig was mostly street noise and mumbling. Over a year after his release from prison, the old Party Monster still fumbled with ending calls on his iPhone and couldn't get into one of the city's best nightspots. Why the hold up? The doorman apparently believed that he was impersonating Michael Alig.

Earlier that night he threw shade when I told him that I wasn't going to The Box. The fact that I was sick with an awful cold meant nothing to Michael compared to the inconvenience that my absence might cause in getting into the club. He desperately wanted to impress his visiting brother by taking him to the scandalous space. Knowing that I was a regular at the venue, Michael no doubt craved the spectacle of casually breezing past the velvet rope, leaving his West Coast big bro agape at just how fabulous his little sibling still was. Listening to the voicemail I wasn't surprised that two short middle-aged men, dressed shabbily, had a tough time getting in. Given the vicious exclusivity and glam hierarchy of Michael's old parties, the irony was obvious.

I usually go to The Box on Fridays and try to sit front row. And when I say front row, I mean that your shoes rest on the actual stairs of the stage. The venue is as intimate as that. It's perfectly normal for topless female dancers to pull up a male guest, pull down his pants, and wave dildos around his bare ass. Or the gentleman could be fellated while he sat in the audience, or have his face rubbed into a female MC's crotch. My own agent Liz Parker was once pulled on stage during the late act and stripped of her dress by DeeDee Luxe. The act was her topless alien astrowarrior woman making love to a gyrating robotic white horse on stage. (I won't spoil what happens in DeeDee's act with Rose, "The Eunuch and the Princess," except to say that it gets requested a lot, especially for corporate events.)

DeeDee funneled her conservative Catholic upbringing into her Box acts, joining the venue early on thanks to Rose. She nailed her Box audition right off by strutting out as a grinder monkey pretending to shit in a bucket and smear herself with it. While growing up in Philadelphia, DeeDee would sneak to New York and party at Limelight and Tunnel while still in her teens. She immediately felt at ease. "The parties, I felt at home," she told me. "Like, 'Wow, there's other people like me.'" After moving to San Francisco for fashion design school and go-go dancing on the side, she was scouted for a Jane's Addiction tour. Today, DeeDee aspires to give Box audience members like me the same scandalous thrills that she felt at the clubs of her teen years.

Fridays at The Box are hosted by Kayvon and Anna Zand and their goth club kid crowd. Rose Wood explained to me that Kayvon was hired to sit on the famous couch at the center of the club and "populate the room with colorful people." Those colorful people were usually dressed all in black, brooding as they sipped vodka crans and suspiciously eyed you. After Kayvon's epic falling-out with Susanne, the Box gig became the bedrock of his fame game, a chance to hold court and show that he mattered despite professional setbacks. Although he enjoyed early support from RuPaul and Michael Musto and collaborated with Amanda Lepore and Mike Ruiz, a weak voice doomed his ability to transcend nightlife and become a mainstream singer.

Kayvon's cringeworthy audition on the 2015 cycle of *America's Got Talent* was the talk of downtown for a solid month. His turn was disastrous on every possible register. You really need to look it up on YouTube. Kayvon's extravagant rococo-goth image totally clashed with his light, boyish persona and a weak singing voice made it all a spectacular failure. Howard Stern and Heidi Klum straight up refused to acknowledge any modicum of talent in him. His one initial backer was Howie Mandel, whose support hinged on a sympathetic but incorrect reading of Kayvon as a willful, "hysterical" parody. That support soon evaporated with Mandel telling Kayvon, "It's not serious music. You're funny, no."

The nadir was Kayvon's response to Mel B's disapproval. After she criticized his abysmal sound he flipped the script and questioned the veteran Spice Girl's vocal ability. "Do you think that you're a better singer than me?" Jaws dropped and Piers Morgan savaged him further, labeling and hashtagging him an "#ObnoxiousLittleBrat." Backstage, a sweating Kayvon—frustrated but defiant to the last— waved away the cameras, demanding that they stop filming.

Cringing, frozen, hands over my mouth, I watched this all from my living room, absolutely sure that he would be fired from The Box after this nationally televised debacle. He was not.

How did his scramble to get Up There go sour? During our chat in his spacious Midtown apartment, Kayvon told me about learning to play the piano early on and later struggling with his body image in middle school. He remembered, "I was really overweight. I was a really fat kid." He overcame it. Losing the weight and being scouted for modeling gigs gave him a sense of former fatty vindication and a way to escape North Carolina. When we spoke, he still dreamt of pop stardom at the level of The Lady, or even running his own record label.

Back at The Box, our pouty, slightly plump peacock of a promoter yearned to be Master of Ceremonies at The Box. The outrageous gender-blurring looks were there but the voice and presence were missing. Back at Simon's apartment I had asked about Kayvon's MC ambitions. He abruptly asked that I turn my recorder off. For some, the verdict on Kayvon was crystal clear. Rose remembered, "I heard his audition for The Box and it just took ten seconds to say 'No.'" The tall-haired, Iranian American possessed a "light, sweet quality that won't work," Rose explained. "He has no ability to make people feel uncomfortable."

The ultimate result of this frustrated ambition was a lavishly dressed but bitter man, a Friday night face caked in pasty white make-up and a body wrapped in tight black vinyl. Put yourself in his shoes. Wear his plumage for a bit. When you yearn so desperately to be on stage, isn't it a special hell to be paid to just watch from the front rows, week after week after week? When I asked Kayvon about the biggest challenge of nightlife hosting, a long pause followed. Eventually he said, "For me it's the fear of doing it forever."

Within The Box's own social curation, why was it so tricky to cast a Master or Mistress of Ceremonies, the role that Simon described as a shamanic "truth sayer"? Several MCs were bisexual, according to Rose, but there must be some additional component. From the perspective of an audience member, the effect should be, according to Simon, "Let me know that they are in charge. I'm in their house. Tell me what I'm scared to say or scared to think."

To date, only two successful models in the MC role exist. The first is a group of very talented female singers, all African American: Acantha Lang, Kimberly Nichole, Sophia Urista, and Ashley Stroud. Nichole and Urista both went on to compete on NBC's *The Voice*.

The second model consisted of a single man, Raven O, and ever since he fled the harsh New York winters, The Box has refused to install a male heir in that role. Granted, the look of the fifty-something is inimitable, his identity indiscernible. Black tattooed symbols swirl around the Hawaiian's tanned limbs and torso, an oaky hue that complements his short platinum blond hair, brazenly curled into devilish horns. Sartorially Raven mixed tight leather apparel with distressed rock 'n' roll outfits, big chunky rings on each finger approximating the effect of brass knuckles. With a toothy smile brimming with the confidence of a seasoned stage veteran, Raven's look was that of a punk circus master, adorned with shiny safety pins, pearls, studs, and chains aplenty. "I'm an old goth faggot," Raven told me. As a stage character modeled on the Devil and surrounded by topless female dancers, his intro numbers featured bibles and clerical clothing, a good way to get eyes looking, jaws dropping, and phones set aside.

Did Raven O's story reveal anything about the need for the MC to evade easy labeling? To be ambiguous and frightening in a way that Kayvon could not?

During a lull in rehearsals at The Box, I sat with Raven in the second-floor lounge, the one with the stripper pole. Muscles bulging through a tight hoodie, he looked a good decade younger than fifty-something. I asked about the things that pushed him toward the stage. "My feeling of isolation and disconnection," the Hawaiian replied. "My insecurities and my fears drove me to create a world of fantasy and beauty that I want to live in."

While Elvis Presley enraptured his mother musically, his father loved the epitome of manly, old school swagger that was Frank Sinatra, an admiration that he would eventually transmit to his son. Initially, however, Raven clashed with his father, an ex–Air Corps paratrooper and military boxer who wanted to instill in his son the same martial bearing. "But I wanted to be what I am now, whatever that is," Raven said.

After winning a dance competition, he arrived in New York in the middle of winter, knocking on the door of a friend with whom he intended to stay. The friend said that he couldn't crash there after all, starting years of homeless nights spent on streets, parks, and friends' floors. He found a "haven" working in clubs and bars. Although he and a friend became the very first go-go boys at Limelight, there was still the nagging problem of acquiring a roof over his head. So after-hour clubs became a place to go after a night of nearly nude dancing, or he might end up sleeping at a friend's home, or just "end up with some guy I picked up and fuck and then sleep in . . . or whatever," he recalled, candid but not quite proud.

Like Michael Alig, he initially avoided drugs, but eventually fell into a "huge addiction problem." And much like the clownish club kids, he became a version of the nightlife caricature that he was performing in clubs. He remembered becoming his "own little Frankenstein's Monster, but much more gorgeous."

Raven told me that he had sex with Freeze a few weeks before he and Michael killed Angel. "Freeze was a trick I used to fuck," Raven said about his client, before trying to pivot to another subject. Surprised at the revelation, I recalled that Riggs is a PhD student in NYU's Sociology Department, headquartered nearby. It was a fun footnote of downtown fame that the former hustler and his past client found themselves working literally four blocks away from each other decades after their initial trysts. And at downtown's best club and its best university.

After a while Raven announced that he had to leave, but invited me to continue our conversation a few nights later in his dressing room. When I went back, the Friday night turn up was in full swing, the music from upstairs reverberating through the walls. We spoke as he prepared for the night, deftly applying eyeliner and lipliner, while his husband looked on. Stagehands regularly popped in to let him know how much time was left until showtime, all while Fleetwood Mac, New Order, and Madonna remixes beat through the walls.

So what made Raven the perfect Master of Ceremonies "truth sayer"? The gender fluidity and the ambiguity of his MC persona shouldn't be confused with androgyny. Raven made clear that his MC character was very masculine. An aggressive virility marked

Raven's on-stage sexual aura, one that could rattle the straight male bro. The sensual tenor set by Raven stomping through the audience was crucial. Richard Kimmel articulated the bro's intended reaction with glee, "Is he gonna fuck my girlfriend? Is he gonna fuck me? Is he gonna fuck us both? *Who the fuck knows?*" The key lies in frustrating the viewer's attempts to discern, identify, and place him.

But at last a provisional answer to the riddle may rest in the indeterminacy of Raven's identity, his ability to be a *non-identity*, an indecipherable one. Dancing around on stage he could not easily be pegged as gay or straight, white or ethnic, young or old, innocent or threatening. Rose explained, "Raven could be a neither, a nothing, just a character. People would say 'Is he straight or gay? How old is he?' He could walk the line of a lot of things." Downtown stars understand the power of the ambiguous identity, of being a blank onto which others project. From Warhol as a "sphinx without a riddle" and Gaga's "My *ARTPOP* can be anything" to The Box's MC or the venue itself, spectacle is animated by its question marks as much as its couture.

Back in the Box dressing room, I sat with Raven and his husband, thinking about the moments before doing a lecture when I slip into a professorial headspace. In a matter of minutes Raven would be going on stage but showed no sign of jitters. He proudly mentioned that he's always the earliest staff member to arrive at any venue, and spends significant pre-show time walking around the stage and sitting in every seat. Just as his paratrooper father might have bragged about military decorations, Raven crowed about a nearly perfect attendance record. He proudly offered up his badassery as if his father himself was in the room: rather than have laryngitis derail a Box night he just had a doctor inject steroids into his vocal chords. That's so Raven.

•

The clammy stickiness of a New York summer came early in 2015. Down on the Bowery older homeless men staggered around, mildly harassing tourists leaving the New Museum. Turning the corner at Stanton Street, I walked past a shoeless man in a filthy white undershirt who bowed as he gestured down the street. "Thank you, sir," I said, waving back and marching on.

Like The Box just around the corner, there was no sign demarcating Kitty's Canteen. There was no interest in drawing in the clueless wanderer with a *Lonely Planet* sticking out of his backpack. Instead, stilettos, expensive clutches, and the most carefully disheveled haircuts were found inside the restaurant owned by Box co-owner Richard Kimmel. While waiting for him to arrive, I heard a couple discuss furloughs in Aspen and Copenhagen. A handsome bartender asked a cook about the right amount of mint to use in one of their signature cocktails. Russian accents spilled out of a corner booth occupied by three hot blondes and an older man fawning over them.

Having asked to see their boss, the staff eyed me warily while I looked around at the restaurant's cat decor. Porcelain statuettes and wallpaper all referenced the feline. Richard had preserved a faux rustic scheme so prized in today's gilded Manhattan. And like so many downtown spaces, it was hard to tell what was authentically worn out and what had been purposefully distressed. Eventually walked in a stout man with glasses, long, salt-and-pepper hair tied into a ponytail and a dress shirt unbuttoned well below his chest. Richard didn't resemble the swaggering tanned men in starched white shirts who would approach him throughout the evening, whispering mysterious items into his ear.

Though known to cavort around both The Box and Kitty's in a Viking hat and a kimono, during our conversation he was more professorial than playboy. His father—a professor and part-time rabbi— and his mother—a librarian—encouraged a sense of imagination in a thoughtful young Richard. He said, "When I was very young I would create these giant worlds," littered around his house, using blocks, toys, and anything he could grab. He would organize carnivals and haunted houses in his backyard, an adolescent P. T. Barnum charging five cents for entry. Like Michael Alig's early "Candy Man" career in school, Richard understood how to harness a money-making engine to his creative enterprises. When I asked if his creativity was encouraged, Kimmel remembered his parents exclaiming, *"What? You want to pursue this lifestyle? This is crazy!"*

He posed heavy questions with a friendly, gravelly voice: "How could the world be more beautiful, more fabulous, more exciting than the one we're in? How can I share that with more people?" Despite his parents' objections he persisted, playing guitar in heavy metal bands in high school. This was a momentary burst of rebellion of which he was proud, and he excitedly pulled out photos of a handsome younger version of himself in punk, sleeveless T-shirts. A split with his first wife led to an immersion in nightlife around 2000, seeking out theater that could achieve the visceral experience of rock 'n' roll, plus nighttime forays fueled by ecstasy that included partying with vogue legend Kevin Aviance until six in the morning.

His undergrad work at Brandeis and MFA training at Columbia didn't lead to an easy fit with The Wooster Group, a partnership during which he fully soured on traditional theater. In particular he cited "so much lip service [paid] to the idea of reaching the new audience, reaching the younger generation, doing something progressive, and experimental," when their actual approach was "dogmatic" and "preaching to the choir," a sameness that was "insular" and "masturbatory."

Kimmel wanted a "new vocabulary" that could meld music, sound, and experience in a powerful way, citing the primacy of "direct engagement" with the audience. He merged the "production sophistication" of theater with the communion of a dance floor via an "immersive, interactive nightlife-theater happening" called Pleasuredome in Bushwick, eventually moving to the famous Mother. His event sounded like an orgiastic nightlife marathon, lasting forty hours with as many DJs, much of it fueled by drugs. Beaming like a proud parent, he pulled out old flyers to show me, including photos of a dancer wearing a George W. Bush "video-mask" or Saddam Hussein guise. "Those were the days!" he declared, energized by our candlelit reminiscing.

Young straight couples petted each other in Kitty's corners as Richard recalled a costume designer friend who had worked with Simon Hammerstein. The friend insisted that they meet, noting their common obsessions and shared disaffections. To complete the mix, Richard's old Columbia classmate was none other than Diane Paulus, which led to Richard becoming acquainted with her husband Randy Weiner, to whom he eventually introduced Simon.

In finding the building that became The Box, Richard went beyond the usual property-buying tactics: he acquired a real estate license and devoted his Sunday afternoons to Lower East Side strolls, eventually stumbling upon the old sign factory on Chrystie Street (the original SPANJER SIGNS lettering still hangs on their façade). Richard also revealed that the disco ball spinning above the main Box bar was originally from Mother and some of the ornamental lettering at Kitty's was from the now-gone Roseland Ballroom (closed out by Lady Gaga in March 2014). So like organs extracted from the dying to sustain the living, Richard transplanted visual elements from now extinct clubs and incorporated them into his downtown joints.

Like the architecture and décor, Kitty's amazing "Jewish soul food" cuisine was also an act of recombination. The "bisgel," for example, spliced a biscuit and a bagel, sandwiching smoked salmon or pastrami. When set before me it looked absolutely delicious but I didn't know how to consume the miniature sandwiches. *"Eat it however you want, bubuleh,"* Richard said. Devouring the food, I wasn't surprised to hear about Kitty's expansion to the space next door and across the Atlantic in London. Richard emphasized that the project was part of his grander conceptual scheme: if The Box "theatricalized" a club venue, now Kitty's must do the same for a restaurant.

Both The Box and Kitty's could be seen as a product of Richard's rebellion, his dissatisfaction with a "dogmatic" theater scene that was maybe similar to my frustrations with Margaret's pie-in-the-sky crew, the Twenty-third Street Communists, and stuffy academic colleagues. He seemed relieved at having left behind a purist theater world so preoccupied with the writing of grant applications and reports. He preferred the classic patronage system in the arts, citing the case of the Sistine Chapel, and claimed that his sponsor was essentially alcohol, or the sale of it.

But Richard the revolutionary capitalist understood that this wasn't popular with his old purist comrades, who shaded him with a snide attitude of "'Oh really, you're running a bar?'" He recalled, "I've really dealt with a lot of my former friends and colleagues being like, 'Eww, The Box. That's not theater.' Less so now because it's been successful, so . . ." A gloating smile appeared on his bearded face, and rightfully so, throwing in that his old chums had their MFAs proudly displayed on their walls but weren't really doing a whole lot with them.

Theater at The Box doesn't end at last call. It spills outside.

Around four in the morning I sat on a nearby stoop, waiting for a friend working as a Box hostess and watching guests and performers hop into cabs. Julie Atlas Muz, wife of Mat Fraser from *American Horror Story: Freak Show*, smoked a cigarette while chatting with DJ Coleman. MC Ashley Stroud left with two friends, while a patron ran after a woman, her arms folded and clearly uninterested. I watched a young bro so totally drunk that he couldn't take two steps without stumbling to the side. The dude mistakenly walked up to at least three cars, trying to get in. Eventually he gave up and just fumbled with his phone for a while, trying to find a way home. As my former student Dayna Troisi likes to say, what turns up must turn down.

Eventually, my friend popped out of The Box's "Active Driveway" but-not-an-actual-driveway door, having changed out of her cocktail dress and heels and into jeans and flip-flops. We walked over to Sugar, the post-Box haunt where we became regulars. The clerk behind the counter greeted us, joking that our "VIP table" was waiting. He asked about Rose, who was at the London Box at the time. We ordered food but my exhausted friend just dozed into her French fries. Discussing her first few nights of Box labor, I wasn't at all surprised to hear about the rivalries, squabbles, and beefs that she saw, the kind that dominate any human organization.

The sun slowly rose above the Lower East Side as we finished eating and chatted with the Sugar employees who grew accustomed to seeing us during our famished turn-down phase. If you ever run into me on Houston Street at this moment keep in mind that I'm in my most depleted state. My hair is wet after dancing and sweating. My glitter make-up has been smeared across half my face. I'm spent and weary, but, more likely than not, happy.

Wherever it's headed, The Box emerged at a time of transition for post-9/11 New York. The old era of clubland kings like Steve Rubell, Ian Schrager, Rudolf Piper, and Peter Gatien has long since waned. The gritty Gotham that incubated a legendary yesteryear gave way to a more austere metropolis with a shiny skyline that grows taller and spikier each year. This is the age of outdoor farmers' markets, not Outlaw parties.

And yet a nostalgia for the past is as rampant and unavoidable today as all the rats that scurry along the subway tracks. I don't understand it. Until some mechanism for time travel is created, nostalgia is a pointless disposition. But it infects the anguished has-beens, the mournful industry veterans, and even the young upstarts. Craig Klein, now based in Berlin, said of New York, "This isn't a fucking bohemia. This is not a petri dish of creativity anymore." Raven O himself fled to Miami in 2014 but still returned on occasion to what he called a "culturally vapid" New York whose commercialism simply didn't mesh with his mind-set now.

Still, The Box endures as both a last gasp of a fading downtown culture and a hint of its future: new generations of spectacle makers trying to up the ante and stave off the vapidity. They saw what came before and lived it. And now they want to outdo it.

Although I'm sometimes invited back to the dressing room, I try to avoid it. I want to preserve some of The Box's magic in my mind. But I loved my behind-the-curtains moment with Raven and his husband. As we wrapped up our chat, a lovely member of the Hammerstein Beauties came in to catch up with Raven. Despite my presence, she relayed a very personal story of a Box regular who invited her to smoke pot in the bathroom, asked if he could grab her breasts, and proposed that they go over to his apartment to watch porn. Apparently she said yes to all three, telling us the tale as if casually giving driving directions. Only *after* the story did she walk over to me and introduce herself. I looked up and smiled at her beauty, at her unedited persona, at what she and the other dancers and Raven and Rose and DeeDee and everyone else would do on stage at The Box. This place, this night, I thought, someday people will be nostalgic for tonight.

EPILOGUE

A PROFESSOR OF
THE NIGHT

A bright orange ferry rushed toward Staten Island, cutting through tossing black waters. Leaning against the railing of the upper deck, I wondered what plunging into the filthy water might feel like. It was the sunny May afternoon of my Conferral Day, the date in 2009 that I officially received my PhD from Columbia. I should have been uptown for a big ceremony on campus, wearing my baby blue academic regalia and celebrating the end of five long years of work. Instead I was on a heaving ferryboat surrounded by obnoxious tourists and their whiny children, fantasizing about being swallowed by a foamy harbor.

I had the misfortune of finishing my doctorate during the year that the recession hit the universities the hardest. Hiring freezes and canceled fellowships made an already glutted job market even worse. So there I stood, with a fresh Ivy League doctorate in hand and no job. Nothing to show for my efforts. Feeling totally defeated, I had no desire to show up to my own graduation ceremony. A sympathetic grad school friend wanted to cheer me up and we settled on a free

Staten Island Ferry ride for what felt like a post mortem of my sociology career, brainstorming about where and how I could find work.

In the months after the ferry ride, while fighting off some crippling depressive episodes, I made some frumpy new friends. Getting wasted on happy hour martinis at tragic gay bars, our crew ogled the cute boys with perfect hair, skin, and bodies and made fun of the older, potbellied queens sitting in the same corner of the bar week after week. Way in the back of our minds we knew that someday we might occupy those same corner stools, embarrassing ourselves with fumbling overtures toward the younger guys. Hence the shade.

Since none of us were good looking, our happy hour kikis often became tedious pity parties. My pals were sheltered and afraid, so totally miserable in their professional and private lives that they spoke incessantly of vacations, of *getting out, getting anywhere.* And therefore night after night of endless drunken chatter about where to eat in what neighborhood of what foreign locale.

But we were in New York. We were foolishly overlooking so much fabulousness around us, all because here *we* were overlooked and mattered little. Despite solid educations, we limited ourselves to spaces where we felt safe as bland wallflowers, lounging around like Statler and Waldorf, pissing on the pretty people actually enjoying their lives in the city.

Fuck. That.

I pulled away from them as I slowly started going downtown more and more, pouring over gossip columns and social media to map out the networks of big clubland players. My pity pals resented me for wanting new things, belittling and dismissing me as "insecure" or "fake." One of my closest friends in that circle—a late-thirties IT guy who was a Grindr aficionado but still closeted—told me not to worry about growing out my hair or experimenting with glittery make-up. He believed that the only thing that mattered was "character," which, for him, included sarcastically spitting on friends' attempts to find and live their truth, plus endless daydreaming about visiting faraway cities where he could actually be as gay as he wanted to be.

Another friend from the group told me, "I just want to be OK with me." I get it, really. To feel the clawing anxiety of inadequacy is truly awful. I know very few people who can fully escape the sensation. But at the same time, um, NO. That's not what New York is about. It thrives on relentless, everyday revolutions. The skyline above and the streets down under it constantly morph and mutate and so should we, always trying to make real the best versions of ourselves.

Alongside exploring new night worlds, things slowly improved in my professional life. I earned a fellowship working on a professor's research contract with a global consumer goods company. At first it seemed like an amazing gig. I did a site visit at a massive factory, conducted extended phone interviews with company employees all over the world, and even met Mayor Mike Bloomberg, who in his quintessentially technocratic manner, shook my hand, looked me in the eye, and asked what I did. Although it was easy for New Yorkers to loathe his enormous wealth and no-frills managerial style, I always admired his fondness for bold policy experimentation.

Engaging the corporate world via this research contract meant a whole new exercise in butching it up: again trying to drop the register of my voice, slouching more, or slumping in my chair like a gorilla. After a while I could tell that my efforts at straight performances were pretty pointless.

I also quickly discovered that I had a truly awful boss. I'll call her Professor Alf, like the creepy alien puppet on that '80s TV show with a little tuft of hair on his head. And like the ugly puppet, my boss Alf rarely had her hair combed, walking in with a wild, frizzy mass piled on top of her head. I have no clue what kind of classroom teacher she was, but toward the other research fellow and me, she was snide, condescending, and always willing to speak maliciously about our colleagues.

Still, I worked long days in a tiny windowless office, trying my best to make creative contributions. In retrospect, I arrogantly tried to do too much and too soon, in my own voice and style, too eager to show that I could offer more than the corporate babble they wanted. But sometimes Alf talked about the petty games of her own advisor ages ago and apparently lacked enough introspection to realize that she was behaving similarly toward us. The other fellow and I would meet for lunch to commiserate and, like countless workers anywhere, we bonded through our shared hatred of a boss. My colleague had moved to New York just for the job and really wanted to make it all somehow work. She soon quit, and after a year, my contract was not renewed. Alf tried to retain the pretense of a gracious exit. Too late, miss honey. At our goodbye lunch, my hands trembled with anger at all the time and energy I wasted on our projects, unable to calmly express how little I thought of our stupid yearlong fiasco.

I soon found a teaching gig at Hofstra University. Despite spending virtually my whole life in the tristate area I had never set foot on Long Island until I hopped on the LIRR train and rode out to Hempstead, watching the cosmopolitan vitality drain from the landscape as the train sped east. F grew up in neighboring Garden City, so I got a chance to see the affluent blandness in which he was reared, wondering how my flamboyant past crush had survived the stifling sameness of it all.

After three years I left Hofstra when I was offered teaching assignments back in Manhattan. The long commute I'll never miss but I do fondly remember many of my Hofstra students and certainly its campus, especially the very cute feral cats always creeping through the shrubbery.

It was on that campus—best known nationally as a perennial host for the presidential debates—where I really understood how unusual an occupation I was in. As a professor you grow older and hopefully wiser but your "customers," the students who pass through your classroom semester after semester, stay the same age: nervous fresh-faced teenagers or students struggling with senioritis and so many question marks about their future. I adapted well, more or less, to the rather conservative Italian and Jewish Long Island natives in my classes, although for them I was an unusual presence up at the podium: youngish, a bit of red in his dark hair, Latin, gay, and blunt. They reminded me in many ways of the Westchester kids I grew up with. It's not that they were necessarily malicious (although some were), just sheltered and clueless about much of the world outside of their homogeneous island.

So I gave them *Paris Is Burning*, Amanda Lepore, youth culture from postmodern *Heathers* to hypermodern *Mean Girls*, Warhol's drag Superstars, Marina Abramović and Cindy Sherman, club kids, Jack Halberstam, glam LQQKS from Leigh Bowery to Lady Gaga, Jean-Michel Basquiat and Andreja Pejic. Or sometimes I asked downtown stars to make the trek out to Long Island to visit my students, including ex–club kid Lila Wolfe, actress and dancer Jocelyn McBride, and the artist Conrad Ventur, who had filmed new screen test portraits of the old Warhol stars.

The sorority girls or lacrosse jocks often didn't know what to make of it all but most really did try to meaningfully process it. A few students stood out, like the young woman who worked as a part-time model and claimed that she could see my aura, which apparently grew larger when I lectured. Another notable was the TMI student who told excessively personal stories in class while everyone in the room uneasily squirmed. And one even ended up working at The Box for a bit and hosted her birthday party there.

Being a professor showed me that meritocracy exists downtown in ways that it doesn't elsewhere. Despite all the dangers of a life lived in clubland revelry, at least a night worker's performance was quantifiable: how many people went through the door each week, how much money did you pull in at the bar, and so on. If Pat Field's boutique didn't sell well, she would have closed up shop much sooner. If no one bought vodka sodas at the parties thrown by Susanne or Ladyfag, they couldn't keep their dance floor diadems on their impeccably styled heads.

And see what happens at the door of a popular high-end club on a Friday night. A straight male in a plain dude uniform, accompanied by fellow bros but no women, should be ready to drop a thousand dollars or more to sit at a table and drink from liquor bottles that retail for fifty bucks. The bros might be the future kings of Manhattan, ruling the giant finance and tech companies where your kids will want to work. But tonight, all they want is to meet a pretty girl and get wasted with their buddies. Downtown values dictate, however, that it will cost them a pretty penny to do so, while the young queer club kid wearing bright blue make-up, a leather harness, and a golden jock strap will breeze right in and drink for free, all night long. The effort matters.

In academia, meanwhile, qualifications and performance in the classroom seemed to count for little. Student evaluations mattered, yes, but they didn't guarantee promotion, better pay, or even basic job security. As I learned throughout eight years of teaching at various area schools, the arbitrary dictates of a department chair could close a door on you, thereby opening up the possibility for hiring and elevating his or her favorites.

As I settled into teaching, I sustained and managed two distinct versions of my self. A nighttime version chasing a downtown notable for an interview or keeping up with nightlife blogs, checking to see who was photographed, with whom, and what they were wearing. This self had to make sure that he had the right plus-one for an invite-only event, made time to get his hair cut and dyed for a certain party, or knew what colors his eye make-up would be serving. Naturally, there were plenty of misfires, like the time I wore a glistening metal headband for a Fritz Lang *Metropolis* look. F watched me fuss with the band as it dug deep into my scalp, leaving dark, painful welts. There were also poorly considered bandanas, vests, concealers, and even an earring for a hot minute, accessories that were just total mismatches for me.

And then the daytime campus version: the tweedy blazer, black polo, and brown Ted Bakers. The one in professor drag who in eight years of teaching at four different institutions has been late to class only five times. Professor Corona up at the podium, who attended faculty meetings, listened to colleagues complain about administrators, corresponded with useless counselors whenever students were in trouble, and lectured about all the beauty and ugliness that the study of human identity had to offer. Hofstra semesters were especially grueling: a subway to Penn Station for a train out to Long Island, back-to-back classes, office hours, a train ride back to the city, a disco nap, shower, change, and back out into the night. Rinse and repeat.

As I taught classes during the day and explored more nighttime scenes, I found my own would-be superstars, young people like M who seemed touched with rare sparks of ambition and ability. In a certain way, for a certain time, they saw me as a mentor. On a May 2015 episode of his YouTube show, Michael Alig described my own little Warholian reperformance like this:

> Well, Victor picks a different person that he features, he puts them on the marquee as Sophia [Lamar] would call it. They're on the marquee for—I don't know—a month, two months, and then they get booted off and replaced by somebody else.

Michael compared it to Warhol and Sedgwick, but he could have easily invoked himself and his beloved "Superstar DJ" Keoki, or himself and Peter Gatien. Or Starlight and Gaga, Susanne and Kenny, Pat Field and her House children. I enjoyed working with young people whose feverish "Stef infections" pushed them to do bold and creative things, and having benefited so much from mentors like Julio and Harrison, I thought that I could pass on something similar to them. But like Warhol, I was accused of using my superstars like Kleenex—of callously booting them off the marquee—and like him, I didn't see it as a fair criticism. Whenever my uppity little stars spazzed out, I reminded them that no one commanded them to go downtown. We chose to run with these tribes and play by the rules of their fame games.

Many downtown folks assumed that I was sleeping with the male ones. But my work with these mentees had nothing to do with sex or money. (To be clear, I have never had an improper relationship with a student.) Together we were working on new projects and learning from our mistakes. But in a business fixated on scrambling your way Up There, conflicts were often inevitable and resentments and squabbles popped up very easily. To this day I think about what I could have done differently with the young people on my marquee, like being more patient and understanding, and still wish them every possible success.

Chasing the downtown story demanded that my mentees and I budge out of our comfort zones. For a night I was even doorman at the now closed Santos Party House after the original person bailed at the last minute. I was at a dinner with Michael Alig when a party promoter texted to ask if I knew of a replacement. Michael insisted that I give it a try and I had the absolute best time. The big, burly, intimidating bouncers were extremely kind to me as they spilled all kinds of tea about the venue. They even brought out a stool and table so I could sit. It was fabulous fun to be on the other side of the velvet rope, to see people slightly fumble as they approached me. Since there was never a huge line that night, I didn't have to turn anyone away, but inhabiting that social role for a tiny bit was really amusing.

Although I do enjoy a cocktail or two (or three), my night outings never led to a drug problem. Although Steve Lewis told me to never, ever try cocaine, I did in fact "meet Judy," as Gaga's friends call coke in a sly nod to Judy Garland. But I only tried it a handful of times and it just isn't for me. At all. I can't deal with the crash. It was too much of a nightmare the last time I did it back in March 2016. I was at the home of a wealthy clubgoer for an impromptu group kiki after a gallery opening. A friend fixed me a drink and I got into deep chats with some club kids there, all while our host's largesse yielded multiple plates of coke lines being passed around. The first couple of times I politely declined. But there was so much! The plates kept going around and around. Fine, one line. And then another and another. Snort, vodka, snort, vodka. (Bob Colacello's staircase to oblivion!) Around five in the morning the kids were still at it but I was way too fucked up.

I took a cab home and my roommate at the time happened to be awake. He saw how coked out I was and offered me weed to help me come down. It didn't work. I ended up roaming my neighborhood as the sun came up, buying two breakfast burritos at Dunkin' Donuts and chips and soda at the bodega across the street. Still stuck in fast forward mode, I went home and tried to watch my Netflix fave *Daredevil*, fantasizing about the hunky hero beating me up in a hallway. Eventually I passed out and woke up the next morning feeling like complete and total shit. I later learned that the coke was laced with meth, hence the insane daybreak jaunt around my neighborhood. Never again.

On top of everything, living on an adjunct professor's pitiful salary meant meager living throughout a good chunk of the last six years. Plenty of other colleagues were in the same spot, going to free downtown clinics for health care or stuffing our faces on free sushi and empanadas at faculty receptions. Depending on what teaching gigs I had, a few semesters were better than others. Like many fellow citizens of twenty-first-century New York, I knew what it was to start the day with a non-balanced breakfast of two slices of $1 pizza and later on go to bed with your stomach growling. Or have a dinner of chips, crackers, and peanuts because you knew you would need to take a $37 Uber home after a night at The Box.

After devouring that dollar pizza, on social media I would see photos of friends' beautiful homes out in the Hamptons or up in the Hollywood Hills, or posts mentioning jet lag after trips to London or the Italian countryside. After not jumping out my window, I had to push myself back to the simple, unglamorous task of writing. As Rose Wood reminded me, a writer is one who writes. Pure and simple. So while the conception of these pages happened in some of the most Up There places in this city, the birth happened in my little Manhattan bedroom, sitting barefoot at my desk, my hair clipped up like Pebbles Flintstone.

Some nights I'd stay in to Netflix and chill by myself, consuming horror films of the found footage subgenre, superhero shows, or political dramas like *House of Cards*, *The Crown*, *The Borgias*, or *Medici*. Watching recent fave *Reign*, a stylish spin on the saga of Mary, Queen of Scots, left me shaking, holding my knees, sobbing hysterically at four in the morning. Although the shows and movies provided a needed respite and reset from downtown settings, I couldn't avoid picking out elements very similar to my night lessons: lavish looks and lustful longings for sex and power, tribal rivalries, endless plotting and pageantry. It's all the same stuff of human culture, the same building blocks of identity. The resentments of a royal court would resonate well within a queen of the night's rowdy retinue.

Whenever I did go out, each night began by blasting my mandatory pregame song: Lana Del Rey's "Off to the Races," the perfect song to accompany me in an Uber racing along the West Side Highway or the FDR Drive. En route to a party I would check my makeup or face jewels or fix my unmanageable hair, but thanks to Lana those rides also marked how much I changed thanks to the lessons of downtown notables. The jackets and skinny jeans, eye shadow and highlighted hair. *I learned it from watching them.*

The song also pepped me up. As my friends know, the hour before going out I was usually in the foulest of moods. My hair didn't look right. I really needed to lose more weight. Had they seen me in this look before? I needed to catch up on sleep. GOD, I had grading and next week's lecture to finish. Excitement and apprehension on top of the fact that no one could possibly anticipate everything that the night would thrust on us.

Sometimes during the ride back home I would be beyond wasted, or upset if there was drama, other times pumped up by how great the music was (Coleman is my absolute favorite DJ.) You probably know this feeling too: the merry buzz of a hot night out, a sensation you can feel anywhere around the world but that's amplified enormously in New York. Come and see for yourself. As you forget the hours dripping by, you'll spin and grind and bounce and stumble on the dance floor. You might get caught in a bad romance. You might even get famous. Or not.

During my Spill the Tea time, students occasionally asked if there were other professors writing books about nightlife. I told them that academic nightlife tomes were often written by tenured researchers who parachuted into a scene to do interviews. They then fled back to the safety of their quiet offices and university-subsidized apartments. The work would be published and they moved on to another project. Sometimes the parachutists offered significant findings but there always seemed to be a slant: either celebrating nightlife as a space of ecstatic underground church-like convergence, or scolding it as an innately racist and misogynistic capitalist enterprise. It's a literature torn between gushing, fangurling nostalgia and dry attempts at critical political economy.

There are exceptions. Fellow sociologist Ashley Mears has lived the downtown life and bears the scars to prove it. To study bottle-model nightlife, she wrote about wielding a bodily capital that I lacked. A former runway model, Ashley accessed social situations and had conversations with informants that a big-nosed, non-white queer man like me simply couldn't. For example, in an article in a major sociology journal, she mentioned accepting invitations to Miami, the Hamptons, and Cannes, "with most expenses paid by promoters, clubs, and VIP clients." Can you imagine?

David Grazian wrote one of the most popular journal articles that I have assigned in my time teaching. Titled "The Girl Hunt," he showed how straight male undergrads' pursuit of sexual encounters in nightlife was actually about "the performance of normative masculinity." The students always got it. His analysis of the wingman and the pregame made sense in light of their own college experiences. And that's really the goal, isn't it? To show what we can learn about human identity and community from all this midnight madness.

But despite fun titles, the goal of most academics' nightlife books isn't really to understand scene people and why they do what they do. As Mears pointed out in an essay reviewing Richard Ocejo's *Upscaling Downtown* and Reuben Buford May's *Urban Nightlife*, "They describe wet streets with conventionally dry academic prose." Parachutists used the spaces to make grandiose points about the big, huge patterns that so many sociologists love to criticize and discuss among themselves.

Others like Tim Lawrence have focused on subcultural lineages in downtown creative networks in extremely detailed books. His own passion for the story burst through the pages. In describing the legacy of DJ and promoter David Mancuso, for example, Lawrence wrote, "Having come out of the sixties, Mancuso formed a perfect bridge into the seventies by providing the disenfranchised and backpedaling rainbow coalition with a space in which to explore its sameness and difference—like glowworms coming out in the night to produce flashes of light in an otherwise gloomy terrain." This man too is a professor of the night. He knows a party.

Although this community of scholars is small, you still see some shade. In Lawrence's *Love Saves the Day*, he skewered Anthony Haden-Guest's *The Last Party*, describing it in terms like "slobbering detail" and "pointless anecdotes and name-dropping." After attending Lawrence's speaking events at NYU, Columbia, and the Museum of Modern Art, I could easily picture him dropping the mic in poor Haden-Guest's face and stomping away.

The big problem with much of the academic literature is this: to make sense of the night, we need more than parachutists. It's not enough to fly in and interview all the "legends." You also need to see the wannabes trying and failing, but still trying, night after hopeless night. In for a dime, in for a dollar. Wednesday Martin, author of the bestseller *Primates of Park Avenue*, was able to offer such a unique and powerful look inside the rarified realms of elite Upper East Side motherhood because she had real skin in the game. Her own sense of self as a mom and wife, alongside the well-being of her children and the success of her marriage, meant that she saw and felt things that a nosey exposé writer couldn't. The stakes for understanding social structure were far higher than just writing a damn book.

The goal is to get a better sense of the full distribution of downtown outcomes and fame game strategies. Case in point. Near NYU is the hookah club Le Souk. Years ago I stopped by to support Gerry Visco's hosting gig at a party called Ra Ra, named for its creator, a small but lively boy named Sébastien Ra. He did something that's pretty rare downtown: he actually bothered to welcome me to his model-filled party, walking up to my unattractive self and saying hello. In the age of endless social media invites, he would always add a personalized touch to nightlife by posting his flyer on your Facebook timeline or texting you the day of. Say what you will about his parties, Sébastien knew that it helped to add a sense of social obligation when pulling people out.

When we met for dinner to chat, I was curious about his disco name. Did he know the club kids Sebastian Jr. and Armen Ra? He instead pointed to his love of Egypt (his heritage is Egyptian, Puerto Rican, Spaniard, and Romani, he said) and the 1998 sci-fi James Spader hit *Stargate*. Like so many club kids past and present, he rode the subway wearing zany looks involving chains, antlers, leather, and neon plastics, even ending up on the popular Instagram account She

Has Had It! When I asked if he was ever harassed in his neighborhood, Sébastien shook his head, "They just love to watch me walk by, honk the horns in the car."

There was a slight whine to Sébastien's voice, paired with enormous affect, as he described his love of acting, fashion, and dancing. "I'm a Renaissance Man. I do a lot of things," he said. Drinking wasn't really one of them, preferring a single chocolate martini when he hosted. An orphan, Sébastien dropped out of Cooper Union after believing that he couldn't learn anything more. Instead, he cited mythology and history as guiding lights, and our long dinner was peppered with his talk of Elizabeth I, Nefertiti, the Dalai Lama, and Alexander the Great. He compared himself to a snake ("I'm very sneaky") and an onion ("I have a lot of layers to myself").

Sébastien cackled as he namedropped Amanda Lepore, with whom he apparently did yoga from time to time. She didn't sweat at all, he reported. Tarot card readings were a social lubricant for him, a way to open up intimidating clubland heavies. He told me about reading Kenny Kenny's palm: "And from there he fell in love with me." He bonded with Richie Rich over a reading that predicted the end of his coupling with Ross "Saucy Rossy" Higgins. Though not the only interviewee to offer claims of clairvoyance, Sébastien was the first to read my aura, which was apparently blue and "not in a perfect flow right now." After I pressed for details, he murmured, *"There's a lot of mystery behind you."*

Sébastien might consider trading in his clairvoyance for a bit of self-awareness. "In order for me to replenish my energy," he proclaimed, eyebrows arched and nose in the air, "I must know the difference between who I can help and who I cannot help." But his big bravado was a thin veneer hiding loneliness and pain, byproducts of his time with downtown kids also scrambling to make it Up There. He said, "In the spotlight, people hurt you," like the boys who dated him just to get into a party. So what does he want out of his hustle? Pure Oscar gold. "When I see acting, I know I could do better and

I know I can be better than them," he told me, gobbling up several French fries. He would give one heck of an acceptance speech.

When I later did my experimental performance showcase with Lady Starlight and her brother Jason, I booked Sébastien as one of the acts. Right before he went on and read his poetry, we got into a slight tiff and, wagging his finger at me, he told me that he didn't like my negativity. I brushed it off, and after the reading cheered on this clairvoyant sneaky onion. A parachutist would have totally missed out on Sébastien Ra.

Another lesson in the ebbs and flows of the fame game. Ask any New Yorker who loves nightlife and they'll tell you about new relationships springing from totally unexpected circumstances. Through a nightlife photographer who spoke at my Wearable Art panel, I met Ivy Higa, a contestant on two *Project Runway* seasons. The show is hosted by Heidi Klum, who glumly looked on as Kayvon had his *America's Got Talent* meltdown. Before Ivy, I mainly associated *Project Runway* with F, who was a huge fan, as in snarkily-live-tweet-every-damn-episode fan.

A petite and pretty Hawaii native, Ivy attracted cruel scorn as the "villain" of her first run on the show, only to return for an all-stars season. Her tropical moxie was surely wrapped in a thick skin, so I was eager to chat with her. After we braved heavy snow to meet at a restaurant off Bryant Park, Ivy spoke wistfully about her far away island childhood. Her grandparents ran a Honolulu pharmacy whose customers included a very young Barack Obama. Meanwhile she would draw on the walls of her room, dreaming of *getting out, getting anywhere*. Via the Style Network, she discovered Donna Karan as her inspiration. "Something that she said was really poignant," Ivy told me. "She said she became a designer because she wanted to be a woman that designed for women."

It was the spark that Ivy needed to attend fashion school at Parsons, where she pursued a second degree (her first is in ceramics) despite her parents' intense disapproval. She paid for her Parsons education herself. "I think I really made the most of it as much as I could, because I was hungry, literally and figuratively," Ivy recalled. Still, she found time to party at gay bars or Fashion Week afterparties alongside Vanessa Williams and Kristin Chenowyth, and laughed as she wondered how she managed to preserve her liver. She too did a nightlife stint, working at 230 Fifth Avenue, a touristy rooftop hub whose gorgeous skyline view is its main selling point.

Ivy explained to me that there were two sides to the fashion business: the front of the house made up of brand representatives like publicists, buyers, merchandisers, and the sales team—"all those people that make it look like it's so glamorous," she said—and the back of the house, the designers, pattern-makers, and seamstresses, who actually make things.

Ivy strongly preferred the back of the house, despite her clear admiration for the Donna Karan style empire and her notorious time on a hit reality competition. She talked about working for a Zac Posen fashion show until eleven at night, then sewing until four in the morning to finish an Emmy gown commissioned by a cable network president. On the morning of the final fitting with her media elite client, she overslept, and without showering rushed to deliver the product. "That's how fashion really is," Ivy said. "You have to love it to the point where you're willing to bleed, sweat, and smell."

After interning at DKNY, finally affiliated with the brand that she so admired back in Hawaii, she landed a full-time gig there. The universe conspired to bring her there, Ivy told me, and yet when we turned to her *Project Runway* stints, she invoked the age-old warning about being careful what you wish for because you just might get it.

Ivy remembered receiving death threats for her appearances on what was essentially a cable TV sewing contest. But she had asked for it, all in an effort to save her young design business. "I remember I wanted *Project Runway* so badly because at this point I had been down to my last dollar," Ivy said as her tone sharpened. She talked about Heidi Klum's show as a "game" or a "chess match," claiming that it had little to do with fashion or creativity. "It's about who makes a great character rather than who can make the best garment," Ivy explained.

Was Tim Gunn at least a helpful advice giver? "No. Sorry," she said right away, maybe thinking that I was a superfan like F. "I know that [Gunn] doesn't really care for me." What really might have killed F was her final verdict on the show's irrelevance in the business: "Everyone in the industry makes a joke of it. And it's really sad. I mean, it's a game show." It wasn't until long after she started her full-time gig at Donna Karan that her boss bothered to ask, in passing, if she had been on the show.

Ivy's role as a villain emerged from her bluntness and candor, as well as the producers' editing. One of her make-up artists pointed it out to her. "You're kind of a hard bitch," Ivy was told. *"And I find it really hot,"* the artist added. I began to feel as though maybe Ivy and I shared the bitch factor, thinking back to a Columbia professor once calling me a "viper" after one of his workshops. I told Ivy that I benefitted much more from brutally direct criticism than pointless head patting. She replied, "Some people don't work well with that—." I then interjected, "Yeah, they crumble, very easily." Not hesitating, she agreed, "Yeah, they need to move out of New York."

On a night typical of late May, before a Manhattan summer turned unbearably swampy, the light breeze coming off the Hudson River couldn't have felt nicer. Sipping a vodka cran, I looked around the roof of Susanne Bartsch's crowded On Top party, peering through the jumble of flower headpieces, studded corsets, tufts of tulle, long faux braids, and black jockstraps clinging to perfectly shaped, bare asses. A man in a furry penguin costume paraded through it all.

Next to me sat a youngish acquaintance who identified as genderqueer. He wore a black turban and clutched a purse shaped like a chicken, which he had named Henny Penny. After finishing a shift at Food Emporium, he changed into his femme look in the supermarket's basement and dashed over to The Standard. When I asked how he was doing, he informed me that he spent time in the "psych ward" and was doing his best not to go back. He plucked a pill bottle from Henny and dumped three pills into his hand. After I asked if they were his antidepressants, he clarified that they were just Advil. Sticking out his glass toward our host—a woman vigorously discussing depression and gay sex—he asked, "Can I have a splash of vodka, please?"

What the fuck was I doing there? So many years after I packed up my Washington cubicle, what had I learned—as a person and a sociologist—and where had I ended up? Had I traded in all those military IDs just to maybe someday end up traipsing around with a rubber chicken purse?

At least I had figured out where I was welcome and where I wasn't, avoiding most Westgay-type parties that mainly existed to give white muscle queens and twinks, all wearing the same clothes, a chance to worshipfully gawk at themselves—exactly the crowd that Sophia Lamar hated so intensely. Other scene veterans loathed the spaces too. Paul Alexander told me, "I don't enjoy The Cock or that sort of dick in your face, finger in the asshole kind of—it's too raunchy for me." DJ Johnny Dynell remembered a party where a young boy requested a Gaga song with the most unbearably whiny of squeals. Johnny couldn't hold back. "Look, you're a man, OK?" he remembered telling the boy. "You're not an eight-year-old girl. You're a man. You get fucked in the ass. Act like a man." The little boy ran to the bathroom, crying.

Susanne's parties tended to be more of a mix. And The Box definitely was. So although I avoided all-gay parties, it was actually at a Ladyfag night where a crossroads moment helped me to make sense of my place downtown.

The night began at a gay bar in Chelsea called Barracuda. Outside two boys petted each other, their faces illuminated by the red lights installed on the façade in order to add a tinge of naughtiness to the place. Barracuda is a few doors down from Spice, the Thai restaurant where I first met F years earlier. He had been smoking a cigarette when I walked up to him, shook his hand, and knew right away that this skinny little boy would be trouble.

I brushed the memory aside and walked in looking for Ernie Glam. We were pregaming before walking over to Ladyfag's Battle Hymn party at Flash Factory. Wearing one of his own club kid designs, Ernie led me to the back lounge where we started spilling tea right away. Right then different strains of downtown fame-hunger somehow congealed. Chatting with Ernie Glam—an original and beloved club kid, *Project X* editor, and Clara the Chicken herself—I noticed that the Barracuda stage behind him was decorated with Warhol flowers. On the screen flashed a Gaga "Manicure" performance, which was mostly ignored by the gays focused on their eye-fuckings.

Thomas Kiedrowski, my oldest nightlife pal, joined us a bit later and we continued dishing before antsy Ernie wanted to stroll up to Flash Factory. Outside the club I ran into M and his boyfriend, while another friend snorted coke right underneath the scaffolding on Twenty-eighth Street. At the door, Ernie talked to House of Field legend The Connie Girl and we were ushered in without paying a cover.

Inside the jam-packed venue, we slowly made our way to radiant Amanda Lepore's VIP table. She and her clingy male hangers-on all posed for the mandatory selfies to document the fabulous outing. Ladyfag had her long dark braids wrapped around her face and danced happily next to her DJ, hands up high displaying her signature underarm hair. Ernie gave Thomas and me a little tour, pointing out all the ecclesiastical embellishments and motifs that copied Limelight. Model and actress Hari Nef milled about, as did some of the St. Jerome's crowd, while good old Sébastien Ra climbed up onto a VIP booth, whipped out his phone and his duck face pout, and danced wildly for his Snapchat story.

It was a frenzied night of collisions, of familiar faces and scenes as well as bodies. A packed Ladyfag party at one of the few hot megaclubs around was bound to turn into a heaving mass of sweaty, shirtless, very attractive men. Slowly worming our way through wet arms and backs, the pounding music and rainbow-bright lighting systems wound us up, drinking and dancing ecstatically.

I did not bel—

Wait. Wait. I did actually, kind of, sort of belong. I didn't look like the delicious muscle queens and I definitely kept my clothes on. But I still felt like I could claim the space, appreciate and be appreciated by some people in the venue, be a part of the night like everyone else. To invoke Coldplay, *all that noise and all that sound!* They were enough. And the lights and the flesh and the glitter. They were enough. They had to be.

David LaChapelle famously said, "If you want reality, take the bus." The point of culture, all the stuff made by people like him and everyone in these pages, is to transcend the bland tedium of our drab reality. But when I really do need to clear my head or think through something, I get on a Manhattan bus. I ride it for almost the whole line, watching how Gotham's humans exhibit themselves to the world, frumpy and fancy alike. I see the building façades change from the new glass and steel structures of a gentrified downtown to the charming old housing stock uptown, punctuated by banks, Starbucks, supermarkets, more banks, and some of the most special, imposing spaces on the planet.

So when I'm really bummed, that bus ride is my therapy session, all for about three dollars. And toward the end of my downtown forays, what LaChapelle's idol wrote in *POPism* really rang true for me:

"The mystery was gone, but the amazement was just starting." After six years of running around downtown, it's not mysterious anymore. I have access to places that would have been practically forbidden to me during my Gandhi era, and can more or less figure out why a particular party collapses. I can explain why certain looks work better than others, and now join in when laments over a venue's closing rile my social media feeds.

But I'm still amazed at how this island thrives after enduring crime waves, recessions, vast inequality, strikes, crippling traffic, terrorist attacks, bed bug outbreaks, *Sex and the City*, corruption scandals, gentrification, and an ever-climbing cost of living. People still want to make their lives here. *Here*, I tell my students. Think of all the people around the world who save up money to visit for a week, maybe two. But you get to live here, to feel and wield a New York habitus, whether you have to hop on a ferry to Staten Island to get home or a train to Astoria. You live in history's greatest city. I say it each semester, maybe sounding like an ancient uncle, or Nigel lecturing Andrea Sachs in the *Runway* layout room.

In *The Devil Wears Prada*, a favorite film of mine, Andrea reckons with the tough choices made on your way Up There. She is pushed into a storied realm not unlike downtown, one brimming with snobbery, fabulousness, conspiracy, and hierarchy. She ultimately walks away from her fame game, symbolically discarding the identity she worked so hard to achieve by tossing her cell phone into a Paris fountain. I wouldn't have been as hasty as Andrea, although there were definitely moments when I felt like this journey was not worth its many heartaches.

Despite how much I changed and came to love downtown's spectacles, I never believed that fame would somehow save me. Although people crave it so desperately, to me it seems so incompatible with real fulfillment. Such an elusive prize, so slippery and unable to meet the expectations attached to it. In *The Man Who Laughs*, Victor Hugo wrote, "I have not the light, but I have the reflection." For me, the reflection is enough. I have zero desire to stand in the blinding limelight. And yet I remain fascinated by its power and enjoy being proximate enough to marvel at it. During our chat, I almost badgered Ivy Higa with questions about the ineffable aspects of fashion fame. What enabled the stellar success of legends like Donna Karan, Diane von Furstenberg, or Alexander McQueen? "Some people are just touched," she shrugged.

But as McQueen's own tale showed us, being "touched" enough to make it Up There will not guarantee your salvation. During my night lessons I saw how even small bits of access and status could distort and warp relationships in really uncomfortable ways. It's what Vincent Fremont noticed once he stopped being gatekeeper to the profitable Warhol art market. Or what Paul Alexander felt when he discovered that he was no longer welcome at the fashion shows of his beloved old friend Marc Jacobs. And what Gaga painfully learned when her cherished rock muse pulled away as her own Fame grew.

When you're a broke, struggling nobody, your friends seek you out because they genuinely love you and your shared shenanigans. But once the upward climb starts, people want things. They want you to lead them into The Box's front row so they can take yet another selfie with Amanda Lepore. They want you to get them and their ugly boyfriend on a guest list for a hot party, find them a job, introduce them to a downtown notable, or make them "the next Holly Woodlawn." And some will prefer that you stay single forever so that *they* can always be your plus-one to Fashion Week parties. And if they aren't, watch out for the resentment and distance. They want to be Up There just as much as anyone and it's a lot easier to be the sidekick BFF than to find your own way in.

Whenever these things happened to me, I realized that others craved the same magical space that I wanted. It all comes back to a very human need to belong somewhere on this earth, to find a way to live life that doesn't feel quite so alone and empty. M once described it as walking into a place where people are actually happy to see you.

Like *Cheers*. Simple as that. So in M's framework, I did find spaces where I belonged and where I had some of the best times of my life.

In New York, nightlife will always endure as an escape from the stresses of living here, like riding a crowded subway while gripping a greasy pole—a stranger's armpit in your face—after waiting on a filthy platform watching rats munch on garbage. We need to remind ourselves that we're more than anonymous automatons packed together in metallic tubes shooting underground from one end of an island to another. Hence the after-work happy hour to complain about obnoxious bosses or dissect simmering romances. Or a night of dancing and coyly eye-fucking the person across the room. We want a space where we can be the most attractive versions of ourselves, allowing the stresses of the day to evaporate in the shadows of the urban night.

Not everyone will find belonging in nightlife or a big city like New York and that's fine. The space where people are happy to see you could be a sports field or an office. If those spaces give you the sense of belonging that others find on Ladyfag's sweaty dance floor or the House of whomever or a stage covered in fake shit and blood, so be it. But let it be because you willfully chose that life for yourself.

Despite downtown's rampant delusions, disappointments, appropriations, and manipulations, it remains a never-dull, all-absorbing sector of spectacle where I somehow found a home. It offers precious shimmers of community to anyone who simply refuses to be beige. In fabulous settings, the downtown night allows the mingling of the failures, the successes, the almosts, and the wannabes, as Steve Lewis labeled them. Turn your Terminator robo-vision on. Activate StarGaze™ mode and spot your fave celebs but also watch the wild theater of the non-famous around you. Yes, the successes should inspire you. But let the almosts and the failures teach you. Learn from them, pour your whole being into making the best work possible, and hopefully you'll avoid their fates. If you make it Up There, great. The wannabes' proof is always in their pudding.

If you're willing to try, in the process of doing the work and getting to know downtown's people you'll discover and enjoy new possible versions of yourself, just like I did. So I'll end with a few guidelines for your own midnight lessons.

The biggest your posse should be is four people. If you want a larger crew, split them up into groups of four and convene inside the venue.

Gallery openings are fun but aren't the right context for actually looking at the art. You go to see who goes. To connect, to kiki, to meet people. For the art, go back during the day, by yourself, when you can really just absorb it and form meaningful reactions.

Always make an effort with your outfit, even if you're not a looker. No excuse for being plain-Jane. Regardless of your gender, size, race, or face, try some bright eye shadow, a colorful lip, or a loud but chic jacket. Have fun with it. The door person and hosts will appreciate your effort.

This next one is via Rose Wood. Clubs tend to be dimly lit spaces so glitter can pack a sparkly punch that it can't under fluorescent lighting. Wear something shimmery—collar, necklace, eye shadow, face jewels—to add that effect in a club. Gay friends who go out mainly to hook up will ignore me on this, insisting that if they don't look sufficiently masculine they won't get laid. As I tell them, any dude who hates a little glitter is so not worth it.

If you can't go to a party, don't text the host hours before the event to say that you're bailing. They're worrying about assembling the people they hired and what they're going to wear, or finalizing the guest list. The last thing they want to read is your lame apologia about being tired or feeling "under the weather." Like I tell my students, either you show up or you don't.

I realize how great it is to be on the guest list. You don't have to wait in line or pay. I get it. But sometimes you *should* pay in order to support the artists, the promoters, and the venue, especially if it's an ongoing party where you rarely stop by. It's like bringing a bottle of wine to someone's house. Definitely use the drink tickets you're given, but then you and your friends should buy a few rounds to support the party too.

Never argue with a door person. As you know, I understand the humiliation of being turned away or being asked to wait while others are let in. But arguing only aggravates the situation and even hinders your efforts. If you can text a promoter friend to come outside and pull you in, do so discreetly, without making a fuss. And when you finally get in, don't smirk or roll your eyes at the door person. Don't seethe about it all night. Listen to Gaga: "J-j-just dance."

If it's the right moment and the club and your hosts are OK with it, by all means, take a selfie. Do it early on when your make-up is fresh and your hair is perfect. But then put your phone AWAY and please just enjoy it all.

Make sure there's someone to check up on you. To tell you that you have had one too many, and to pour you into a cab if you have. Or double-check your beer goggles and make sure you *really* want to go home with that particular person you've been making out with in the corner. Text each other so you know everyone got home safe and sound.

Never answer last call. If you hear the bartender yell it out or they start turning on the lights, you have stayed way too long. Forget the goodbyes. Run out and jump into a cab. Rare exceptions to this are if the DJ is truly choice and the dance floor is still packed because the music is THAT good.

Never, ever ask for a drink ticket. If you truly deserve one, you'll get one. Like a kiss.

The person who can now pass on these guidelines and the person who had to figure them out almost seem like two different people. Although the price of learning these lessons was high, the dividends made it all worth it. As a person and as a professor, I understand the city and myself so much better. And the pull of the night is as intense as ever. There's still so much to learn.

ACKNOWLEDGMENTS

My greatest debt is to all those who shared their stories with me. They are without a doubt the most fascinating people that I have ever come across.

I'm also grateful to Carly Altomare, Susanne Bartsch, Lendita Berisha, Roland Betancourt, Cynthia Bogard, Lisa Brubaker, Alexander Cavaluzzo, Gary Comenas, Dalton Conley, Andrew Barret Cox, Derek Fearon, Ramon Fernandez, Reanna Flores, Ernie Garcia, Monique Girard, Ava Glasscott, Frédéric C. Godart, Julio Gonzalez, Kevin Gray, J. Jack Halberstam, Bibbe Hansen, Suzie Hart, Ivy Higa, Jacques Hyzagi, Olivia Kendall, Joe Kerr, Thomas Kiedrowski, Richard Kimmel, Elena Krumova, Steve Lewis, Katherine Lloyd, DeeDee Luxe, Oliva Martinez, David Maurici, Jocelyn McBride, madison moore, Shira Mor, Muffinhead, Joe Polsonetti, Ingrid Praniuk, Corey Rae, Cannon Schaub, Jeannie Stapleton Smith, David Stark, Marcos Tejeda, Bharti Tiwari, Dayna Troisi, Gerry Visco, Harrison C. White, Christel Wiebenga, Kimberly Wilkens, and Michael Womack. And so many students at NYU, Columbia, Hofstra, and FIT who supported me with encouragement and suggestions, especially my inequality and sexuality seminars at NYU in 2016. A special note of appreciation and gratitude is owed to the very talented writer, thinker, performer, and designer Alexandra Warrick, my former Barnard student and now dear friend, collaborator, and fellow Box regular.

Jack Shoemaker and Andy Hunter had faith in the work and made it a reality. My editor Mensah Demary expertly provided valuable guidance during the final revisions, while Wah-Ming Chang adeptly managed the design and layout. Alex Gigante at Cowan, DeBaets, Abrahams & Sheppard delivered helpful legal counsel.

My agent Liz Parker steadfastly supported this book from the early stages, patiently endured my frustrations and musings, and pushed me to become a better writer.

Wednesday Martin is a true trailblazer and a brilliant mentor with a powerfully incisive mind. Tough and fiery, while also generous and inspiring, she is a role model for what a scholar could be.

Rose Wood is a transcendent post-human, a true artist, a disco mother, a muse, and an endless font of hard wisdom and wonderful stories. She possesses a wildly creative and sharp mind, seeing so much. I will forever be in awe of her.

My mother once said that my best friend Talal Alfayez deserves a medal for putting up with me. She's right. Chic, hilarious, and a wonderful singer, no one has faithfully accompanied me in both carousing and crisis like Talal, whom I consider my sister. Talal always cheered me up during the worst moments of the last six years. Without him there might not be a book to read. I met him at Susanne Bartsch's On Top party one summer and should thank her for providing the context where we met.

No one realizes the frustrations and joys that accompanied this project like my brother Joel. He has always shown remarkable patience in listening to stories of my defeats and strong support of my happiness whenever something fabulous happened. Our Sunday night phone catch-ups, often ending with my ribs aching from laughter, always pushed me to keep going. Visits with him, my sister-in-law-to-be Liz, and nieces Sophie and Maya in sunny LA were extremely fun respites from Gotham's grit.

My parents, Guadalupe and Victor M., have patiently supported the six years of this journey. It led me to places that they couldn't possibly have imagined when they moved to the United States in 1983, accompanied by a one-year-old version of me. But they never really protested and instead simply worried about my health and happiness. My debt to them is enormous.

SOURCES

Abrams, Margaret. "Costume Designer Patricia Field Chats About Closing Her Namesake Store." *Observer.* December 10, 2015.

Anger, Kenneth. *Hollywood Babylon.* New York: Dell Publishing, 1981.

Arnold, Sarah and Georgina Dickinson. "The Woman Who Invented Lady GaGa." *Mirror.* February 21, 2010.

Bockris, Victor. *The Life and Death of Andy Warhol.* New York: Bantam Books, 1989.

Buford May, Reuben A. *Urban Nightlife: Entertaining Race, Class, and Culture in Public Space.* New Brunswick, NJ: Rutgers University Press, 2014.

Callahan, Maureen. *Poker Face: The Rise and Rise of Lady Gaga.* New York: Hyperion, 2010.

Colacello, Bob. *Holy Terror: Andy Warhol Close Up.* New York: Harper-Perennial, 1990.

Danto, Arthur C. *Andy Warhol.* New Haven, CT: Yale University Press, 2009.

Feitelberg, Rosemary. "Susanne Bartsch Filming Documentary About New York Nightlife." *WWD.* March 20, 2016.

Felsenthal, Julia. "Nightlife Icon Susanne Bartsch on Why You Should Kickstart a Documentary About Her Life." *Vogue.* March 9, 2016.

Ferguson, Michael. *Joe Dallesandro: Warhol Superstar, Underground Film Icon, Actor.* Self-published, 2011.

French, Alex. "The Impresario of Smut." *New York.* November 23, 2008.

Glueck, Grace. "The Artist as Icon, Busybody and Chief Executive." *New York Times.* August 9, 1990.

Gonsalves, Rebecca. "Patricia Field Interview: The Costume Designer Who Dressed Carrie Bradshaw and Now Caitlyn Jenner." *The Independent.* September 11, 2015.

Grazian, David. "The Girl Hunt: Urban Nightlife and the Performance of Masculinity as Collective Activity." *Symbolic Interaction* 30(2): 221–43, 2007.

Haden-Guest, Anthony. *The Last Party: Studio 54, Disco, and the Culture of the Night.* New York: It Books, 2009.

Halberstam, Judith Jack. *Gaga Feminism: Sex, Gender, and the End of Normal.* Boston: Beacon Press, 2012.

Harrity, Christopher. "Susanne Bartsch: The Mother of All Club Kids." *The Advocate.* March 15, 2016.

Hebdige, Dick. *Subculture: The Meaning of Style.* New York: Routledge, 1988.

Highberger, Craig. *Superstar in a Housedress: The Life and Legend of Jackie Curtis.* New York: Chamberlain Bros. 2005.

Jung, E. Alex. "*RuPaul's Drag Race*'s Phi Phi O'Hara on RuPaul: 'We're Just Game Pieces for Her Show.'" *Vulture.* September 22, 2016.

Kiedrowski, Thomas. *Andy Warhol's New York City: Four Walks, Uptown to Downtown.* New York: The Little Bookroom, 2011.

Koch, Stephen. *Stargazer: The Life, World and Films of Andy Warhol.* New York and London: Marion Boyars, 2002.

Lawrence, Tim. *Love Saves the Day: A History of American Dance Music Culture, 1970–1979.* Durham and London: Duke University Press, 2003.

Martin, Wednesday. *Primates of Park Avenue: A Memoir.* New York: Simon & Schuster, 2015.

Mears, Ashley. "Ethnography Goes Out on the Town." *Sociological Forum* 31(1): 253–57, 2016.

Mears, Ashley. "Working for Free in the VIP: Relational Work and the Production of Consent." *American Sociological Review* 80(6): 1099–22, 2015.

Ocejo, Richard E. *Upscaling Downtown: From Bowery Saloons to Cocktail Bars in New York City*. Princeton, NJ: Princeton University Press, 2014.

Owen, Frank. *Clubland: The Fabulous Rise and Murderous Fall of Club Culture*. New York: St. Martin's Press, 2003.

Resnick, Marcia. *Punks, Poets & Provocateurs: New York City Bad Boys, 1977–1982*. San Rafael, CA: Insight Editions, 2015.

Rockwell, Donna and David C. Giles. "Being a Celebrity: A Phenomenology of Fame." *Journal of Phenomenological Psychology* 40: 178–210, 2009.

Schickel, Richard. *Intimate Strangers: The Culture of Celebrity*. Garden City, NY: Doubleday & Company, 1985.

Schulman, Michael. "Not Going Gentle Into That Good Night." *New York Times*. July 10, 2013.

Schulman, Michael. "Patricia Field Hangs Up Her Retail Wig." *New York Times*. December 26, 2015.

Stein, Jean. Edited with George Plimpton. *Edie: American Girl*. New York: Grove Press, 1994.

St. James, James. *Party Monster: The Fabulous but True Tale of Murder in Clubland*. New York: Simon & Schuster, 2003.

Sullivan, Brendan Jay. *Rivington Was Ours: Lady Gaga, the Lower East Side, and the Prime of Our Lives*. New York: It Books, 2013.

Violet, Ultra. *Famous for 15 Minutes: My Years with Andy Warhol*. Lincoln, NE: iUniverse, 2008.

Virshup, Amy. "Club Kids: Rocking with the New Music of the Night." *New York*. March 1988.

Warhol, Andy. Edited by Pat Hackett. *The Andy Warhol Diaries*. New York: Warner Books, 1989.

Warhol, Andy and Pat Hackett. *POPism: The Warhol Sixties*. Orlando, FL: Harcourt, 1980.

Watson, Steven. *Factory Made: Warhol and the Sixties*. New York: Pantheon Books, 2003.

White, Harrison C. *Identity and Control: How Social Formations Emerge*. Princeton, NJ: Princeton University Press, 2008.

Woronov, Mary. *Swimming Underground: My Years in the Warhol Factory*. Boston, MA: Journey Editions, 1995.

Yuzna, Jake (ed). *The FUN: The Social Practice of Nightlife in NYC*. Brooklyn, NY: powerHouse Books, 2013.

Author photograph by Bharti Tiwari

About the Author

VICTOR P. CORONA, PhD, is a sociologist at New York University. He has been mentioned in *The New York Times*, *New York Post*, *The Times* (London), *Glamour*, *Town & Country*, *Black-Book*, *Daily Beast*, and *The Washington Post*. Born in Mexico City, Corona grew up in the New York suburb of White Plains. He now lives in Harlem.